To my dearest grandchildren, Hannah and Max.

May their lives be filled with creativity, excitement and a love of learning.

FOREWORD

Ros, her inspirational writings, continual support and challenging ideas have been a profoundly deep influence on my thinking and in extending my leadership for learning. I have been extremely fortunate to know Ros for some fifteen years. In my first headship, as curriculum and assessment advisor, she was instrumental in supporting the development and implementation of an inclusive, inspirational curriculum and assessment provision across the primary phase .This led to significant achievement gains for all learners.

Ros has developed many curriculum models, used extensively across schools, and was co-writer of the Primary Curriculum Organiser, a former Kirklees best seller which in turn strengthened curriculum entailment and provision across many schools.

Ros continually demonstrates that unshakeable capacity to provide clarity of thinking that focuses on pedagogical strategies which support schools in providing the very best of learning opportunities .This book is a valuable addition to assist in the creation and advancement of an innovative curriculum model.

Darran Lee, B.Ed, MA
Headteacher
Regional Leader NCSL

THE CREATIVE CURRICULUM
SUMMARY OF CONTENT

INTRODUCTION

This publication reflects and promotes the principles of 'Excellence and Enjoyment' (DfES Publications 2003).

THE OBJECTIVES FOR THIS PUBLICATION ARE:

To provide a model for curriculum planning that:

» Reflects the needs of society for the twenty-first century

» Reflects the principles of 'Every Child Matters' (DfES:2005)

» Enables development of strong cross-curricular links

» Incorporates the QCA Units of Study for those schools wishing to retain them as an underpinning body of planning

» Encourages schools to identify their own priorities and curricular content

» Enables tracking and monitoring of curriculum coverage within the curriculum

» Builds on the strengths of the Primary National Strategies

» Promotes independence and creativity for learners

To provide models for posing curriculum challenges that:

» Promote the principles of 'Every Child Matters' (DfES:2005)

» Promote independence and creativity for learners

» Are based on intrinsic cross-curricular links

» Reflect the diverse learning needs and styles of pupils

» Promote collaboration and communication

» Promote assessment of generic learning skills that are transferable across the curriculum

» Reflect and promote the principles of Assessment for Learning

To provide a hierarchy of learning skills that:

» Are rooted in the National Curriculum Level Descriptions for all subjects

» Promote a model for learning to be a learner in all aspects of the curriculum

» Complement and promote the principles of Assessment for Learning

To provide curriculum models that promote the application of the skills of self-assessment, peer-assessment and Assessment for Learning, teaching through talk and valuing talk, questioning skills and visual literacy.

The debate on the creative curriculum and what it might look like is dominating much of educational thinking currently. The following are summaries of recent publications describing the characteristics of this curriculum and what learning within it may need to look like.

'All our Futures' (QCA, 1999) states that in order to meet the challenges of a new society there is a need to foster creative education that will:

'…Develop young people's capacities for original ideas and action…forms that enable young people to engage positively with the growing complexity and diversity of social values and ways of life.'

(‘All Our Futures’, QCA 1999)

The published outcomes of the funded project to explore models for the creative curriculum in primary schools, 'Creative Partnerships' states that the characteristics of creative learning are that:

» It is long term and collaborative in nature

» It demands a joint commitment, a shared vision and a willingness to embrace open-ended outcomes, challenge and risk

» It helps to equip young people with the skills, ability, confidence and attitudes to enable them to work creatively, to transfer and apply knowledge in different contexts towards new and valuable goals

» It encourages creative, critical and reflective thinking and produces excited, enthusiastic, enquiry-driven learners

THE FOLLOWING ARE FURTHER EXCERPTS FROM THIS PUBLICATION:

1. Key characteristics of creative learning include use of:

» imagination

» flexibility

» curiosity

» independence

» tolerance for ambiguity

» trust in one's own senses

» openness to subconscious material

» an ability to work on several ideas / address problems in different ways

Creative learning encourages a climate for young people to explore how to apply their knowledge in original ways and with purpose.

Creativity is not the preserve of a gifted few, but something that, given the right conditions, can be developed in anybody. By the same token, it is not something that can simply be mined from a prescribed body of knowledge, but is dependent upon the way in which students interact with the content of creative programmes.'

2. Five characteristics evidenced in effective 'creative partnership schools'

1 - LEADERSHIP

» visionary and ambitious leadership
» high levels of autonomy
» confidence to take risks and operate with open-ended outcomes
» a whole-school approach to embedding creative teaching and learning strategies
» an emphasis on a creative stimulus
» strengthening pupils' knowledge and skills by delivering an enriched curriculum
» an openness that welcomes individuals from the creative professions
» a strong emphasis on personalised learning.

2 - CAPACITY

» school commitment to timetable staff and pupils' involvement
» staff willing and able to engage with innovative ideas and think creatively
» pupils' enjoyment of the programme and their educational and personal progress
» teacher morale
» capacity to deliver high quality and enriched projects
» commitment to professional development from all partners
» quality of creative programme and evidence and research produced.

3 - CULTURE

» culture of the school shapes the environment within which creative learning can take place
» the approach of the school towards risk taking
» the extent to which the school is open-minded
» the strength of communication within the school
» the approach to partnership working
» the importance placed on core-values such as trust and respect.

4 - PLANNING

» the ability to plan effectively and in partnership with others
» the setting of shared aims and objectives and clearly identified roles at the outset
» recognition of the significance and impact of long-term projects, with continuous joint planning that enables creative learning opportunities to be built into the curriculum.

5 - ENVIRONMENTS FOR CREATIVE LEARNING

» the right environment physically
» emotional literacy and awareness
» ability to take risks
» the right practitioner with the right skills and language
» trust
» a value system based on enabling young people as opposed to the 'talent' led approach which focuses on those who already 'can do'

('Creative Partnerships': 'First Findings' 2005)

The Qualifications and Curriculum Authority (QCA) has been staging a wide debate into how and why the curriculum may need to evolve to better prepare young people for life in the future. They have identified five forces for change to the curriculum:

1. Society and the nature of work.
2. New technology
3. New understanding about learning
4. The need for greater personalisation and innovation
5. The increasing global dimension to work and life.

This debate is not confined to review of the primary curriculum. The skills identified as necessary for young adults in the 21st century are to be:

Active Investigators

- » Make decisions
- » Identify questions to answer and problems to resolve.

Creative Contributors

- » Generate ideas
- » Ask questions to extend their thinking
- » Connect their own and others' ideas and experiences in inventive ways
- » Challenge conventions and stereotyping
- » Adapt their ideas as circumstances change.

Reflective Learners

- » Recognise their achievements
- » Set clear objectives with success criteria for their development and work
- » Invite feedback and deal positively with praise and criticism
- » Evaluate learning and make changes to achieve success.

Practical Self-managers

- » Achieve their goals, showing initiative, commitment and perseverance
- » Prioritise actions, anticipating and overcoming difficulties
- » Respond positively to change by taking on new responsibilities and learning new skills
- » Show flexibility.

Confident Collaborators

- » Contribute openly, working with others to common objectives
- » Try out different roles within a group
- » Take responsibility for their contribution to the outcome
- » Provide constructive support and feedback to others
- » Manage conflict to achieve results.

('14 to 19 Skills Framework Consultation', QCA 2005)

R RATIONALE

The National Curriculum (NC), is a statutory body of subject knowledge, skills and content organised into Programmes of Study that schools are legally required to plan and teach in full. There are ten subjects within the National Curriculum and, in addition, state schools are required to teach Religious Education. At the end of the original Programmes of Study for each subject there are Level Descriptions through which the assessment process is to take place.

The statutory National Curriculum is only part of a school's curriculum. Schools are further required to address pupils' personal, social and health education and the issues of citizenship (PSHCE), their religious education, and should consider whether the needs of their particular community require further inclusions in the curriculum.

Furthermore, schools are now required to root their curriculum and all associated activity within the principles of 'Every Child Matters' (2005). The implications of this are an education that enables children to:

» Be healthy
» Stay safe
» Enjoy and achieve
» Make a positive contribution
» Achieve economic well being

The challenge is for schools to design a curriculum that will meet the needs of current and future generations, rather than the historic curriculum of the twentieth century. Head teachers and Senior Managers must ask themselves:

» What sort of adults will we need in the year 2020?
» What skills and abilities will they need?
» What is in our curriculum that is already not relevant?
» What is likely to become less relevant as time passes?

The purpose of education will probably remain consistent in the twenty-first century to that of the late twentieth century, i.e. "… a route to the spiritual, moral, social, cultural, physical, and mental development, and thus the well-being, of the individual…(and)… a route to equality of opportunity for all, a healthy and just democracy, a productive economy, and sustainable development" (DfEE / QCA 'The National Curriculum Handbook' 1999)

The current National Curriculum has a significant amount of content-driven knowledge. Furthermore, the prescriptive content has been increased by the introduction of the QCA Schemes of Work, which do have the principles and processes of the subject within them but, being too overloaded for achievement within the time available, have led many teachers and schools to focus on the contexts through which the skills and processes were intended to be developed rather than the skills and processes themselves. Thus teachers have understandably placed their emphasis even more heavily on 'What we are learning?' and 'What we have made?' rather than

on 'How we have learned?' and 'How might we use this in our daily lives?'

The pupils we educate need to become active, informed, creative and intelligent learners. They should have full awareness of their own intelligences and those of others they need to interact with. They should know how they can influence and shape their own lives and those of others. Being empowered by this knowledge, learners should develop a sense of well-being and an eagerness to support and sustain the well-being of their community and the wider community. To achieve this they need a curriculum that will develop the following:

» Communication
» Application of Number
» Information Technology
» Working with Others
» Improving own learning and performance
» Problem Solving
» Thinking Skills
» Information Processing Skills
» Reasoning Skills
» Enquiry Skills
» Creative Thinking Skills
» Evaluation Skills

Through this curriculum they will need to develop:

» Functional skills including literacy, numeracy and ICT
» Personal skills
» Thinking skills
» Learning skills

(National Curriculum Orders 1999)

Pupils will need to develop positive attitudes and dispositions, becoming adaptable and flexible learners who are determined and unafraid to take risks.
Furthermore, pupils will need to know and understand the areas and aspects in which their particular strengths and talents lie, and how they can utilise these strengths in order to compensate for other areas that may be less well developed.

'In schools young people need to articulate for themselves what they have learned, make explicit links between different areas of experience, and reflect on how something from one area can be applied to another.

Where young people are failing to develop in one area, they need active encouragement to draw on their resources in other areas. …. Transferable skills are sometimes not transferred simply because their relevance to new areas of learning has not been thought through….

This is why it is crucial that the school's common objectives are woven through all subjects, that teachers see themselves as teachers of language, thinking, culture and values as well as of science or history….'

(Dr. Nicholas Tate, TES, March 2006)

Currently too many pupils leave school with a feeling of having failed. The words 'I can't…' are embedded in the psyche of far too many of the population we have educated. Pupils need to learn how to transfer skills and bring their strengths and talents from areas of confidence, to areas where they are experiencing more difficulty. Pupils of today do not always have sufficient awareness of their personal strengths and the skills involved within them to draw upon them in other situations, and the curriculum of today does not generally support this process. Furthermore, the present structure and organisation of many schools renders the adults within them deskilled in awareness of the skills and abilities developed and applied in all aspects of the curriculum. They may be unaware of those in which a particular pupil may have the potential to develop a particular ability, and how that pupil might later draw upon these skills to strengthen areas in which he / she is experiencing difficulty.

The curriculum model in this publication is based upon the need for linkage across subjects of the National Curriculum. It has reduced significantly the current overload, however, it is still too demanding to allow teachers the time and flexibility they need in order to shift the focus of teaching from content and product, to learning outcomes and personal and social self-awareness. It has been designed, however, to promote radical further reduction in accordance with the priorities of the school and its locality.

Head teachers and Senior Managers will need to make further reductions to the model provided here.

In particular, the model here provides exemplification of cross-curricular challenges that promote the skills of independent and small group reasoning, decision making, hypothesis, investigation, recording, analysis and presentation that will empower pupils in self-motivated and self-managed learning in order to produce the self-confident and self-aware citizens of the future.

Schools of the future will rapidly move into the zone of e-learning and home or locality based education. Pupils need to be independent learners, resourceful and curious, willing and unafraid to take risks and aware of their own capabilities and those of others they need to work with. The current curriculum is not specifically designed to produce this type of individual, and its interpretation in some schools continues to lead to the development of a learner who is adult or resource dependent. The challenge for the school is to design a curriculum that does empower pupils as independent learners!

Finally, the curriculum of the twenty-first century must produce pupils who are healthy, safe, contribute positively, have the potential for economic well-being, enjoy learning and, above all, achieve well.

'Every Child Matters' should be at the heart of the principles of the primary curriculum for the twenty-first century.

'YOUNG PEOPLE WILL ENJOY AND VALUE A CURRICULUM THAT ENABLES THEM TO ENJOY AND VALUE THEMSELVES.'

EILEEN MARCHANT,
(POLICY DIRECTOR, AFPE, MAY 2006)

'AN EFFECTIVE CURRICULUM WOULD ENABLE ALL PUPILS TO FEEL THAT THEY ARE GIFTED AND TALENTED AND THAT THEY HAVE SOME FLEXIBILITY TO CHOOSE THEIR OWN LEARNING PATHWAYS.'

ROS. GARSIDE
(EDUCATION BRADFORD MAY 2006)

S SUMMARY

The rapid pace required to cover as much as possible of an overloaded curriculum has been a deterrent to developing investigative approaches, enquiry learning and the use of extended discussion. It has encouraged many teachers to depend on direct delivery of content through limited resources and instructional input.

'Excellence and Enjoyment', (Department for Education and Skills, (DfES) 2003) urges teachers to restore creativity and excitement to the curriculum. Some teachers, however, are afraid to make bold decisions in reshaping the curriculum, and some Head Teachers actually discourage significant change, fearing reprisals from external agencies, despite the permission implicit in 'Excellence and Enjoyment', (Department for Education and Skills, (DfES) 2003).

The above publication states that it wants schools to feel they have the freedom to:

'Take a fresh look at their curriculum, their timetable and the organisation of the school day and week, and think actively about how they would like to develop and enrich the experience they offer their children.'

('Excellence and Enjoyment' 2003, Page 12)

Teachers can sometimes be resistant to major curricular change because it means changing their planning and taking on board new subject knowledge. The writer maintains that without significant curricular change it is unlikely that teachers will re-invigorate their teaching and bring excitement back into the classroom.

'Excellence and Enjoyment' states that;

'Children learn better when they are excited and engaged – but what excites them best is truly excellent teaching, which challenges them and shows them what they can do.'

(Foreword)

This publication, 'Planning and Organising The Creative Curriculum', provides a curriculum model that enables teachers to identify clear links across subjects. It supports teachers in designing learning opportunities that bring the skills and knowledge of more than one subject area together.

Too many schools and teachers are still delivering a twentieth century curriculum to the citizens of the twenty-first century, and on the whole there is too little guidance for Senior Managers and teachers on how to change this situation. This publication aims to contribute to that debate in a positive and supportive way.

Curriculum support provided in the following chapters consists of:

» Assessment for Learning
» Questioning Skills
» The Cruciality of Talk
» Visual Literacy
» The Creative Curriculum Long Term Plan
» The Medium Term Creative Curriculum Maps (CCMs)
» The Creative Curriculum Challenges
» The Optional Mini Challenges
» The Hierarchy of Learning Skills
» Taking the Issues Into Planning
» Taking the Medium Term into the Short term
» Three Case Studies
» A Model for Embedding Literacy Into a Thematic Curriculum

NB: Only the subjects contributing to the thematic subject links as driving or supporting subjects, have been defined on the CCMs and the remaining subjects might be recorded in a similar format or in subject boxes on the rear of the map.

(Models for adapting CCMs, and for identifying links within the subjects unplanned on the CCMs, are provided in Chapter 12).

There are more opportunities for the foundation subjects planned than teachers are required to deliver, (especially for history and geography) and thus this enables further choice for the teachers and Senior Managers of a school, prioritising according to the needs of their pupils and the opportunities available in the community in order to personalise the curriculum. All foundation subjects need not be running at the same time every half term.

(Models for reducing content in CCMs are provided in Chapter 13).

By enlarging the maps onto A3 paper, teachers are able to add subject references, notes or key questions for those subjects not planned here, and to add other aspects such as PSHCE.

1 A BRIEF HISTORY OF DEVELOPMENTS IN THE CURRICULUM SINCE 1989

The first draft orders for English and mathematics came into schools in 1987. The actual National Curriculum was launched through a staggered 'rolling programme' across the subjects and years, commencing in Years 1 and 7 in the academic year 1989

– 1990. The following is an illustration of the 'roll out' of the original curriculum:

THE FIRST FIVE YEARS OF THE NATIONAL CURRICULUM

Year	1989 /1990	1990 / 1991	1991 / 1992	1992 / 1993	1993 / 1994	1994 / 1995	1995 /1996
1	MSE	MSET	MSETG H	MSETG HAMPE	MSETG HAMPE	MSETG HAMPE	MSETG HAMPE
2		MSE	MSET	MSETG H	MSETG HAMPE	MSETG HAMPE	MSETG HAMPE
3		MSET	MSETG H	MSETG HAMPE	MSETG HAMPE	MSETG HAMPE	MSETG HAMPE
4			MSET	MSETG H	MSETG HAMPE	MSETG HAMPE	MSETG HAMPE
5				MSET	MSETG H	MSETG HAMPE	MSETG HAMPE
6					MSET	MSETG H	MSETG HAMPE
7	MS	MSET	MSETG H	MSETG HAMPE ML	MSETG HAMPE ML	MSETG HAMPE ML	MSETG HAMPE ML
8		MS	MSET	MSETG H	MSETG HAMPE ML	MSETG HAMPE ML	MSETG HAMPE ML
9			MS	MSET	MSETG H	MSETG HAMPE ML	MSETG HAMPE ML
10				MSE	MSET	MSET	MSET
11					MSET	MSET	MSET

M	mathematicsics	S	science	E	English
T	technology*	G	geography	H	history
A	art**	PE	physical education	M	music
ML	modern languages***				

* became D&T ** became A&C *** became MFL (modern foreign languages)

It should be noted that ICT was not originally an NC subject in its own right.

The original National Curriculum was not generally well received in primary schools. Teachers had traditionally identified their own areas for study based on personal interest, resources available and personal knowledge. Planning in most schools was often brief and usually took the form of a flow chart identifying the subject foci to be taught under an 'umbrella' topic title and brief notes to clarify the content. Teachers then usually kept a one weekly or two weekly record of what had been taught. 'Differentiation' and 'objectives' were largely unknown words.

Because the launch was staggered, upper Key Stage 2 teachers and Key Stage 4 teachers had three to four years to witness the stress of adopting an unfamiliar and overwhelming volume of curricular planning and assessment requirements, and many anticipated that the rolling programme would never reach them as it would have been abandoned long since as unworkable. However, the launch continued relentlessly.

The content of the original National Curriculum Orders (as the ten ring binders, one for each subject, were called), was grossly overloaded, with unworkable assessment targets defined through the Statements of Attainment found in the Attainment Targets. Even before the roll out in Years 1 and 7 was complete, the mathematics and science orders had been recalled for a major rewrite because of their complete lack of realism, having seventeen and eighteen Attainment Targets respectively. Schools were finding the assessment systems, based on Statements of Attainment to be assessed, unmanageable. In the primary phases alone there were 1,010 Statements of Attainment to be assessed by the end of Year 6.

By 1993 it was widely recognised that the National Curriculum was unworkable in its original form and a review was called for, which was to be led by Sir Ronald Dearing. In his report, which stated that the original curriculum was unmanageable and that a vastly simplified version was to be published and implemented in schools, Sir Ronald pledged that there would then be five years without curricular change.

Teachers eagerly awaited the new edition of the National Curriculum, however in the main it was received with disappointment. Although the volume of words had undoubtedly been reduced, (the entire ten subjects could now be housed in one compendium and the Statements of Attainment had been replaced by simple paragraphs defining the levels, known now as Level Descriptions), nevertheless the bulk of the content remained within a paraphrased form. Current National Curriculum test and task criteria are required to match the levels as defined in the Level Descriptions.

Despite Sir Ronald Dearing's promise, the five years from 1995 to 2000 probably saw a greater increase in volume and prescription than in any previous period following the original release of the first draft orders. Firstly there was the arrival of the revised curriculum, followed by the launch of the National Strategies (formerly the National Literacy Strategy (NLS) and the National Numeracy Strategy (NNS). Then there followed a further revision of the National Curriculum, which coincided with the launch of the Q.C.A Schemes of Work (also known as the Q.C.A. Units) in 1999.

WHAT ARE THE QCA SCHEMES OF WORK?

OFSTED and HMI inspections had identified that many schools were struggling to produce good quality Medium Term Plans from the simplified National Curriculum, thus the integrity of subjects was being jeopardised when teachers did not have adequate subject knowledge. Soon after the launch of the revised National Curriculum, therefore, QCA responded to schools' complaints about the amount of time required and the difficulties experienced in converting the Programmes of Study into workable Medium Term Plans. This led to the production of the QCA Schemes of Work (often also referred to as the QCA Units).

These Schemes of Work quickly became the whole curriculum for many teachers and schools, and indeed many young teachers have been encouraged to become completely dependent upon them. Although they remained optional, the pressure to adopt a range of the Units of Study was great, as OFSTED inspections were frequently critical of schools' own Medium Term Plans.

The intention was good, however in the reality most QCA Schemes are too overloaded with content to be taught in their entirety, and this has led to teachers playing at 'pick and mix', taking the bits they like from a Unit and leaving the rest. This can lead to fragmentation, and some aspects that are actually key elements of the NC Programmes of Study, which remain the legal requirement of the National Curriculum, being neglected.

HOW DO THE QCA UNITS SOMETIMES CAUSE CONFUSION AS WELL AS OVERLOAD?

The QCA Units often create a confusing assessment picture due to conflicting assessment foci in the units, which sometimes have not only lesson objectives, but also learning outcomes and End of Unit expectations that do not always complement one another.

The following is an example of this confusion:

QCA GEOGRAPHY SCHEME OF WORK, UNIT 4 : 'GOING TO THE SEASIDE'

Different Parts of the Unit	Targets for Learning
Key Questions (In the dividing strips)	Who has visited other places? Where are they? How far away are they? How did they get there?
Objectives (Left of teaching activities)	To name and investigate places. To use geographical terms. To use maps and atlases. To conduct a survey.
Learning Outcomes (Right of teaching activities)	Identify places and relate them to different environments. Organise a survey. Use ICT to present findings. Research conclusions from evidence. Know where the seaside is in relation to the locality.
Suggested activities (main column)	Ask children what places they have visited and compile a list. Help the children to locate the places by using a map and an atlas, and group them into different types of environment eg…. Help the children to design and carry out a school survey to find other places that children have visited and find out, for example, which is the most popular place. Help the children to enter this information into a database, using a data file with structure that you have created.
End of Unit Expectations (on the back)	Most children will: Recall information about their local area and use this to help them study a contrasting area e.g. the seaside. Recognise how each environment is different and changing. Use a variety of resources to find out information.

Clearly there are many potential pitfalls here for the conscientious teacher. How does s/he answer the following questions?

1. Am I to assume that the objectives are the learning targets to be assessed?

2. If I help children to design and carry out a survey, can I now say they can conduct a survey and tick that objective?

3. If children can say how far away a place is and how their family happened to get there, have they now investigated places?

4. If they can say how far away a place is and how their family happened to get there, can they now relate those places to different environments?

5. Why aren't the Key Questions the same as the objectives? In this unit might the Key Questions be:

5.i Can you name six (four? ten?) popular seaside resorts in England?

5.ii Can you use books, pamphlets, videos and the internet to find out at least four (six?) things that are always found at the seaside?

5.iii Can you use the following terms in your presentation and explain what each means?

» Coast
» Cliff
» Promenade
» Beach
» Sea
» Waves
» Rocks
» Hotels
» Caves
» Amusements

5.iv Can you say:

» Which of the above are man made and which are natural?
» Which would you almost always see and which only sometimes?

5.v Can you list the steps we went through to:

» Make up our questionnaire?
» Collect the answers?
» Organise the answers?
» Store the answers in the data base?
» Use the print out to decide the following…..etc?

6. Why aren't the learning outcomes the same as the objectives? In this unit shouldn't the learning outcomes be:

» They can now name places and describe their main characteristics
» They can now use the following geographical terms (list)
» They can now use maps and atlases to show where the places are
» They can now inform others how to conduct a survey?

The QCA Units have deskilled many teachers, causing them to lose confidence in their ability to think creatively 'outside the box' and to adapt the curriculum to better reflect the needs of their pupils and the community that the school serves. Indeed, the QCA Schemes have replaced the National Curriculum (NC) as the dictate of teaching for many teachers, who have sometimes been heard to say, 'We can't do that, it isn't in the QCA'.

2 CONSTRUCTING THE CURRICULUM FOR 2020

The OFSTED publication of findings on the impact of the National Strategies during 2004 / 2005, released Spring 2006, states that many schools have not yet taken on board the messages of 'Excellence and Enjoyment', which urge schools and managers to review and restructure the curriculum in order to increase opportunities for creativity, and to address the different learning styles preferred by pupils we teach.

'Many schools have made only limited changes to the way in which they manage the curriculum since the publication of Excellence and Enjoyment. In schools where management and leadership are most successful, leadership teams are prepared to challenge and modify current practice and take every opportunity to use the PNS to improve provision….. Although there is a commitment to the principles embodied in Excellence and Enjoyment, a few schools lack the practical knowledge of ways in which to implement change and bring about improvement in line with these principles. Consequently such schools agree with the underlying messages but are hesitant to make changes.'

(Primary National Strategy – An evaluation of its impact in primary schools 2004 / 05, OFSTED 2005)

WHAT DO SENIOR MANAGERS NEED TO DO TO CONSTRUCT THE CURRICULUM OF THE FUTURE?

1. Decide what SORT OF INDIVIDUALS adults might need to be in order to build our future.

2. Decide what sort of school might educate these individuals.

3. Decide what are the core skills needed by current and future generations.

4. Decide what are key experiences, knowledge and understanding for current and future generations.

5. Determine what the local and surrounding community can contribute to the education of current and future generations.

6. Construct a curriculum that enables the delivery of these priorities in creative and exciting ways, enabling repeated, but creative and exciting teaching, consolidation and re-cycling across the curriculum.

WHAT MIGHT THE CORE SKILLS INCLUDE?

1. The ability to talk confidently, using a sophisticated range of language structures and vocabulary to discuss, debate, explain, justify, describe and recount.

2. The ability to use ICT confidently for the full range of purposes, including processing, presenting, researching, analysing, computing, illustrating and communicating.

3. Physical and mental well being, good health and an active life style.

4. The ability to work and play with others, co-operating and collaborating, responding and communicating successfully.

5. The ability to work alone and with others to hypothesise, plan , investigate, record, analyse, conclude and re-hypothesise.

6. Reading skills that include:

» The ability to read at progressively more challenging levels.
» The ability to synthesise out information from texts, to interpret information and to use and apply information.
» Higher order reading comprehension skills including the ability to infer and deduce from text.

7. Writing skills that include:

» The four Basic Skills of Writing including the ability to use accurate grammatical structures, a neat and accurate cursive style, accurate spelling both through basic sight vocabulary and phonic skills and the ability to construct and punctuate sentences accurately. (See: 'Write on Target' – the 'gold book', Chapter 8, Ros. Wilson, 2006)
» The ability to accurately apply the characteristics of the full range of text types and genre.
» The ability to respond appropriately to a wide range of stimuli
» A higher level writing voice as achieved through the VCOP of Big Writing, (see 'Strategies for Immediate Impact on Writing Standards', 2003, and 'Write on Target', Chapters 3 and 8, 2006).

8. Be numerate and use and apply a high level of numeracy skills confidently and accurately in their work across the curriculum.

9. Be creative through music, art, gymnastics, dance, design and construction.

10. Confidently tackle and solve problems involving some or all of the core skills.

11. Confidently make decisions and choices without fear of risk taking.

12. Be creative learners who are inquisitive, determined and able to work independently through self-motivation.

WHAT MIGHT THE LOCAL AND SURROUNDING COMMUNITY CONTRIBUTE TO A SCHOOL'S CURRICULUM?

The extended school agenda is leading many schools to be even more in tune with their communities and to draw members of the wider communities into their community. An integral aspect of this process must be the identification of the many skills and talents available within the community that might enrich the school's curriculum and the life experiences available for their pupils. Sports people, poets, writers, mathematicians, scientists, craftsmen, artists, musicians and other performers live within most communities and their crafts frequently reflect the culture and/or ethnicities of the community within which they live. Many schools already access this great wealth of educational opportunities and in the future this should be a natural source of curricular opportunity for all.

In general, schools should make full use of their immediate and wider locality, using them as a source for:

1. Positive role models in all aspects of learning, including crafts, literature, the arts, sport, religion, commerce and industry.

2. Field study, research and investigation within the environment.

3. Cultural enrichment and learning opportunities through museums, galleries, centres for religions, theatres, stately homes and other facilities.

4. Work experience and learning opportunities within the world of business and commerce.

5. Citizenship and enrichment through understanding of the importance of rules, trust and mutual respect for life in a civilised society, and ways in which membership of a complex society requires skills of interdependence.

6. Support, services and networks.

7. Community links.

HOW MIGHT THE DEVELOPMENT AND CONSOLIDATION OF THE CORE SKILLS BE ACHIEVED?

1. Develop a flexible curriculum model that:

» Promotes learning through investigation and research.
» Promotes hypothesis and curiosity.
» Promotes risk taking and a lack of fear of being wrong.
» Promotes the use and application of the full range of core skills across all curriculum areas.
» Promotes creativity.
» Promotes choice and decision making.
» Is not heavily content laden but promotes exciting and challenging learning opportunities.
» **Has in-built re-cycling of opportunities for learning, consolidating, using and applying the core skills for life in a wide range of interesting, relevant, exciting and challenging situations across the curriculum.**

3 THE THREE FORMS OF
ASSESSMENT IN SCHOOLS

There are three quite distinct forms of assessment in schools: summative assessment, formative assessment, and Assessment for Learning.

Summative assessment is quite different in purpose and form from the other two. Its purpose is to make a judgement on the current standard of performance of an individual at the moment in time that it is applied. It is normally in the form of a test or a pre-planned assessment activity. It may contribute information to future planning; however, that is not its primary purpose.

Formative assessment has some elements of Assessment for Learning in that its primary purpose is to inform the next and future learning but it does not always explicitly involve and inform pupils in the ways that Assessment for Learning does, nor does it necessarily empower pupils to assess their own achievement and to know explicitly what they should do next.

The following table defines the three forms of assessment.

THE THREE FORMS OF ASSESSMENT

Summative Assessment	Formative Assessment
Makes a judgement on a pupil's attainment at a given point in time: Use of assessment to make a specific judgement on the actual level of a pupil's performance, usually either by calculation based on accumulated short term assessments or through an assessment activity or test.	**Informs teaching:** Use of assessment in the short term, usually within a week, or even a lesson or piece of work, in order to plan the next step of teaching so that progression is ensured. It is informed by knowing how well pupils understood or could do the previous learning.

Assessment for Learning
Involves pupils in their own learning and achievement: Incorporates the principles of formative assessment, but explicitly involves the pupils in the process. Pupils are enabled to know what success looks like, what skill levels are required and how to judge whether they have actually been successful. They are, therefore, able to form an opinion on the level of their own achievement through self assessment, or to support and advise their peers. Pupils are able to verbalise their learning, saying how they might use and apply that learning in other contexts and what they now need to do in order to progress further. In addition, pupils have their own precise small -step targets matched to their individual needs that will ensure they are moving forward in a progressive way through the sub-levels of the National Curriculum, in order to move up the levels.

WHAT ARE THE PRINCIPLES OF ASSESSMENT FOR LEARNING?

The principles of Assessment for Learning (AfL) should be applied to the delivery of all Units of Work. They are that:

1. Pupils should always know where they are currently in terms of skills, knowledge and understanding, i.e. 'I can…', 'I know…' and 'I understand that…'

2. Pupils should always know and understand how their skills, knowledge and understanding will be different when they have completed the learning cycle (usually a Unit of Work) i.e. 'I will be able to…', 'I will know that…' or 'I will understand that…'

3. Pupils should always know and understand what they need to do next in order to achieve well, i.e. 'Now I need to…'

4. Pupils will always know what the key learning objective/s of the lesson are and how they will demonstrate success at achieving it or them.

5. Pupils will be able to verbalise what they have learned or are learning and how they can use it, either within mini-plenaries throughout a lesson and/or in the final plenary.

6. Pupils will talk confidently about learning, stating what they have learned, how it might be used in the future and what else they need to learn in order to progress.

NB: it is only when children can transfer learning to another situation that you know they know and understand it.

On the following page there is a basic model for teaching that reflects the principles of assessment for learning and will ensure those principles are met.

There is currently national debate as to the necessity of a rigid lesson structure and the writer is not advocating this approach. However, there is undoubtedly a need for clearly planned structures when there are to be changes of focus within the same session such as an adult taught input and an activity for pupils' application of skills. If a lesson is a continuation of such a session and pupils are spending the majority or all of the time available on activity, there is still a great need for planned talk at the opening of the lesson for review and refresh purposes, mini-plenaries and a final review and discussion with some sharing of outcomes. These talk sections should still include the 'What have we learned?' and 'How are we using it?' and 'Is this successful? How do we know?' type of questions.

Teachers have frequently been advised to plan and organise their lessons into a structure described as either a three or a four part lesson. To ensure Assessment for Learning is securely planned into practice we probably should think in terms of a five part structure. Planning the explanation and demonstration of the activity as a separate element in its own right will help to ensure that talk is securely embedded as an AfL tool in both the taught input and the explanation of the activity. The following is a framework for building talk into learning, followed by a model for the five part lesson.

ASSESSMENT FOR LEARNING IN PRACTICE

What	When	Examples
1. Key Learning Objective/s	Introduction to lesson	This is what we are going to learn. This is why we are learning it. Might include a brief activity.
2. Teach the learning	Body of Introduction	Explain and show. Model. Demonstrate.
3. Pupils talk	During and after teaching	What have we learned? Did we all know? (Assess as they talk) Peer restates what has been learned in simple terms.
4. Explain the activity	When sure all know what they are expected to have learned (i.e. after introduction)	Explain what has to be done. Model and demonstrate. Explain how it will successfully demonstrate the learning. Give success criteria if appropriate.
5. Pupils talk	After explanation of activity is complete	What have we got to do? Why are we doing it? How can we show success? (Assess if all understand through their talk) Peer restates simply what has to be done. This is how long you have to complete.
6. Activity	Body of lesson	Monitor all are working confidently. Support as needed but maintain oversight of class. Conduct mini-plenaries if working for more than ten minutes. Give time prompts to ensure all work at pace and complete on time.
7. Mini-plenaries	Every 8 to 10 minutes during activity	Stop. Tell your friend – What have you learned? How are you using it? Is this one going to be successful? How do you know?
8. Plenary	Final ten minutes of lesson	What have we learned? How did we use it? These are successful – how do we know? The big 'What if…?' question
9. Summary of plenary and 'What if….?'	Closing	We learned this…. We used it this way. What if I had asked you to do that instead? Would it have been the same or would it have been different?
10. Where next…	End	Respond to pupils' confidence in response to 9.3 with either: We learned this and now we know how to use it, OR We learned this and we used it this way. Next week we shall use it that way and see if it is the same or different.

THE FIVE PART LESSON

Support for Less Able Pupils	What?	Support for More Able Pupils
» Access through closed questions for some pupils.	**1. WARM-UP** Quick-fire questioning and/or activities to: Activate learning, thinking, interest and excitement Review prior learning Assess readiness for next learning	» Extend through open questions for some pupils
» What is the minimum ALL pupils must learn?	**2. TAUGHT INPUT** Sections 1 to 3 of Assessment for Learning model above. Teach, explain, model and demonstrate. What do we know?	» Should some pupils know more? » Use open questions.
» Will all pupils understand the language? » Will all be able to do all of this or should some do less?	**3. EXPLAIN ACTIVITY** Sections 4 and 5 of Assessment for Learning model above. Model and demonstrate. Explain how pupils will know if they have been successful. 'How are we using it?' 'How will we know if we have been successful?' 'How long have we got to complete?'	» Is this challenging enough for all pupils? » Should some be doing more or tackling it in a more investigative way?
» Should some pupils have peer or adult support? » Should they be expected to do less or do it in a simpler way?	**4. ACTIVITY** Sections 6 and 7 of Assessment for Learning model above. Monitor and support. Mini-plenaries. Time prompts and encouragement for good pace. Adjust activity if need is identified through assessment of performance or observation of pupils' attitudes and degree of challenge exhibited.	» Should some pupils work independently when rest are not? » Should some be expected to do more or do it in a more challenging way?
» Do you KNOW if everyone has learned at least the minimum you expected within this lesson?	**5. PLENARY** Sections 8 to 10 of Assessment for Learning model above. What have we learned? How have we used it? These are successful – how do we know? What if….? Where next?	» Do all pupils know what they have learned and can they say how their learning, skills and/or understanding are now different from the beginning of the lesson?

4 THE IMPORTANCE OF QUESTIONING

WHAT ARE QUESTIONING SKILLS?

Questioning skills are generally used as an element of assessment to determine pupils' understanding. Questioning is also a useful and effective form of differentiation that enables pupils of all abilities, and of different ages if necessary, to fully participate in the lesson. Not all teachers, however, fully develop the art of questioning in order to maximise the potential of this skill. Questioning skills do not usually come naturally to teachers and time spent in planning or considering potential questions to be used is good practice. Nevertheless, there are clear types and purposes for questions that should be known to all professionals and whole staff consideration of this issue may be a wise investment.

There are generally regarded to be three main types of questions; closed questions, optional questions and open questions.

WHAT ARE CLOSED QUESTIONS?

Closed questions usually involve the responder in only having to make one decision, 'Is it or isn't it?'

Thus the question usually involves only one variable, for example 'Is this a red pen?' or 'Can you see a duck?' These types of questions usually only require the responder to reply 'Yes' or 'No'. The challenge level is varied through the degree of difficulty there is in deciding which reply to use.

Closed questions are useful for involving less able pupils in more challenging discussions, or as part of a lead into more challenging questions.

WHAT ARE OPTIONAL QUESTIONS?

Optional questions usually give the responder two or more choices for response. The challenge level can range from low, operating more like a closed question, to high, operating more like an open question. At the basic level, if the respondent has the knowledge then the question is very easy, if s/he does not, s/he has a 50-50 chance through a guess.

Example 1 (optional):

'Is this pen red or blue?' = low level because the challenge level is similar to closed questions as the responder has a 50-50 chance of being right through a guess and the answer is modelled within the question. If the respondent has the knowledge the answer is very easy.

Example 2 (optional):

'Would you like a pizza or a burger?' = low level because although more thought may be required there is no wrong answer so the responder cannot be wrong.

Example 3 (optional):

'Was Guy Fawkes a hero or a villain?' = may be high or low according to whether this question had ever been posed and/or answered explicitly in previous lessons. If it had been discussed previously the respondent has only to recall and the question is low level. However, if the respondent has to deduce from a body of evidence that does not include an explicit answer, the question's difficulty increases in direct proportion to how explicit the evidence is.

Example 4 (optional):

'Which of these two XXXXX would demand the greatest skill?' = may be high or low in the same way as the previous example.

The challenge level of optional questions may be increased by asking pupils to justify their answers. Depending on the age and/or ability of the pupil, teachers may say things like;

'Can you use the 'because' word please?'

'Can you explain how you know?'

'Can you justify your answer please?'

WHAT ARE OPEN QUESTIONS?

Open questions usually demand that the respondent must reason or use logic to arrive at an answer. They should require some extension in the answer that might include opinion or justification. These questions are very good for all pupils but can be an excellent form of differentiation for the more able children. These questions often fall into the 'why?', 'how?' or 'what if…?' variety that demands reasoning.

Caution is needed as questions that can appear to be high in challenge may be low if the answer has been discussed previously and all the respondent is required to do is recall the answer.

Example 1 (open):

1. 'Why do you think this might be that way?' = degree of difficulty is still influenced by prior experience and learning. If the answer has been given previously this is recall, but if the learning aspect is new to pupils the challenge level may be high. The teacher's mental success criteria should be influenced by this. In addition, the teacher should consider whether the better response is the correct one or the one that shows greater reasoning and logic. Creative thinkers may see things from a different perspective to the majority and can put an interesting but different slant on an issue. Literal adults may see this as being a 'wrong' response rather than it being a potentially higher order response. If the respondent arrives at a combination of both reasoned and valid, this may be very high achievement.

2. 'How might this be improved?' Again the degree of challenge is influenced by prior exposure and learning.

Example 2 (open):

'Should parents be allowed to take their children on holiday at any time of the year, regardless of whether school is open?' or 'Are recent natural disasters a result of global warming?' Both these questions might be answered as though closed i.e. by 'Yes' or 'No'. However, there is an implied expectation of justification for the answer and the teacher should tell pupils that s/he expects an explanation for their opinion.

'What if…' questions can be extremely challenging because they imply that the respondent has to address a change in the variables. For example:

'We learned this and used it this way. What if I had asked you to do that instead? Would it have been the same or different?'

'A warning was sent to the stricken country's government prior to the onslaught of the tsunami. What if a radio operator had received the warning? How might the outcome have changed? What if a farmer had received the warning? Would the outcome have been the same?'

These types of questions have no right or wrong answer (at this point) and are a matter of opinion, although there may be clearer evidence for one opinion than another. The 'correct' answer could either be deemed to be the one the teacher expects or the one that is better reasoned, regardless of its final judgement. The best answer in this case might be the one that gives both points of view and then concludes with a final judgement.

However, the same cautions exist. All the above could be simple recall if the issues have already been explored, opinions formed and justification learned.

See also 'What might we do on a daily basis?' which includes further examples of open questions.

HOW DO WE USE QUESTIONS FOR DIFFERENT PURPOSES?

There are different types of questions that may be used for different purposes. Knowing what sort of skill a teacher is interrogating will inform her/his ability to use the answers formatively in order to plan better for the needs of the pupils. There are six main purposes for questions:

QUESTIONING FOR PURPOSE

Purpose	Examples
Recall of Facts	What are…? How many…? What is the name of…? Who was…?
Application of Facts	Is this a…? How much…? What pairs of numbers make…?
Procedural / Designing Ways	How are you going to…? What are you going to…? When are you going to…? How might we…? How could we…?
Predictive / Hypothesising	What do you think will…? How is it going to work? Why do you think…? Can you estimate…? Is … linked to…? Can you continue the pattern?
Observational	What is happening to it? How is it working? How are these different?
Interpretive	What made that happen? What did your results show? How do you know…? What does that tell you about…?
Speculative	What do you think might happen if…? Why do you think that might happen? How do you think you could…? Can you reason why…?
Conclusive	What do your results tell you? Why do you think that happened? How do you think that happened? What have we found out about…?

Clearly there are overlaps here, conclusive questions may still be speculative and interpretive questions may depend on observation, however the better the teacher understands the skills involved in answering the better s/he will know what to do next in order to better meet the needs of a pupil or class.

Furthermore, explicit teaching and explanation of the types of questions may support pupils in improved interpretation of and response to test questions.

5 THE IMPORTANCE OF TALK

'In schools young people need to articulate for themselves what they have learned, make explicit links between different areas of experience, and reflect on how something from one area can be applied to another.'

(Dr. Nicholas Tate, TES, March 2006)

Both the previous chapters emphasised the crucial role of talk in the teaching process.

IN ASSESSMENT FOR LEARNING TALK IS:

» the means by which the teacher knows whether what pupils think they have learned matches what s/he thinks has been taught

» the means by which the teacher knows whether pupils understand what they have to do in the activity

» the means by which the teacher knows whether pupils understand how the activity will demonstrate their understanding of what has been learned

» the means by which the teacher knows whether pupils understand how they can be successful, if that is not already explicit in the objectives

» the means by which the teacher knows whether pupils are applying that knowledge during the task

» the means by which the teacher knows whether pupils can still recall what they have learned and how and why they were doing what they were doing, at the end of the lesson or in a subsequent lesson

» the means by which the teacher knows whether pupils are able to transfer their knowledge to a new situation

IN CHAPTER 4, 'THE IMPORTANCE OF QUESTIONING SKILLS', TALK IS THE MAIN VEHICLE THROUGH WHICH A TEACHER IS ABLE TO ASSESS PUPILS' ABILITY TO DEPLOY ANALYTIC SKILLS OF:

» procedure
» prediction
» observation
» interpretation
» speculation
» conclusion

In addition, questioning skills may be used as an effective form of differentiation in the teaching process. However, the teaching and development of the skills of interactive talk and effective communication should also be planned for explicitly across the range of subjects and learning opportunities within the curriculum.

HOW CAN TALK BE FULLY UTILISED IN TEACHING AND LEARNING?

The issue of how and when talk is to be used as a planned teaching and learning tool in the classroom is one that should be addressed as a whole school priority. The truly creative curriculum will be talk driven in every sense as its priorities do not just allow but REQUIRE pupils to: collaborate, co-operate, hypothesise, research, plan, investigate, record, analyse, and present outcomes. This has to be done not only as individuals and in pairs, but also as members of a group.

Former HMCI David Bell observed that there was too much teacher talk and not enough pupil talk in primary classrooms. The creative curriculum should lessen the demand for paper outcomes to evidence achievement and should rely, more often, on pupils' capacity to verbalise their knowledge and understanding or demonstrate their skills.

Many OFSTED inspectors use the strategy of pupil interviews to confirm learning. These usually take place towards the end of the inspection and have potential impact on final judgements on teaching and learning. This is particularly true both when there is little evidence or inconclusive evidence in exercise books but pupils are able to talk confidently and in detail about their learning and ALSO when, despite copious recorded outcomes, pupils clearly have retained little knowledge or understanding of what has been taught.

In 'Write on Target' (2006) the writer says, 'If a child can't say it a child can't write it' when addressing the issues of teaching both correct grammar and the writing voice.

This publication asks the following question:

"If a child (able to speak) cannot say what he / she knows or understands then how do we know he / she truly does know or understand it?"

Recorded outcomes may be arrived at in many ways, not all of which ensure that the pupil knows, understands and will retain the learning in the future.

Teaching pupils to verbalise their knowledge and understanding through the ten steps of Assessment for Learning and the Five Step Lesson (pages 23 to 26) not only allows adults to assess what has been learned but also requires the pupil to clarify and summarise her / his learning in order to verbalise it. The act of verbalising the learning consolidates it and provides a 'hook' for the child to hang the learning on in order to find it again when required.

'Hooks' are planned strategies that enable pupils to make links to previous learning or to recall and access previous learning. Examples of effective hooks are:

> » Visual prompts such as seeing a previously used visual aid or work completed, use of the same resource or scaffold, or use of a trigger visual such as a title, caption, colour, logo, character, font or emblem that, having been explicitly explained, represents the learning.
>
> » Oral / aural prompts such as slogans, captions, chants, learned phrases, a significant piece of music, chorus or musical phrase or a song…..
>
> » Kinaesthetic prompts such as a particular brain gym activity, arm, hand or finger action.'

('Write on Target', Page 49, Ros. Wilson 2006)

Skills of oral communication are a crucial feature of life for most people. To give a pupil the skills of confident oratory and debate is a great gift to give. These skills, however, require teaching and 'expecting' pupils to discuss an aspect of learning several times a week will not necessarily improve these skills. Fifty years ago most homes had no television and to eat a meal on one's knee was unheard of. Meals were taken round a table, whether in a dining room or in a kitchen, and were almost always accompanied by lively conversation. Young children often listened to adults engaged in extended discussion and as they grew up they increasingly became a part of these debates.

In this era of television meals and eating at the desk the art of conversation is not always developed naturally within the home. Schools would do well to advise parents to insist on at least one family meal a week around a table without the television turned on. In addition, the giving of at least one 'talk' homework a week will promote this valuable skill.

In 'Write on Target' (the 'gold' book, Ros. Wilson, 2006) the writer recommends that pupils take home a weekly slip of paper upon which is written, 'My homework is to talk about…………..'. This is then repeated with the subject or stimulus for that week's 'Big Writing' topic. Parents will have had this process explained at induction and parents' evenings, and will know that this means they are to help their child to explore their ideas through talk and thus to scaffold their work for the next day.

HOW MIGHT THE TIMETABLE BE ADJUSTED FOR TALK?

We need to commit time for talking about aspects of talk as a valid activity in its own right. This might include the following:

> » How do we express different moods visually and through vocal expression?
>
> » How do we structure language for different purposes such as chatting to friends, talking to the teacher, asking a stranger for help and presenting information to a large gathering?
>
> » How do we use physical stance and gesture to compliment what we are saying?
>
> » How do we comment and respond, showing awareness of other participants, in different discussion opportunities such as informal conversations over a meal or a formal debate with strangers on a current issue?
>
> » How do we create links between earlier contributions to debate for courtesy and/or coherence; for example through using phrases such as, "As previously mentioned…." or "To refer to your earlier point…".

We need to timetable opportunities for pupils to participate in real and imagined situations that call for different types of talk, and provide them with a range of strategies and phrases for communicating appropriately. These opportunities can be planned both within the PSHE curriculum and citizenship as they are crucial aspects of personal, social and mental health skills and also of the successful social interaction that can contribute to an individual assuming a positive role in the society within which s/he lives.

There are, however, many opportunities within the academic curriculum for planned talk, focused discussion and debate. The modified Creative Curriculum Maps (Chapter 8), and the Optional Challenges and Mini-Challenges (Chapters 9 and 10) in this publication provide some examples of such opportunities, however there may well be an argument for re-introducing some of the following into the curriculum on a regular timetabled basis:

> » Formal debate on relevant curricular issues such as global warming, air pollution, the national smoking or fox hunting ban, local issues or created but plausible issues such as 'Should the council build a chicken farm on our school playground?' or 'Should all Year 5 and 6 pupils attend Saturday morning lessons for PE in order to free up more time for SAT practice during the week?' *
>
> » Formal oral presentation of findings as an individual or member of a group in one subject every week or two weeks.
>
> » Opportunities not only for role play and the reading and writing of play scripts but also to analyse and learn speeches or parts in a play.
>
> » Opportunities for role play and presentation skills to demonstrate knowledge and understanding within a specific aspect of learning in all subjects.
>
> » Opportunities to learn verse or poems by heart.
>
> » Opportunities to perform for different audiences such as their own class, a younger class, parents, the school or residents of a local retirement home.

The writer does NOT agree with this but it is a good issue to stimulate discussion!

Every timetable should include an identified opportunity for planned talk at minimum every two or three weeks, however talk should also be an integral aspect of learning on a daily basis.

It should be noted that the origional NLS promoted a strong model of dialogic teaching that has not generally been widely adopted. Reshaping a school's curriculum is a good opportunity to include this type of methodology.

WHAT CAN WE DO ON A DAILY BASIS?

Besides utilising talk as an assessment tool (see 'Assessment for Learning' and 'The Five Part Lesson') teachers should examine their personal attitudes to pupil talk. Some teachers are intrinsically opposed to pupil discussion and debate in lessons. This may be for some of the following reasons:

» because they were not 'allowed' to do that when they were young

» because they are afraid that it may get out of control

» because they are afraid that some pupils may just be 'chatting' and off task

» because they are worried that others may pass by and think there is no 'work' going on

» because they believe it is time wasted

» because they believe that learning should be evidenced through recorded outcomes

» because they are afraid that the Senior Managers in the school will feel time is being wasted

» because the ethos and the culture of the school does not value talk

These attitudes can take a long time to change and the head teacher and other Senior Managers must ensure that the vision of the school promotes the value of talk, that parents are aware of this and subscribe to it, and that it is a key aspect of the school's culture. This should include promoting and praising good use of talk both within the curriculum and in other areas of pupils' lives.

Above all, teachers must learn to value talk as an intrinsic aspect of every lesson and learning opportunity. They should regularly ask pupils to discuss what has just been said or experienced, to verbalise what they have just learned. In addition they should ask questions about their pupils' responses to many aspects of their learning, listening closely to their pupils' answers and responding appropriately.

IS THE WAY WE LISTEN IMPORTANT?

The way all adults listen to children is crucial. Listening should always be patient and respectful. Children should feel their opinion is valued and should not feel under pressure to answer briefly or quickly. For some people, verbalisation not only confirms and consolidates learning but it also inspires

further thinking and leads to the extension of ideas. Thus the thinking process is continuing WHILE the responder is speaking and this may lead to a hesitant or drawn out answer. Adults should wait patiently for the child to develop her / his thinking and then sometimes ask if she / he would like to re-verbalise it in a more succinct form.

As far as possible the listener should indicate involvement in the speaker's contribution. This might be done through maintaining eye contact (unless culturally inappropriate), through nodding and sometimes through small sounds of agreement. As far as possible the listener should avoid interrupting or 'cutting the speaker off' and children should be taught that this is rude.

As in all other aspects of teaching:

ADULTS SHOULD PRACTISE WHAT THEY PREACH!

We should talk with and listen to children in the way we would want others to talk with or listen to us!

ARE THERE SOME QUESTIONS THAT ARE PARTICULARLY HELPFUL IN DEVELOPING DISCUSSION AND CONVERSATION SKILLS?

Lists of questions for assessment of learning and understanding have already been provided. However, there are a range of questions that can encourage continued dialogue or extension of ideas and contributions.

The sorts of questions that encourage continued participation might include:

» How did you feel when you heard that / did that / saw that?

» Did you enjoy that or not? Why?

» What was hardest thing in doing that and why?

» How might we / you have improved that?

» Can you think of a different way we might have done that?

» What did you enjoy most about that activity / lesson / today / the visit?

» What might you learn next in order to improve?

» How else might you have shown that you have learned and understood that?

» Which of those did you prefer doing and why?

» Which of these do you like best and why?

» Have you always thought that? Why?

» Do you think most people would agree with that and why?

» Do you think older people / people from another place / people who are… would agree with that? Can you say why?

» Can you think of anyone who might not agree with that and why?

» Could there be any worrying or wrong result of that? Why?

» Would EVERYONE do that / say that / like that?

» Why do you think that?

HOW CAN WE MAKE DISCUSSIONS MORE FOCUSED?

Teachers should also consider ways of focusing the role of discussion in learning and of maximising its impact. Too often we ask pupils to 'discuss' an aspect of learning without focusing their discussion sufficiently to ensure a positive outcome. Giving pupils an outcome to achieve in their discussions often leads to more productive outcomes, although for more able pupils an open discussion can be a fruitful and sometimes surprising experience. The important questions are:

» 'Is the teacher clear about WHY the pupils are being asked to discuss and what is the intended outcome?'

» 'Will unfocused / open discussion ensure that outcome is achieved?'

If the intended outcome is creative thought such as might be achieved through a free 'brainstorm' then there may be no structure to the discussion. However, if there is a pre-determined outcome required the discussion may be scaffolded. The following are just two examples of the many ways a discussion might be scaffolded:

1. History: Year 6 Term 3 'Tudor Exploration'

Give each question AFTER the previous one has been discussed. Decide whether to take feedback before giving the next question.

i) Please discuss how life might have been on board the Santa Maria after several months at sea and before the mutiny. (5 minutes)

ii) What might Columbus have been thinking after the mutiny? (5 minutes)

iii) What must the sailors have been thinking as they were forced to sail on across the ocean? (5 minutes)

iv) Why do you think Columbus might have insisted on keeping going, instead of turning back as the sailors wished? (5 minutes)

v) How might events have been different had it happened in the year 2000?

2. Geography: Year 2 'Our Locality'

Children should be looking at a road that contrasts with the road their school is on i.e. if school is on a quiet street, then a busy main road, if the school is on a busy main road, then they should study a quiet lane. Ideally, they should have visited the contrasting road, although they may be looking at photographs (which they may have taken) for the purposes of discussion.

Alternatively they may be watching a video clip (visual literacy opportunity, see Chapter 6 'Visual Literacy').

In addition they should have been outside to the school's boundary and should have studied the road their school is on. During this activity they might discuss questions such as:

i) 'Is it usually busy or quiet?'

ii) 'What can you see on the road?'

iii) 'What can you see along the sides of the road?'

iv) 'What can you hear?'

When these pre-discussion activities have all taken place the teacher might ask questions such as:

i) Close your eyes please. Think of the road outside our school as you saw it when we went out to look this morning. How did it look? Was it busy or quiet? What was moving on the road? What was parked along the road? Were there any people around? What were they doing? Talk to your friends and see how much you can all remember please.' (5 minutes) Take feedback.

ii) What words would describe our school's road? Quiet? Busy? Can you think of any more? Can you think of some 'wow' words? (3 to 5 minutes with feedback).

iii) Now let's look at the road we visited (or 'in the video'). What is the SAME about this road as the one our school is on? (2 minutes)

iv) Now, see how many things you can find that are different. (5 minutes)

v) What words would you use to describe this road? Can you find some 'wow' words? (5 minutes with feedback).

vi) Now here is the big talk…. Which road would you most want to live on and why? (5 minutes – more if very engaged).

vii) Let's find out how many of us would like to live on the busy road and why.

viii) Let's see who wants to live on the quiet road and why.

ix) Could we think of a sort of chart that we could make to show these answers? (Mathematics and possible ICT opportunity).

6 VISUAL LITERACY

WHAT IS VISUAL LITERACY?

Visual literacy is the ability to 'read', interpret and understand information that is presented in pictorial or moving image media.

Sources of visual literacy can be found in many forms, including:

- » Video
- » DVD
- » Digital image
- » Photograph
- » Sound
- » Electronic text
- » Other animation
- » Performance

WHY SHOULD WE USE VISUAL LITERACY TO ENHANCE PUPILS' LEARNING?

Children of today usually experience a high level of exposure to television, DVDs, videos and other animations and it would be foolish to ignore the potential impact of these media on their lives and the opportunities they present for contributing to a child's education. If we ask children whether they have more books than videos and DVDs at home we might be surprised to discover that moving images are gaining in popularity over the traditional texts.

Many children, particularly boys, may lack the motivation to write, especially if the writing appears to have no purpose or audience. Incorporating visual literacy into the teaching sequence can be a real motivator for both writing and discussion.

Films and television play a central role in the lives and cultural understanding of many of our children and it is becoming increasingly widely accepted that good teaching should acknowledge and build upon children's existing experiences. Videos are often motivating and can make an exciting way to start a Unit of Work or a lesson as opposed to using a piece of text. Talented teachers plan a range of ways to introduce learning across a Unit of Work or a term or half term. These might include:

- » Big Books
- » Electronic text
- » Video
- » Photograph
- » Newspaper or magazine articles
- » Shared text

The use of a range of contrasting examples of visual literacy offers pupils both variety and enhancement.

Many young children enjoy sharing their personal experiences in watching films and videos and can quickly learn the codes and conventions through which stories are told in these media. This knowledge is easily transferable to both reading and writing. The following literary skills can be enhanced and scaffolded through watching moving media:

- » Description
- » Retell
- » Interpretation
- » Prediction
- » Further development of a story
- » Drawing conclusions
- » Inferring
- » Deducing
- » Sequencing events
- » Paragraphing skills through scene changes

In other words, the strengths of learning through one media can create conceptual structure and a scaffold around the weaknesses of another.

"…television and video are key components in the toolkit children use on their journey towards decoding the abstractedness of written language."

(N. Browne, 'Young Children's Literacy Development and the Role of Televisual Texts', Falmer Press, London, 1999)

HOW MIGHT WE USE VISUAL LITERACY?

Before we use a visual stimulus we should always be clear about:

1. The reason for selection of the image
2. How we will make clear the intended learning outcome
3. What success in the learning outcome will look like

It is good practice to give pupils a key question to steer their learning before they watch or see an item of media. This sharpens their observations and helps to ensure that they achieve the intended outcome.

Greatest success may be achieved through selecting items that are not too time intensive so that learning can take place through repeated viewings and discussion. The following structure can be a powerful model:

Viewing	Depth	Possible Outcomes
1.	May be unprepared with no key questions.	Simple recount / retell / did we like it or not?
2.	Given first key question, for example, 'How did they make it seem exciting or scary?'	Recall detail, for example, 'It was dark and then there was a big crash.'
3.	Given more specific key question to achieve desired learning. For example, 'How did they use sound in particular, to get that effect?'	Recall more detail, for example, 'There was spooky music and the sound of heavy footsteps and then there was the loud crash.'

Questions may focus around technical aspects similar to the following:

» Use of light
» Use of colour
» Use of sound
» Use of camera angle
» Characterisation
» Setting
» Plot
» Prediction

Discussion may be focused through either:

» Giving the whole class the same key question/s
» Using the envoy or snowball techniques where different groups having different key questions and then 'experts' travelling to other groups so that all move forward on all aspects.

Interesting dimensions can be added through the early viewing being through listening to the sound or dialogue only, initially, without visual support and seeing what conclusions or predictions might be made. Alternatively, it may be through seeing the visual only and suggesting what sound track might be added or what plot may be unfolding.

ARE THERE SIMPLE WAYS TO USE VISUAL LITERACY?

In order to use visual stimulus effectively the adult does not have to have sophisticated technical knowledge or access to advanced technology. The following are some of the simple ways we can use visual literacy:

» Photographs
» Advertisements (newspapers and magazines)
» Advertisements (television)
» Excerpts from popular soaps and children's tv
» Video clips

It is possible to buy a small piece of equipment called a 'Freeview USB stick' for less than fifty pounds (currently available on Amazon.com). This quickly and easily captures short excerpts from television for use in the classroom.

The following two photographs represent simple ways to use challenging and stimulating images for different purposes.

Questions for pupils might include any of the following:

» What do you think is happening here?
» What might have happened before this photograph was taken?
» What might this person be saying or thinking?
» What might happen next?
» Do you think this event is the outcome of a man-made or natural disaster?
» How many possible causes can you think of for this event?
» What questions might you want to ask about this?
» What are the environmental implications of this?
» How could you describe the actual images you can see here?
» What sort of sound track / music might be used to enrich this picture?
» How could we use this picture to raise environmental awareness?
» Which of these two pictures causes you most concern and why?

CONCLUSIONS

Visual Literacy can provoke responses that are not always possible through the written word alone. They promote discussion and the development of oral and aural skills. Visual media can enhance both fiction and non-fiction based writing in all year groups and can complement or strengthen cross-curricular links.

When teachers first take on board the use of visual media they can be amazed by the changes in attitude, motivation, attainment and contribution of many of their pupils.

They also report a remarkable impact on all aspects of learning, including:

» Oral
» Aural
» Written
» Read
» Observation
» Interpretation

With acknowledgements to:

Michelle Wraith, (Big Writing / Teaching and Learning Consultant, Andrell Education)

Michael Thorp, (Deputy Head Teacher, Swain House Primary School and Boys' Achievement / Visual Literacy Adviser, Andrell Education)

From bfi Education; www.bfi.org.uk:

'Look Again! A teaching guide to using film and television with three to eleven year olds'

'Starting Stories – A film and literacy resource for three to seven year olds'

'Story Shorts – a resource for Key Stage 2'

Browne N. 'Young Children's Literacy Development and the Role of Televisual Texts', Falmer Press, London (1999)

Robinson M. 'Children reading Print and television', Falmer Press, London 1997)

Oldham J. 'The book of the film: enhancing print literacy at Key Stage 3, English in Education, NATE, Sheffield, (1999)

Parker D. ' You've Read The Book Now Make the Film: Moving Image Media, Print Literacy & Narrative, English in Education, NATE, Sheffield, (1999)

The National Strategies

7 THE 'CREATIVE CURRICULUM' LONG TERM PLAN

The model for 'The Creative Curriculum' Long Term Plan provided here has been planned to reflect the coverage legally required by the National Curriculum. The linking opportunities across subjects and the content foci suggested are referenced to the QCA Schemes of Work, but with considerable reduction. This is to give confidence to those teachers for whom the Schemes of Work are currently their primary curricular knowledge and enables a teacher to refer back to the referenced Scheme for further subject knowledge or ideas for activities if s/he is unclear about an aspect.

HOW MIGHT A TEACHER OR TEAM PHYSICALLY ORGANISE AND MANAGE THE CURRICULUM PLANS?

The class or year team's curriculum might be organised within plastic pockets in a ring binder. The Long Term Plan would be in the front pocket with the school's rationale / policy for the curriculum inserted back-to-back. A cover page naming the term and the focus title would be placed forward facing in the second pocket. The medium term map for the first term would then be inserted in the left hand pocket (back of second pocket) facing backwards with the actual plan on the school's format facing forwards in the third pocket. The appropriate QCA Unit/s could then be inserted behind the plan for reference if needed. The map for the second term would now be placed in the backwards facing position of the third pocket, with the plan and QCA Units forwards in the fourth pocket. The map for the third term would now be placed in the backwards facing position of the fourth pocket, with the plan and QCA Units forwards in the fifth pocket.

Schools are encouraged, however, to replace the content foci of all models provided here with their own priorities, whilst retaining the intrinsic process of the subject as defined in the statutory National Curriculum orders.

WHAT IS THE ROLE OF A SCHOOL'S LONG TERM CURRICULUM PLAN?

A school's Long Term Plan organises the whole curriculum into a series of Units of Work, (both continuous and blocked – see page 49) that enable the school to ensure full coverage and management of time. The plan should be simple and clear and its aim should be to provide a coherent overview only, so that all may easily see how the curriculum is managed across an academic year or cycle of years. It is not the purpose of a long term plan to provide the detail of the curriculum but it should incorporate a simple system of headings and references to enable easy access to the detail which will be in the Medium Term Plans.

The following are the usual audiences for a school's Long Term Plan:

» The head teacher
» All teachers and Teaching Assistants
» Governors of the school
» LEA officers
» HMI and OFSTED inspectors
» Consultants
» Parents (in many primary schools)

A tension for schools at the current time of urgent curricular reorganisation is the fact that the National Curriculum remains the legal requirement of all state schools and until the law is amended or repealed the amount of freedom available remains unclear.

Schools are being urged to free up curricular time for increased opportunities for creativity, to increase creativity within the existing curricular content and also within the way pupils learn and develop as learners. In addition schools are being urged to make subject content more relevant for their pupils. These priorities could be seen to imply dispensing with some of the legal requirement.

HOW CAN THE LITERACY AND NUMERACY UNITS OF THE NATIONAL STRATEGIES COMPLEMENT THIS PROCESS?

As the rigidity of the literacy and numeracy strategies is freed up through the revision of the Primary National Strategies, schools must take care not to lose the huge strengths gained from the original strategies in terms of rigour and improved subject knowledge.

The skill is to restructure these aspects of the strategies to give them coherence and purpose, not to abandon them.

Pupils (and particularly boys) like to see a purpose for learning a skill and to have stimulating and purposeful reasons to use and apply it.

One of the great strengths of the National Literacy Strategy, for example, is the focused teaching of the characteristics of text types. Prior to the introduction of the NLS few of us had ever been taught these characteristics, and we wrote different text types with a degree of success commensurate only to our intuitive understanding of how that text should be constructed.

The writer suggests that, having redeveloped a coherent and relevant long term plan for their school, managers re-sequence the units that teach, develop and consolidate these characteristics so that they may be used and applied in relevant and coherent contexts (see Chapter 12 and Appendix 1).

'We think that school communities can meet the curriculum specification, stick within the regulations and devise the best fit with the local need.

The willingness is infectious: schools want to know they have permission to do things differently. Press the play button; we have been on pause for long enough. The learner needs to engage. You don't need permission or an invitation. Let's make learning irresistible!'

(Mick Waters, Director of Curriculum QCA, TES, May 2006)

HOW CAN WE ACHIEVE REDUCTION IN THE EXISTING CURRICULUM?

The National Curriculum is a mix of predominantly PROCESS driven subjects, predominantly CONTENT driven subjects and subjects with a reasonable balance of both.

It is important to note that all subjects have a process and that the process is a crucial aspect of the subject, often the most crucial; however it is process that often becomes neglected in a heavily content- overloaded curriculum.

Process may be described as, 'Behaving like a......'

E.g. Behaving like a scientist, historian, artist or geographer.

It is the process of the subject that requires pupils to be actively involved in hypothesising, planning, resourcing, investigating, producing, observing, recording, evaluating, adapting, reviewing and re- hypothesising. It is the creative implementation of opportunities for this process within every subject that enables teachers to cater for pupils' different learning styles, preferences and creative thought. The contexts for that implementation cater for their personal interests and response to stimulus.

The following is a generalisation and it MUST be born in mind that there is a mix of both in all subjects.

THE NATIONAL CURRICULUM AND RELIGIOUS EDUCATION

Currently Predominantly Content Driven:
History
Geography
Religious Education

Currently Predominantly Process Driven:
English
Art
Music
Physical Education
Design and Technology
ICT

Currently Balanced:

Mathematics
Science
Modern Foreign Languages

NB Religious Education is not a subject of the National Curriculum but is required by law. It is mainly content in the majority of Local Authority Syllabi.

Although this is the current structure of the actual curriculum orders, the QCA Schemes of Work have converted the process driven subjects into heavily content laden subjects through appearing to prescribe a large amount of content through which to achieve the process.

As previously stated, the impact of this is for many teachers to plough a furrow through content whilst forgetting the essence of the process.

If we revert to our original hypothesis as to the needs of citizens in the twenty-first century:

WHAT MIGHT THE CORE SKILLS INCLUDE?

1. The ability to talk confidently, using a sophisticated range of language structures and vocabulary to discuss, debate, explain, justify, describe and recount.

2. The ability to use ICT confidently for the full range of purposes, including processing, presenting, researching, analysing, computing, illustrating and communicating.

3. Physical and mental well being, good health and an active life style.

4. The ability to work and play with others, co-operating and collaborating, responding and communicating successfully.

5. The ability to work alone and with others to hypothesise, plan , investigate, record, analyse, conclude and re-hypothesise.

6. Reading skills that include:

» The ability to read at progressively more challenging levels

» The ability to synthesise out information from texts, to interpret information and to use and apply information.

» Higher order reading comprehension skills including the ability to infer and deduce from text.

7. Writing skills that include:

The four Basic Skills of Writing including the ability to use accurate grammatical structures, a neat and accurate cursive style, accurate spelling both through basic sight vocabulary and phonic skills and the ability to construct and punctuate sentences accurately. (See: 'Write on Target' – the 'gold book', Chapter 8, Ros. Wilson, 2006)

» The ability to accurately apply the characteristics of the full range of text types and genres

» The ability to respond appropriately to a wide range of stimuli

» A higher level writing voice as achieved through the VCOP of Big Writing, (see 'Strategies for Immediate Impact on Writing Standards', 2003, and 'Write on Target', Chapters 3 and 8, 2006).

8. Be numerate and use and apply a high level of numeracy skills confidently and accurately in their work across the curriculum.

9. Be creative through music, art, gymnastics, dance, design and construction.

10. Confidently tackle and solve problems involving some or all of the core skills.

11. Confidently make decisions and choices without fear of risk taking.

12. Be creative learners who are inquisitive and able to work independently through self-motivation.

WHAT MIGHT THE LOCAL AND SURROUNDING COMMUNITY CONTRIBUTE TO A SCHOOL'S CURRICULUM?

1. Positive role models in all aspects of learning, including literature, the arts, sport, religion, commerce and industry.

2. Field study, research and investigation within the environment.

3. Cultural enrichment and learning opportunities through museums, galleries, centres for religions, theatres, stately homes and other facilities.

4. Work experience and learning opportunities within the world of business and commerce.

5. Citizenship and enrichment through understanding of the importance of rules, trust and mutual respect for life in a civilised society, and ways in which membership of a complex society is interdependent.

6. Support, services and networks.

7. Community links.

HOW MIGHT THE DEVELOPMENT AND CONSOLIDATION OF THESE CORE SKILLS BE ACHIEVED?

Develop a flexible curriculum model that:

1. promotes learning through investigation and research

2. promotes hypothesis and curiosity

3. promotes risk taking and a lack of fear of being wrong

4. promotes the use and application of the full range of core skills across all curriculum areas

5. promotes creative behaviour

6. promotes choice and decision making

7. is not heavily content laden but promotes exciting and challenging learning opportunities

8. Has in-built re-cycling of opportunities for learning, consolidating, using and applying the core skills for life in a wide range of interesting, exciting and challenging situations across the curriculum.

Three of the subjects of the National Curriculum are core subjects, English, mathematics and science, and thus are subject to national testing. The remainder are known as the foundation subjects.

The overloading of content in the foundation subjects through the introduction of the QCA Schemes of Work has resulted in many teachers having to take a 'pick and mix' approach to their interpretation. As a result aspects of some foundation subjects have become fragmented and occasionally incoherent.

In order to provide pupils with rich opportunities for the development of the above core skills through as wide range of varied learning opportunities as possible, schools need to re-identify the process of the subject and teach the core skills through pupils' development within the process.

The process of all subjects is embodied within the Level Descriptions through which a subject is to be assessed in the National Curriculum. These skills have been synthesised out and listed in the hierarchy of skills provided in this publication. However, the following is a simplified summary:

Within any subject pupils should be taught the following processes:

1. How to speculate or develop a hypothesy

2. How to collect evidence

3. How to experiment or investigate

4. How to observe and draw conclusions

5. How to see things from different perspectives

6. How to improve or suggest improvements for their work

7. How to record or present their learning outcomes

8. How to use their learning to extend learning or develop a new hypothesis

9. How to achieve outcomes through working alone, as a pair and as a member of a group.

If the creative curriculum enabled the teaching of the core skills through the above processes within each subject, we would better enable pupils to enjoy and enthuse about learning, achieve well and ultimately to achieve economic well-being. These are the aspirations of 'Every Child Matters'.

This publication is intended to provide a bridge for teachers and schools who wish to develop a more flexible curriculum that builds on existing curricular models and subject knowledge, the links potentially available across subjects and the potential for creativity in delivery of the short tem curriculum.

WHAT ARE THE THREE STAGES OF CURRICULUM PLANNING AND HOW DO THEIR PURPOSES DIFFER?

Long Term Curriculum:

Duration:

» A year or longer (Long Term Plan)

Purpose:

» To ensure coverage of the statutory curriculum
» To organise curricular priorities and responsibilities
» To communicate the above

Medium Term Curriculum:

Duration:

» A term, half term or specific number of weeks (Units or Schemes of Work)

Purpose:

» To determine the process and content to be covered within the Unit
» To organise the teaching sequence for the Unit
» To ensure coverage of the subject's requirements
» To inform teaching / subject knowledge
» To ensure all pupils have equal entitlement and access if more than one class in a year
» To inform resourcing
» To inform others

Short Term Curriculum:

Duration:

» A lesson, day, week or two weeks (Lesson Plans)

Purpose:

» To inform teaching and learning
» To ensure achievement of planned learning outcomes
» To ensure access and achievement for all pupils
» To inform subject knowledge
» To inform resourcing
» To inform others

Generally reduction is best achieved within the foundation subjects by:

» reducing the number of content driven units to be delivered
» reducing the amount of content within a given unit

Schools should look at the FACTS being taught within foundation subject units and decide if they are all relevant and important for their pupils. They should remember that the PROCESS is the most important element of a subject. If an individual knows how to research, investigate, draw conclusions etcetera s/he is able to develop or identify content for her / himself.

The Hierarchy of Learning Skills promotes process driven assessment.

How is the Creative Curriculum Long Term Plan constructed?

'The Creative Curriculum' Long Term Plan provided below has been planned to reflect the coverage legally required by the National Curriculum, however the linking opportunities across subjects and the content foci suggested are referenced to a selection of the QCA Schemes of Work. This is to give confidence to those teachers for whom the Schemes of Work are currently their primary curricular knowledge and enables a teacher to refer back to the referenced scheme for further subject knowledge or ideas for activities if s/he is unclear about an aspect. However, schools are encouraged to replace the content foci with their own priorities when more appropriate, retaining the PROCESS of the subject as defined in the National Curriculum statutory orders. (Models for this are provided in Appendices 1 and 2).

Clusters of subject skills, content and knowledge have been given a summarising title, (usually already existent in the National Curriculum) followed by the National Curriculum, (NC) references to allow teachers to refer back to the NC and see precisely what is required to be covered.

For example, the first cluster on the Year 3 Term 2 section is science and has a title of 'Variation and Classification'. The reference is Sc 2. 1c, 4abc.

Sc 2 refers the reader to the second Attainment Target, (AT) in the science Programmes of Study, (PoS). This AT is entitled 'Living Things' and the content is about the life cycles and impact of plants and animals, including humans. The references 1c and 4abc, (4a, 4b,4c) refer the reader to the precise items of the PoS suggested for inclusion in this term. All numerical references are taken directly from the National Curriculum.

The whole termly allocation has been given an umbrella title that enables the main focus for the term to be described simply and that promotes the development of other thematic links.

Year 3 Term 2 has been given the title 'Animal Kingdoms' and science, geography, design and technology, art, music and P.E. have all been identified as having subject content that links well to this theme.

ARE THE UMBRELLA TITLES AND THE SUGGESTED CONTENT OPTIONAL?

The entire Long Term Plan provided below is only a model. It has been successfully adopted and implemented by many schools but in all cases the school has been urged to adapt it and reduce the content or the number of some foundation subject opportunities.

The umbrella titles are entirely optional and should be changed whenever that would increase coherence for either teachers or pupils.

Further opportunities for potential thematic links with other subjects, particularly literacy, mathematics and Personal, Social, Health and Citizenship studies, (PSHCE) should be identified by the teaching team, possibly in a similar form on the rear of the plan. The format of the Long Term Plan could be reproduced on the back and the additional subjects recorded there.

The existing plan could be separated into 3 pages covering Key Stage 1, Lower Key Stage 2 and Upper Key Stage 2 allowing expansion of the boxes to include other subject references, both further thematically linked subject foci and discrete ongoing and blocked subject content.

Alternatively the modified plan could be re-presented in a revised form. The foci for subjects that do not have natural links and need to be taught discretely should also be included.

Continuous or ongoing subject content is the strands of certain subjects that are taught in a continuum that starts or ends according to the dictate of the total phase time available or the achievement of a whole body that requires long term development, rather than a fixed, medium or short term block of time. Examples of this might be skills such as planning and evaluation in Science, D & T or PE, aspects of number in Mathematics A.T. 2, and the basic skills of reading and writing.

Blocked subject content is any body of skills, content or knowledge that can usefully be started at a set point and taught for a predicted number of weeks, at which point it can be successfully concluded, although a more advanced level of knowledge or understanding may be planned in a new unit at a later point. Most referenced subjects on the Long Term Plan provided as a model are blocked units that may be taught within a number of weeks, a half term or term.

These often include the content of the subject and provide the contexts through which the key or core skills, often ongoing, may be learned.

Schools should make their own decisions as to whether to change termly umbrella titles and suggested termly content. They should decide whether to add further links as suggested above, and which other subjects might be taught discretely, running alongside within the time frame but not linking in any way.

Finally they should decide how long each subject focus is to run, bearing in mind the Dearing recommendation for light touch and heavy touch subject foci.

For example, in Year 3 Term 2, 'Animal Kingdoms', a school may wish to disregard the QCA Unit for Art, 'Can we change places?' and develop their own art unit through study of animals in works of art, or study of patterns in coats and camouflage, or life studies of small pets.

It is perfectly acceptable for some foundation subjects not to be running within a given half term or even, occasionally, a term. Subjects like history, geography and design and technology lend themselves very well to being taught in intensive blocks of study and then might not appear on the next half or full term maps.

Art and music may also lend themselves to this in terms of blocked content, although in the spirit of the creative curriculum the skills of both subjects should be applied throughout the thematic link whenever possible.

HOW MIGHT A SCHOOL ADAPT THE LONG TERM PLAN?

The staff of a school should discuss the Long Term Plan, as it is written, and its implications. They should ask themselves the following questions:

1. Should all these subjects be running all term?

2. Might some subjects only run for a short, blocked period e.g. five weeks or one half of the term?

3. Are all these Units appropriate for our pupils?

4. Might we replace this suggested Unit with a more appropriate alternative that still enables delivery of the intended National Curriculum PROCESS through a more relevant content?

5. Are these suggested links the best links we can identify?

6. Can we improve the linkage by moving or substituting Units?

7. Can we plan further opportunities in other subjects not planned here, that would link well under this title? E.g. English or mathematics?

HOW CAN WE ADAPT THIS PLAN FOR MIXED-AGE CLASSES?

A school with mixed-age classes needs a cycle of planning that matches the number of ages within the class.

Thus:

- » Two years within a class requires a two year plan
- » Three years within a class requires a three year plan
- » Four years within a class requires a two year plan with changed CONTENT focus in the third and fourth years for the foundation subjects when repeated.

The following is a model for adapting The Creative Curriculum Long Term Plan for a pure Year 1/2 , 3/4, 5/6 mix:

1. Rename Year 1 on the plan as KS1 Year A

2. Rename Year 2 as KS1 Year B

3. Rename Year 3 as LKS2 Year A (Lower Key Stage 2)

4. Rename Year 4 as LKS2 Year B (Lower Key Stage 2)

5. Rename Year 5 as UKS2 Year A (Upper Key Stage 2)

6. Rename Year 6 as UKS2 Year B (Upper Key Stage 2)

All classes run Year A plans the first year and Year B plans the second year.

NB: Ensure the process and skills are differentiated across the two years in short term planning.

The following is the overview of the Long Term Curriculum Plan for Key Stages 1 and 2, organised under thematic titles that enable the medium and short term planning of strong cross-curricular links (see Chapter 8), and the addressing of the core skills across the curriculum through cross-curricular links.

All allocations and titles are models only and should be changed to meet the needs of pupils, schools and the community.

Examples of changes to thematic titles might include:

Year 2 Term 1: name the locality to be studied e.g. 'Linthwaite', 'Halifax' or 'West Yorkshire'.

Year 2 Term 2: 'Our World'

Year 2 Term 3: name the resort to be studied e.g. 'Scarborough' or 'Brighton'

Year 5 Term 1: 'The Victorians'

Year 5 Term 2: 'The Calder', 'The Amazon' or 'The Thames'

Year 5 Term 3: 'Transport' or 'Travel'

The core subjects of English, mathematics and I.C.T. should be planned in through the medium term plans and then mapped to ensure full coverage (see chapter 12 for model).

EXEMPLAR LONG TERM CURRICULUM PLAN

Yr.	Autumn Term		Spring Term		Summer Term	
1	**"OURSELVES"**		**"HOMES LONG AGO"**		**"AROUND OUR SCHOOL"**	
	Sc.2abcd	Ourselves	Sc4.3ab	Light and Dark	Sc2.4ab	Variation/Classification
	Sc4.2ab	Pushes and Pulls	Sc3.1abcd	Grouping Materials	Sc2.1ab,2de	Lifecycles
	Hist1-5	Changes in Our Lives	Hist U 2	Homes Long Ago	Geo U1	Around Our School
	Art U1A	Self Portrait	D&T U1D	Homes	D&T U5	Playgrounds
	D&T U1C	Eat More Fruit & Veg	Art U1B	Investigating Materials	Art U2C	Can Buildings Speak?
	Music U2	Sounds Interesting	MusU3	The Long & The Short of It	PE	Gymnastics, Dance, Games
	PE	Dance, Gymnastics, Games	PE	Dance, Gymnastics, Games	Music U4	Feel The Pulse
2	**"OUR LOCALITY"**		**"THE WORLD AROUND US"**		**"THE SEASIDE"**	
	Sc2.2g/Sc4.3cd	Senses	Sc2.3abc	Growing Plants	Sc3.2ab	Changing Materials
	Sc4.1abc	Electricity	Sc2.5abc,1c	Living Things	Sc4.2c	Speed & Movement
	Geo U2(link)	Our Locality	Hist U4/5	People/Place Study	Hist U3	Seaside Holidays
	Hist U1	Toys	ArtU2B	Mother Nature, Designer	Geo U4	Going to the Seaside
	Art U1C	What is Sculpture?	D&T U2B	Puppets	D&T U2A	Vehicles
	D&T U2C	Winding Up	U2D (Link)	Joseph's Coat	Art U 2A	Picture This!
	PE	Dance, Gymnastics, Games	PE	Dance, Gymnastics, Games	Music U7	Rain, Rain, Go Away
	Music U6	What's The Score?	Music U5	Taking Off	PE	Dance, Gymnastics, Games
3	**"SETTLEMENT"**		**"ANIMAL KINGDOMS"**		**"TUDOR TIMES"**	
	Sc3.1a2a	Grouping/Mixing Materials	Sc2.1c,4abc	Variation and	Sc2.1ab,2ab	Teeth & Diet
	Sc4.3abcd	Light & Sight		Classification	Sc4.2ae	Pushes & Pulls, Magnets
	Hist U6	Invaders	Sc3.1^e	Solids, Liquids & Gases	Geo U24	Passport to the World
	Geo U9	Village Settlers	Geo U18(Link)	Animal Environs	HistU8 (U7 Link)	Tudor Times
	Art U3B	Investigating Pattern	D&T U3C	Moving Monsters	ArtU3A	Portraying Relationships
	D&T U3A	Packaging	Art 3C	Can We Change Places?	D&T 3D	Photograph Frames
	PE U1	Invasion Games	Music U9	Animal Magic	PE U1	Athletic Activities
	U3	Gymnastics	PE U3	Dance	U1	Striking/fielding
	Music U10	Play It Again	U1	Net/wall	Music U11	The Class Orchestra
4	**"CHANGE"**		**"CONTRASTING UK"**		**"LIGHT & SOUND"**	
	Sc2.5abcde	Food Chains & Adaptation	Sc2.3abc	Plant Growth/Nutrition	Sc4.1abc,Sc3.1c	Electricity
	Sc3.2bcdfg	Changing State	Sc3.2bde	Evaporation& Condensation	Sc4.3efg	Sound
	Geo U6	Our Local Area	Geo U22(link)	UK Locality	Hist U9	Children in 2nd World War
	U19(link)	Spending Time	Hist U10	Ancient Civilisation	D&T U4D	Alarms
	D&T U4A	Money Containers	Art U4C	Journeys	Art U4A	Viewpoints
	Art U4B	Take A Seat	D&T U3B	Sandwich Snacks	Music U13	Painting With Sound
	PE U4	Gymnastics	Music U12	Dragon Scales	PE U4	Gymnastics
	U1	Outdoor & Adventurous	PE U2	Invasion Games	U4	Dance
	Mus U14	Salt, Pepper ,Vinegar	U2	Outdoor & Adventurous	U2	Athletic Activities
5	**"THE WAY WE LIVE"**		**"WATER"**		**"PLANET EARTH"**	
	Sc2.1ab,2cdefgh	Life Processes	Sc3.1bde	Rocks & Soils	Sc4.4abcd	Earth & Beyond
		Humans & Exercise		Keeping Warm	Sc2.1b,3d	Plant Lifecycles
	Sc3.3abcde	Separating Mixtures	Sc4.2bcde	Forces & Friction	Sc2. 5f	Micro-organisms
	Hist U11/12	Victorian Times	Geo U11	Water	Geo U20	Local Traffic
	Geo U12	High Street	U14 (Link)	The River	Hist U13	Change Since 1948
	D&T U4E	Lighting it Up	Art U5B	Containers	Art U5C	Talking Textiles
	Art U5A	Objects & Meanings	D&T U5D	Bread (or Biscuits)	D&T U5A	Musical Instruments
	PE U1	Net/wall Games	Mus U16	Cyclic Patterns	Mus U18	Journey Into Space
	U5	Gymnastics	PE U3	Invasion Games	PE U3	Athletic Activities
	Mus U17	Roundabout	U5	Dance	U3	Outdoor & Adventurous
6	**"THE GREEKS"**		**"BOOKS"**		**"THE CARIBBEAN"**	
	Sc	Review Audit & Priorities	Sc2,3,4	Revision	Sc2	Flora & Fauna
	Hist U 14/15	Ancient Greeks	Hist U20 (Link)	Famous People	Geo U22(Link)	Caribbean Study
	Geo U15	Mountain Environs	Art U6C	A Sense of Place	Hist U19	Tudor Exploration
	Art U6A	People in Action	D&T U6D	Controllable Vehicles	D&T U6A	Shelters
	D&T U5C	Moving Toys	Mus U20	Stars, Hide Your Fires	Art U6B	What a Performance
	PE U6	Gymnastics	PE U3	Outdoor & Adventurous	PE U6	Dance
	U2	Striking/fielding	U4	Invasion Games	U2	Net/wall
	Mus U19	Songwriter			U3	Athletic Activities

8 THE MEDIUM TERM CREATIVE
CURRICULUM MAPS

The Medium Term 'Creative Curriculum Maps' (CCMs) enable teachers to see curricular links at a glance and thus to use the key questions, (medium term objectives) to inform their short term planning. Again, the subject content should be changed or adapted as appropriate; to reflect the school's revised Long Term Plan, whilst retaining the process.

NB: Only the subjects contributing to the thematic subject links as driving or supporting subjects, have been defined on the CCMs and the remaining subjects might be recorded in a similar format or in subject boxes on the rear of the map or adapted map.

WHAT MIGHT THE LOCAL AND SURROUNDING COMMUNITY CONTRIBUTE TO A SCHOOL'S CURRICULUM?

1. Positive role models in all aspects of learning, including literature, the arts, sport, religion, commerce and industry.

2. Field study, research and investigation within the environment.

3. Cultural enrichment and learning opportunities through museums, galleries, centres for religions, theatres, stately homes and other facilities.

4. Work experience and learning opportunities within the world of business and commerce.

5. Citizenship and enrichment through understanding of the importance of rules, trust and mutual respect for life in a civilised society, and ways in which membership of a complex society is interdependent.

6. Support, services and networks.

7. Community links.

HOW MIGHT THE DEVELOPMENT AND CONSOLIDATION OF THESE CORE SKILLS BE ACHIEVED?

Develop a flexible curriculum model that:

» Promotes learning through investigation and research

» Promotes hypothesis and curiosity

» Promotes risk taking and a lack of fear of being wrong

» Promotes the use and application of the full range of core skills across all curriculum areas

» Promotes creativity

» Promotes choice and decision making

» Is not heavily content laden but promotes exciting and challenging learning opportunities

» Has in-built re-cycling of opportunities for learning, consolidating and using and applying the core skills for life within a wide range of interesting, relevant, exciting and challenging situations across the curriculum.

IT IS CRUCIAL THAT THE FOLLOWING MAPS ARE REGARDED AS A MODEL ONLY AND ARE ADAPTED TO SUIT THE NEEDS OF THE PUPILS AND COMMUNITY OF THE SCHOOL.

NB if a school wished, the key questions/content of any individual map could be lifted off into a standard planning format to form a Medium Term Plan, with activities, resources and differentiation added.

PLANNING ACTIVITY:

1. Copy a map onto the middle of a sheet of A3 white paper.

2. Use pen or fine highlighter to extend the map oputwards, identifying things like:

» field study opportunities

» visitors

» texts or books

» creative opportunities

» further links

» literacy/numeracy opportunities

» ICT oportunities/programmes etcetera

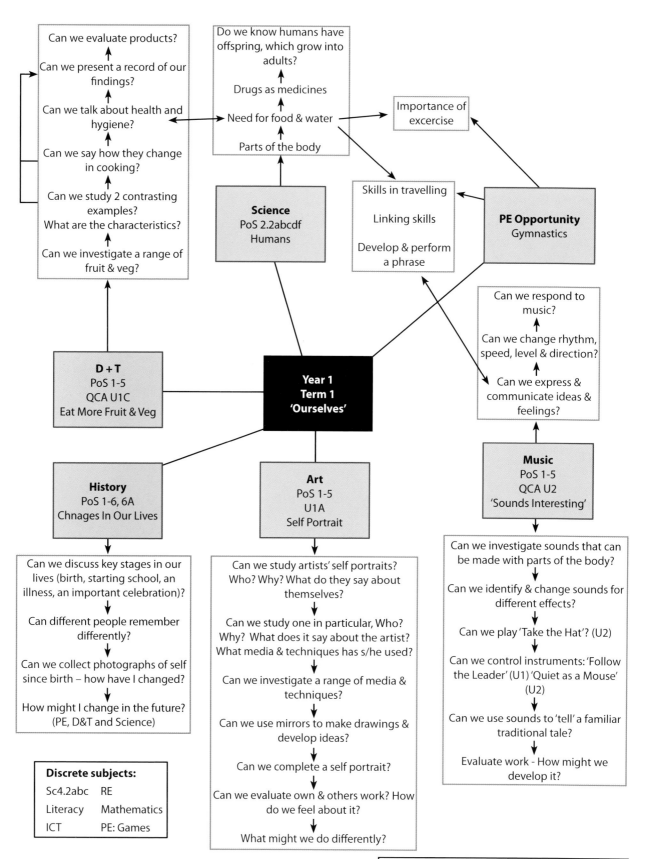

Can we evaluate products?

Can we present a record of our findings?

Can we talk about health and hygiene?

Can we say how they change in cooking?

Can we study 2 contrasting examples? What are the characteristics?

Can we investigate a range of fruit & veg?

Do we know humans have offspring, which grow into adults?

Drugs as medicines

Need for food & water

Parts of the body

Importance of excercise

Science
PoS 2.2abcdf
Humans

Skills in travelling

Linking skills

Develop & perform a phrase

PE Opportunity
Gymnastics

Can we respond to music?

Can we change rhythm, speed, level & direction?

Can we express & communicate ideas & feelings?

D + T
PoS 1-5
QCA U1C
Eat More Fruit & Veg

**Year 1
Term 1
'Ourselves'**

Music
PoS 1-5
QCA U2
'Sounds Interesting'

History
PoS 1-6, 6A
Chnages In Our Lives

Art
PoS 1-5
U1A
Self Portrait

Can we discuss key stages in our lives (birth, starting school, an illness, an important celebration)?

Can different people remember differently?

Can we collect photographs of self since birth – how have I changed?

How might I change in the future? (PE, D&T and Science)

Can we study artists' self portraits? Who? Why? What do they say about themselves?

Can we study one in particular, Who? Why? What does it say about the artist? What media & techniques has s/he used?

Can we investigate a range of media & techniques?

Can we use mirrors to make drawings & develop ideas?

Can we complete a self portrait?

Can we evaluate own & others work? How do we feel about it?

What might we do differently?

Can we investigate sounds that can be made with parts of the body?

Can we identify & change sounds for different effects?

Can we play 'Take the Hat'? (U2)

Can we control instruments: 'Follow the Leader' (U1) 'Quiet as a Mouse' (U2)

Can we use sounds to 'tell' a familiar traditional tale?

Evaluate work - How might we develop it?

Discrete subjects:

Sc4.2abc	RE
Literacy	Mathematics
ICT	PE: Games

Plan for: Citizenship, PSHE, Themes & Links, S&L

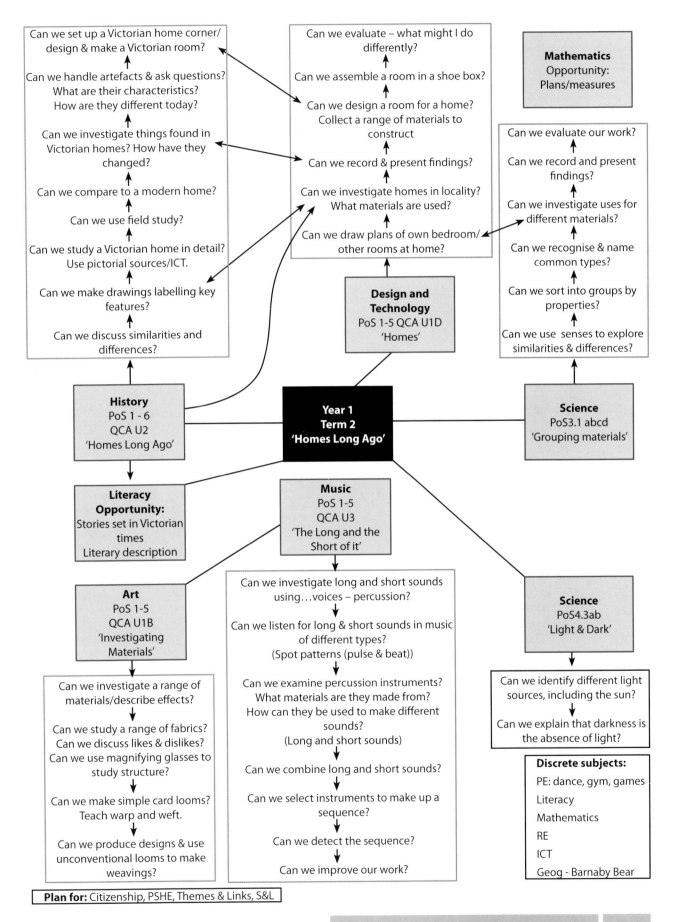

Can we set up a Victorian home corner/ design & make a Victorian room?

Can we handle artefacts & ask questions? What are their characteristics? How are they different today?

Can we investigate things found in Victorian homes? How have they changed?

Can we compare to a modern home?

Can we use field study?

Can we study a Victorian home in detail? Use pictorial sources/ICT.

Can we make drawings labelling key features?

Can we discuss similarities and differences?

Can we evaluate – what might I do differently?

Can we assemble a room in a shoe box?

Can we design a room for a home? Collect a range of materials to construct

Can we record & present findings?

Can we investigate homes in locality? What materials are used?

Can we draw plans of own bedroom/ other rooms at home?

Mathematics
Opportunity:
Plans/measures

Can we evaluate our work?

Can we record and present findings?

Can we investigate uses for different materials?

Can we recognise & name common types?

Can we sort into groups by properties?

Can we use senses to explore similarities & differences?

Design and Technology
PoS 1-5 QCA U1D
'Homes'

History
PoS 1 - 6
QCA U2
'Homes Long Ago'

**Year 1
Term 2
'Homes Long Ago'**

Science
PoS3.1 abcd
'Grouping materials'

**Literacy
Opportunity:**
Stories set in Victorian times
Literary description

Music
PoS 1-5
QCA U3
'The Long and the Short of it'

Art
PoS 1-5
QCA U1B
'Investigating Materials'

Can we investigate a range of materials/describe effects?

Can we study a range of fabrics? Can we discuss likes & dislikes? Can we use magnifying glasses to study structure?

Can we make simple card looms? Teach warp and weft.

Can we produce designs & use unconventional looms to make weavings?

Can we investigate long and short sounds using…voices – percussion?

Can we listen for long & short sounds in music of different types?
(Spot patterns (pulse & beat))

Can we examine percussion instruments? What materials are they made from? How can they be used to make different sounds?
(Long and short sounds)

Can we combine long and short sounds?

Can we select instruments to make up a sequence?

Can we detect the sequence?

Can we improve our work?

Science
PoS4.3ab
'Light & Dark'

Can we identify different light sources, including the sun?

Can we explain that darkness is the absence of light?

Discrete subjects:
PE: dance, gym, games
Literacy
Mathematics
RE
ICT
Geog - Barnaby Bear

Plan for: Citizenship, PSHE, Themes & Links, S&L

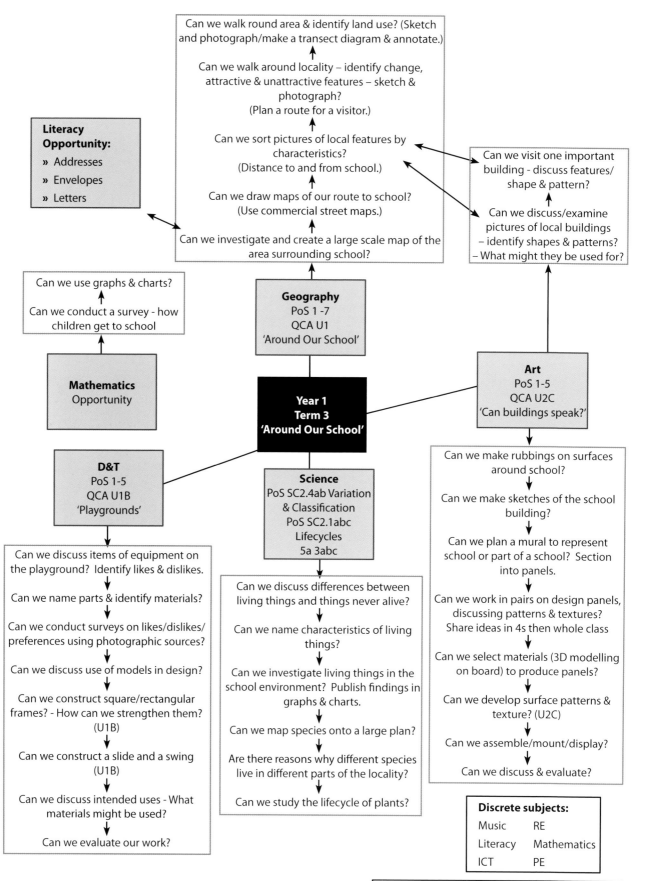

Can we walk round area & identify land use? (Sketch and photograph/make a transect diagram & annotate.)

Can we walk around locality – identify change, attractive & unattractive features – sketch & photograph?
(Plan a route for a visitor.)

Can we sort pictures of local features by characteristics?
(Distance to and from school.)

Can we draw maps of our route to school?
(Use commercial street maps.)

Can we investigate and create a large scale map of the area surrounding school?

Literacy Opportunity:
» Addresses
» Envelopes
» Letters

Can we visit one important building - discuss features/ shape & pattern?

Can we discuss/examine pictures of local buildings – identify shapes & patterns? – What might they be used for?

Can we use graphs & charts?

Can we conduct a survey - how children get to school

Geography
PoS 1 -7
QCA U1
'Around Our School'

Mathematics
Opportunity

**Year 1
Term 3
'Around Our School'**

Art
PoS 1-5
QCA U2C
'Can buildings speak?'

D&T
PoS 1-5
QCA U1B
'Playgrounds'

Science
PoS SC2.4ab Variation & Classification
PoS SC2.1abc
Lifecycles
5a 3abc

Can we make rubbings on surfaces around school?

Can we make sketches of the school building?

Can we plan a mural to represent school or part of a school? Section into panels.

Can we work in pairs on design panels, discussing patterns & textures? Share ideas in 4s then whole class

Can we select materials (3D modelling on board) to produce panels?

Can we develop surface patterns & texture? (U2C)

Can we assemble/mount/display?

Can we discuss & evaluate?

Can we discuss items of equipment on the playground? Identify likes & dislikes.

Can we name parts & identify materials?

Can we conduct surveys on likes/dislikes/ preferences using photographic sources?

Can we discuss use of models in design?

Can we construct square/rectangular frames? - How can we strengthen them? (U1B)

Can we construct a slide and a swing (U1B)

Can we discuss intended uses - What materials might be used?

Can we evaluate our work?

Can we discuss differences between living things and things never alive?

Can we name characteristics of living things?

Can we investigate living things in the school environment? Publish findings in graphs & charts.

Can we map species onto a large plan?

Are there reasons why different species live in different parts of the locality?

Can we study the lifecycle of plants?

Discrete subjects:
Music	RE
Literacy	Mathematics
ICT	PE

Plan for: Citizenship, PSHE, Themes & Links, S&L

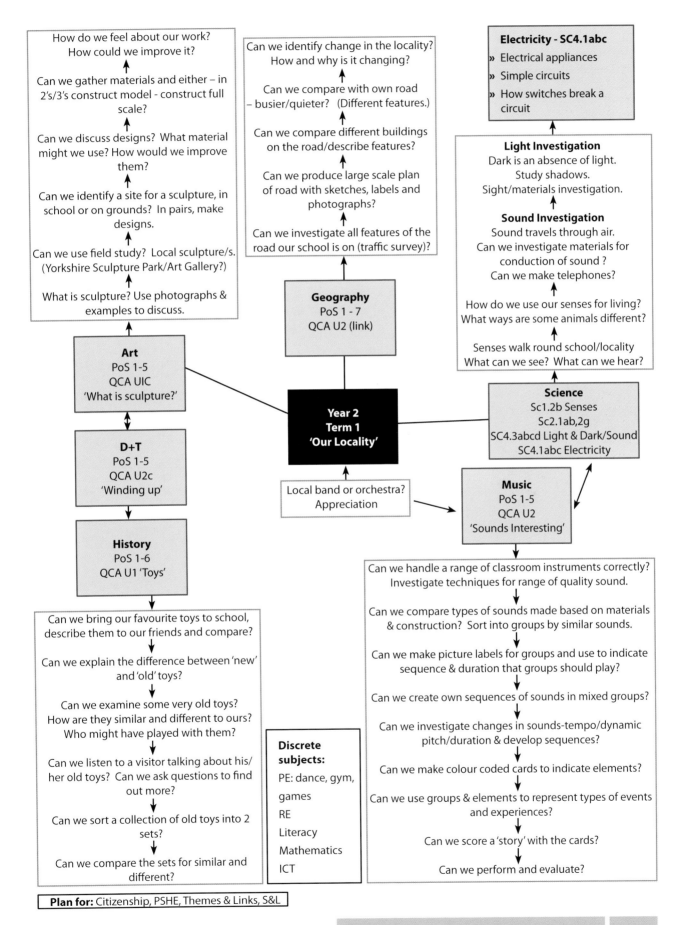

How do we feel about our work?
How could we improve it?

Can we gather materials and either – in 2's/3's construct model - construct full scale?

Can we discuss designs? What material might we use? How would we improve them?

Can we identify a site for a sculpture, in school or on grounds? In pairs, make designs.

Can we use field study? Local sculpture/s. (Yorkshire Sculpture Park/Art Gallery?)

What is sculpture? Use photographs & examples to discuss.

Can we identify change in the locality?
How and why is it changing?

Can we compare with own road – busier/quieter? (Different features.)

Can we compare different buildings on the road/describe features?

Can we produce large scale plan of road with sketches, labels and photographs?

Can we investigate all features of the road our school is on (traffic survey)?

Electricity - SC4.1abc
» Electrical appliances
» Simple circuits
» How switches break a circuit

Light Investigation
Dark is an absence of light.
Study shadows.
Sight/materials investigation.

Sound Investigation
Sound travels through air.
Can we investigate materials for conduction of sound ?
Can we make telephones?

How do we use our senses for living?
What ways are some animals different?

Senses walk round school/locality
What can we see? What can we hear?

Art
PoS 1-5
QCA UIC
'What is sculpture?'

Geography
PoS 1 - 7
QCA U2 (link)

Science
Sc1.2b Senses
Sc2.1ab,2g
SC4.3abcd Light & Dark/Sound
SC4.1abc Electricity

D+T
PoS 1-5
QCA U2c
'Winding up'

**Year 2
Term 1
'Our Locality'**

Local band or orchestra?
Appreciation

Music
PoS 1-5
QCA U2
'Sounds Interesting'

History
PoS 1-6
QCA U1 'Toys'

Can we bring our favourite toys to school, describe them to our friends and compare?
↓
Can we explain the difference between 'new' and 'old' toys?
↓
Can we examine some very old toys? How are they similar and different to ours? Who might have played with them?
↓
Can we listen to a visitor talking about his/her old toys? Can we ask questions to find out more?
↓
Can we sort a collection of old toys into 2 sets?
↓
Can we compare the sets for similar and different?

Discrete subjects:
PE: dance, gym, games
RE
Literacy
Mathematics
ICT

Can we handle a range of classroom instruments correctly? Investigate techniques for range of quality sound.
↓
Can we compare types of sounds made based on materials & construction? Sort into groups by similar sounds.
↓
Can we make picture labels for groups and use to indicate sequence & duration that groups should play?
↓
Can we create own sequences of sounds in mixed groups?
↓
Can we investigate changes in sounds-tempo/dynamic pitch/duration & develop sequences?
↓
Can we make colour coded cards to indicate elements?
↓
Can we use groups & elements to represent types of events and experiences?
↓
Can we score a 'story' with the cards?
↓
Can we perform and evaluate?

Plan for: Citizenship, PSHE, Themes & Links, S&L

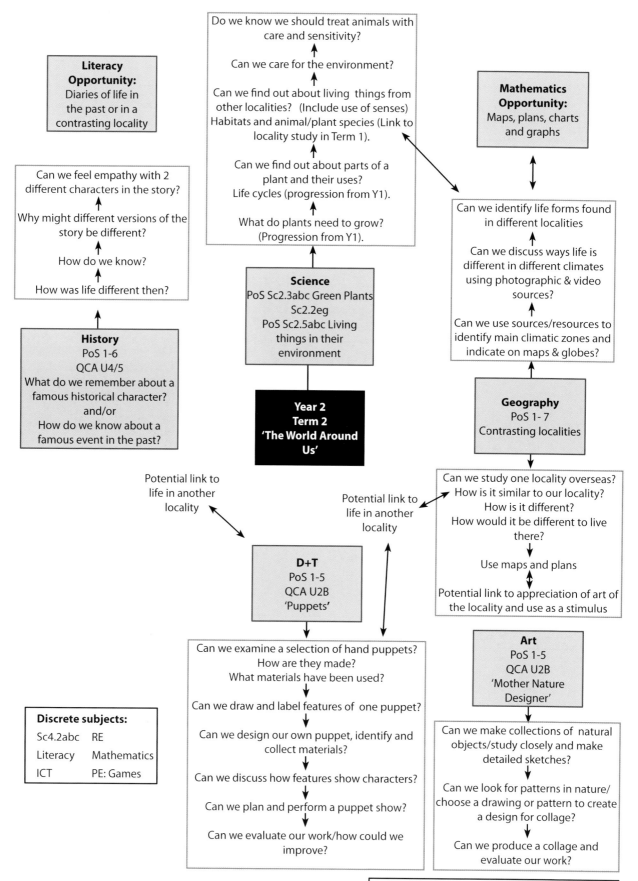

Literacy Opportunity: Diaries of life in the past or in a contrasting locality

Can we feel empathy with 2 different characters in the story?
↑
Why might different versions of the story be different?
↑
How do we know?
↑
How was life different then?

History
PoS 1-6
QCA U4/5
What do we remember about a famous historical character? and/or
How do we know about a famous event in the past?

Do we know we should treat animals with care and sensitivity?
↑
Can we care for the environment?
↑
Can we find out about living things from other localities? (Include use of senses)
Habitats and animal/plant species (Link to locality study in Term 1).
↑
Can we find out about parts of a plant and their uses?
Life cycles (progression from Y1).
↑
What do plants need to grow? (Progression from Y1).

Science
PoS Sc2.3abc Green Plants
Sc2.2eg
PoS Sc2.5abc Living things in their environment

**Year 2
Term 2
'The World Around Us'**

Mathematics Opportunity: Maps, plans, charts and graphs

Can we identify life forms found in different localities
↑
Can we discuss ways life is different in different climates using photographic & video sources?
↑
Can we use sources/resources to identify main climatic zones and indicate on maps & globes?

Geography
PoS 1- 7
Contrasting localities

Can we study one locality overseas? How is it similar to our locality? How is it different? How would it be different to live there?
↓
Use maps and plans
↕
Potential link to appreciation of art of the locality and use as a stimulus

Potential link to life in another locality

Potential link to life in another locality

D+T
PoS 1-5
QCA U2B
'Puppets'

Can we examine a selection of hand puppets?
How are they made?
What materials have been used?
↓
Can we draw and label features of one puppet?
↓
Can we design our own puppet, identify and collect materials?
↓
Can we discuss how features show characters?
↓
Can we plan and perform a puppet show?
↓
Can we evaluate our work/how could we improve?

Discrete subjects:
Sc4.2abc   RE
Literacy   Mathematics
ICT   PE: Games

Art
PoS 1-5
QCA U2B
'Mother Nature Designer'

Can we make collections of natural objects/study closely and make detailed sketches?
↓
Can we look for patterns in nature/ choose a drawing or pattern to create a design for collage?
↓
Can we produce a collage and evaluate our work?

Plan for: Citizenship, PSHE, Themes & Links, S&L

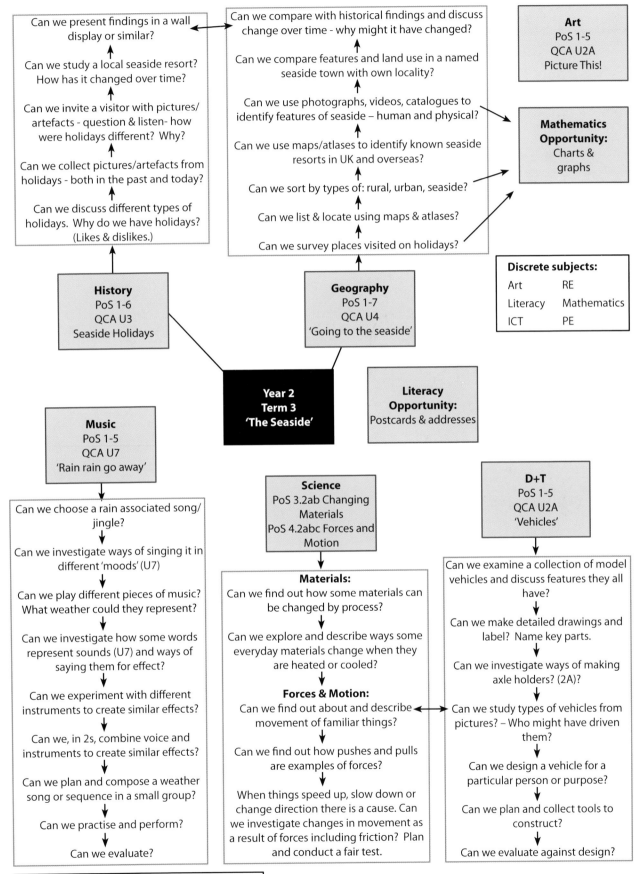

Can we present findings in a wall display or similar?

Can we study a local seaside resort? How has it changed over time?

Can we invite a visitor with pictures/artefacts - question & listen- how were holidays different? Why?

Can we collect pictures/artefacts from holidays - both in the past and today?

Can we discuss different types of holidays. Why do we have holidays? (Likes & dislikes.)

History
PoS 1-6
QCA U3
Seaside Holidays

Can we compare with historical findings and discuss change over time - why might it have changed?

Can we compare features and land use in a named seaside town with own locality?

Can we use photographs, videos, catalogues to identify features of seaside – human and physical?

Can we use maps/atlases to identify known seaside resorts in UK and overseas?

Can we sort by types of: rural, urban, seaside?

Can we list & locate using maps & atlases?

Can we survey places visited on holidays?

Geography
PoS 1-7
QCA U4
'Going to the seaside'

Art
PoS 1-5
QCA U2A
Picture This!

Mathematics Opportunity:
Charts & graphs

Discrete subjects:

Art	RE
Literacy	Mathematics
ICT	PE

**Year 2
Term 3
'The Seaside'**

Literacy Opportunity:
Postcards & addresses

Music
PoS 1-5
QCA U7
'Rain rain go away'

Can we choose a rain associated song/ jingle?

Can we investigate ways of singing it in different 'moods' (U7)

Can we play different pieces of music? What weather could they represent?

Can we investigate how some words represent sounds (U7) and ways of saying them for effect?

Can we experiment with different instruments to create similar effects?

Can we, in 2s, combine voice and instruments to create similar effects?

Can we plan and compose a weather song or sequence in a small group?

Can we practise and perform?

Can we evaluate?

Science
PoS 3.2ab Changing Materials
PoS 4.2abc Forces and Motion

Materials:
Can we find out how some materials can be changed by process?

Can we explore and describe ways some everyday materials change when they are heated or cooled?

Forces & Motion:
Can we find out about and describe movement of familiar things?

Can we find out how pushes and pulls are examples of forces?

When things speed up, slow down or change direction there is a cause. Can we investigate changes in movement as a result of forces including friction? Plan and conduct a fair test.

D+T
PoS 1-5
QCA U2A
'Vehicles'

Can we examine a collection of model vehicles and discuss features they all have?

Can we make detailed drawings and label? Name key parts.

Can we investigate ways of making axle holders? (2A)?

Can we study types of vehicles from pictures? – Who might have driven them?

Can we design a vehicle for a particular person or purpose?

Can we plan and collect tools to construct?

Can we evaluate against design?

Plan for: Citizenship, PSHE, Themes & Links, S&L

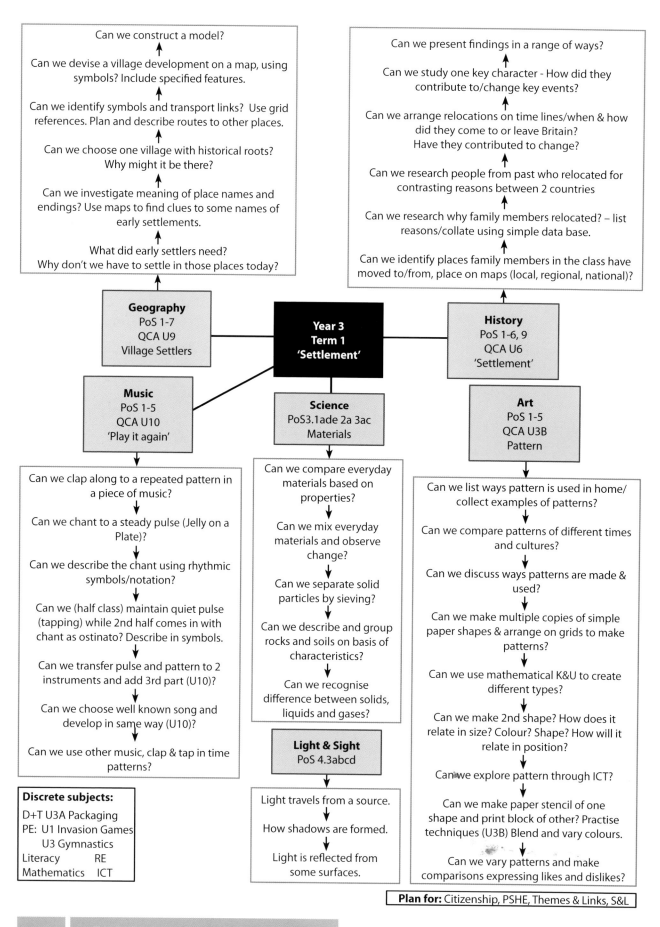

Geography
PoS 1-7
QCA U9
Village Settlers

Can we construct a model?

Can we devise a village development on a map, using symbols? Include specified features.

Can we identify symbols and transport links? Use grid references. Plan and describe routes to other places.

Can we choose one village with historical roots? Why might it be there?

Can we investigate meaning of place names and endings? Use maps to find clues to some names of early settlements.

What did early settlers need? Why don't we have to settle in those places today?

History
PoS 1-6, 9
QCA U6
'Settlement'

Can we present findings in a range of ways?

Can we study one key character - How did they contribute to/change key events?

Can we arrange relocations on time lines/when & how did they come to or leave Britain? Have they contributed to change?

Can we research people from past who relocated for contrasting reasons between 2 countries

Can we research why family members relocated? – list reasons/collate using simple data base.

Can we identify places family members in the class have moved to/from, place on maps (local, regional, national)?

Year 3 Term 1 'Settlement'

Music
PoS 1-5
QCA U10
'Play it again'

Can we clap along to a repeated pattern in a piece of music?

Can we chant to a steady pulse (Jelly on a Plate)?

Can we describe the chant using rhythmic symbols/notation?

Can we (half class) maintain quiet pulse (tapping) while 2nd half comes in with chant as ostinato? Describe in symbols.

Can we transfer pulse and pattern to 2 instruments and add 3rd part (U10)?

Can we choose well known song and develop in same way (U10)?

Can we use other music, clap & tap in time patterns?

Science
PoS3.1ade 2a 3ac
Materials

Can we compare everyday materials based on properties?

Can we mix everyday materials and observe change?

Can we separate solid particles by sieving?

Can we describe and group rocks and soils on basis of characteristics?

Can we recognise difference between solids, liquids and gases?

Light & Sight
PoS 4.3abcd

Light travels from a source.

How shadows are formed.

Light is reflected from some surfaces.

Art
PoS 1-5
QCA U3B
Pattern

Can we list ways pattern is used in home/ collect examples of patterns?

Can we compare patterns of different times and cultures?

Can we discuss ways patterns are made & used?

Can we make multiple copies of simple paper shapes & arrange on grids to make patterns?

Can we use mathematical K&U to create different types?

Can we make 2nd shape? How does it relate in size? Colour? Shape? How will it relate in position?

Can we explore pattern through ICT?

Can we make paper stencil of one shape and print block of other? Practise techniques (U3B) Blend and vary colours.

Can we vary patterns and make comparisons expressing likes and dislikes?

Discrete subjects:
D+T U3A Packaging
PE: U1 Invasion Games
        U3 Gymnastics
Literacy   RE
Mathematics   ICT

Plan for: Citizenship, PSHE, Themes & Links, S&L

Literacy Opportunity:
Communication with other school

Literacy Opportunity:
Story with animal theme, (Wind in the Willows?)

Can we identify 2 contrasting localities and study animal life? How are they different? Are there environmental threats?

Can we identify animal species in locality through research? Study habitat and life patterns. Are there environmental threats? Human threats?

Can we analyse data for 2 weeks? Discuss impact on human activity. Suggest reasons for variations. Locate on maps and globes, identify routes to get there.

Can we either 'twin' with another school & exchange data by fax/email daily or study weather through 'w.w.w' or a programme such as MyLO? Record for one contrasting locality.

Can we discuss faxes & emails coming in to school? Track sources using spreadsheets/database. From? Why? Compare with letters.

Can we study ways 2 different animals are suited to their habitats?

Can we identify habitats for a range of animals?

Why do some living things need protection? How can we help?

Can we study animal forms in a contrasting environment & classify using keys/assigning in groups. Why do we need groups?

Music
PoS 1-5
QCA U9
Animal Magic

Geography
PoS 1-7
QCA U18
'The World'

**Year 3
Term 2
'Animal Kingdom'**

Science
PoS 2.1c, 4abc, 5abc
Variation & Classification

Can we listen to piece of music that describes animals, compare animals with sounds used.

Can we refine comparison to use of rhythm and melody (U9).

Can we sing animal songs. Vary pace and dynamic. Which works best? Vary timbre & discuss.

Can we make movements to describe first song thinking about height, length, rhythm and quality – Combine 2 more features.

Can we work in pairs to create sounds & movements for 1 animal. Select an untuned instrument to describe way it moves. Work out a sequence – one plays/one moves – change over. Explore melody patterns.

Can we perform – can we guess the animal? Add a narrator for voice over of what is happening.

Can we compose a piece for 2 animals interacting – in pairs choosing appropriate instruments. Perform, evaluate and review.

D+T
PoS 1-5
QCA U3C
Moving Monsters

Science
PoS 3.2e
Water Cycle

Can we investigate familiar things that use air to make them work. How does air do this?

Can we construct simple pneumatic system with balloon, 5mm tubing and washing up liquid bottle. What happens when you squeeze the bottle? When you let go? What can it lift?

Can we use 2 syringes and plastic tubing to create alternative model & answer some questions? Make comparisons.

Can we collect pictures of monsters. Design own monster and collect materials to make. Construct with pneumatic system to open mouth.

Can we discuss how made and how features work?

Can we evaluate our work?

Role of evaporation and condensation in the water cycle

Discrete subjects:
Art: U 3C - Can we change places?
PE: U3 Dance
     U1 Net/Wall Games
Literacy   ICT
Mathematics   RE

Plan for: Citizenship, PSHE, Themes & Links, S&L

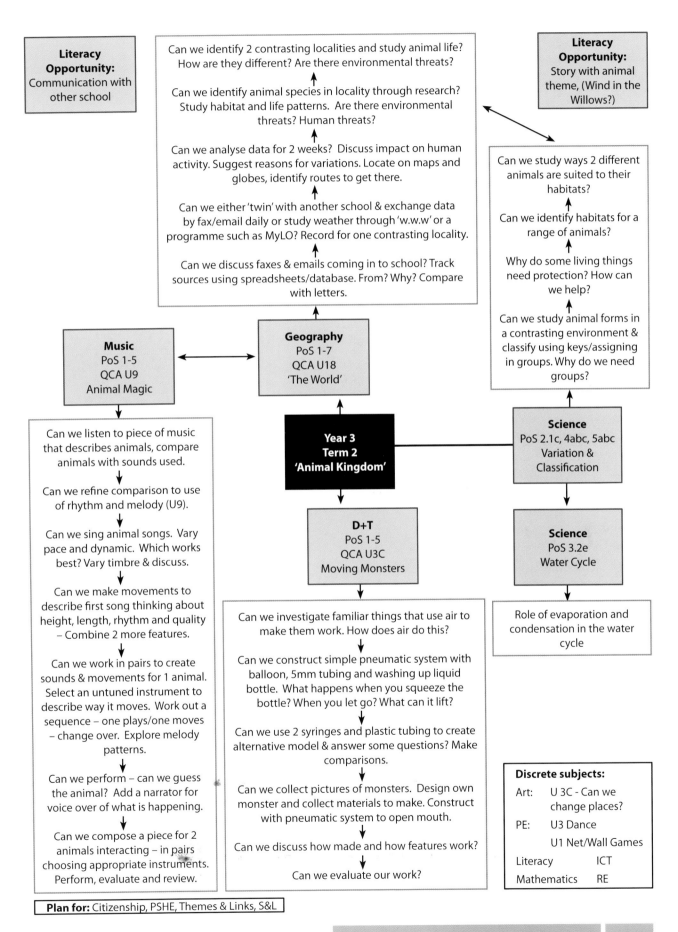

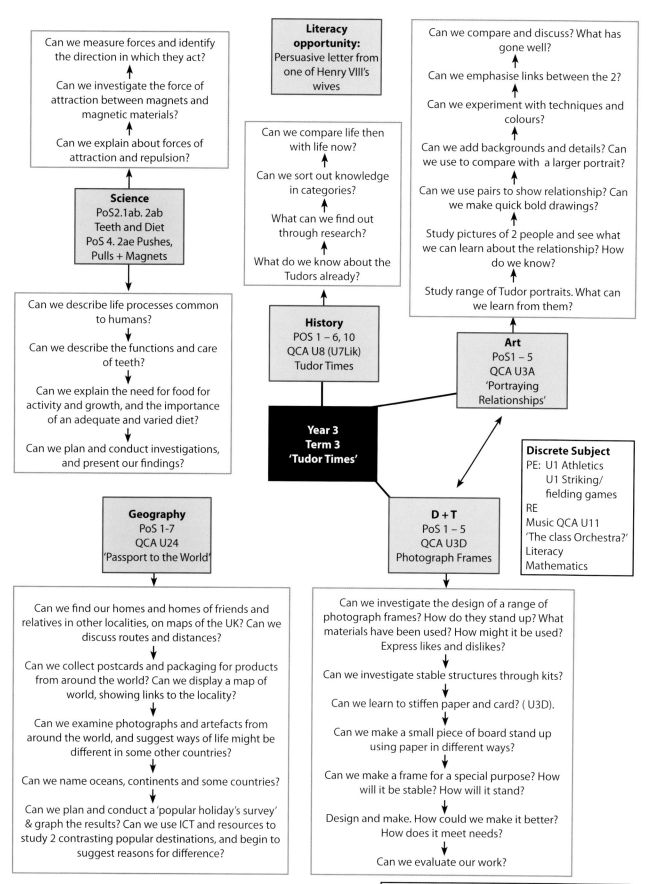

Can we measure forces and identify the direction in which they act?

↑

Can we investigate the force of attraction between magnets and magnetic materials?

↑

Can we explain about forces of attraction and repulsion?

Science
PoS2.1ab. 2ab
Teeth and Diet
PoS 4. 2ae Pushes,
Pulls + Magnets

Can we describe life processes common to humans?

↓

Can we describe the functions and care of teeth?

↓

Can we explain the need for food for activity and growth, and the importance of an adequate and varied diet?

↓

Can we plan and conduct investigations, and present our findings?

Literacy opportunity:
Persuasive letter from one of Henry VIII's wives

Can we compare life then with life now?

↑

Can we sort out knowledge in categories?

↑

What can we find out through research?

↑

What do we know about the Tudors already?

History
POS 1 – 6, 10
QCA U8 (U7Lik)
Tudor Times

Can we compare and discuss? What has gone well?

↑

Can we emphasise links between the 2?

↑

Can we experiment with techniques and colours?

↑

Can we add backgrounds and details? Can we use to compare with a larger portrait?

↑

Can we use pairs to show relationship? Can we make quick bold drawings?

↑

Study pictures of 2 people and see what we can learn about the relationship? How do we know?

↑

Study range of Tudor portraits. What can we learn from them?

Art
PoS1 – 5
QCA U3A
'Portraying Relationships'

**Year 3
Term 3
'Tudor Times'**

Discrete Subject
PE: U1 Athletics
U1 Striking/ fielding games
RE
Music QCA U11 'The class Orchestra?'
Literacy
Mathematics

Geography
PoS 1-7
QCA U24
'Passport to the World'

Can we find our homes and homes of friends and relatives in other localities, on maps of the UK? Can we discuss routes and distances?

↓

Can we collect postcards and packaging for products from around the world? Can we display a map of world, showing links to the locality?

↓

Can we examine photographs and artefacts from around the world, and suggest ways of life might be different in some other countries?

↓

Can we name oceans, continents and some countries?

↓

Can we plan and conduct a 'popular holiday's survey' & graph the results? Can we use ICT and resources to study 2 contrasting popular destinations, and begin to suggest reasons for difference?

D + T
PoS 1 – 5
QCA U3D
Photograph Frames

Can we investigate the design of a range of photograph frames? How do they stand up? What materials have been used? How might it be used? Express likes and dislikes?

↓

Can we investigate stable structures through kits?

↓

Can we learn to stiffen paper and card? (U3D).

↓

Can we make a small piece of board stand up using paper in different ways?

↓

Can we make a frame for a special purpose? How will it be stable? How will it stand?

↓

Design and make. How could we make it better? How does it meet needs?

↓

Can we evaluate our work?

Plan for: Citizenship, PSHE, Themes & Links, S&L

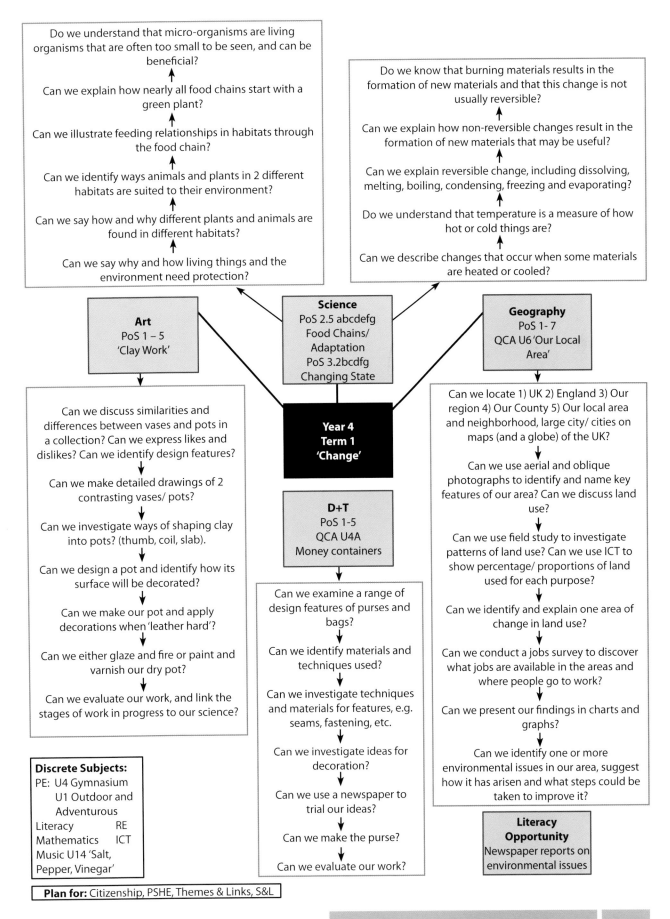

Do we understand that micro-organisms are living organisms that are often too small to be seen, and can be beneficial?

↑

Can we explain how nearly all food chains start with a green plant?

↑

Can we illustrate feeding relationships in habitats through the food chain?

↑

Can we identify ways animals and plants in 2 different habitats are suited to their environment?

↑

Can we say how and why different plants and animals are found in different habitats?

↑

Can we say why and how living things and the environment need protection?

Do we know that burning materials results in the formation of new materials and that this change is not usually reversible?

↑

Can we explain how non-reversible changes result in the formation of new materials that may be useful?

↑

Can we explain reversible change, including dissolving, melting, boiling, condensing, freezing and evaporating?

↑

Do we understand that temperature is a measure of how hot or cold things are?

↑

Can we describe changes that occur when some materials are heated or cooled?

Art
PoS 1 – 5
'Clay Work'

Science
PoS 2.5 abcdefg
Food Chains/
Adaptation
PoS 3.2bcdfg
Changing State

Geography
PoS 1- 7
QCA U6 'Our Local Area'

**Year 4
Term 1
'Change'**

D+T
PoS 1-5
QCA U4A
Money containers

Can we discuss similarities and differences between vases and pots in a collection? Can we express likes and dislikes? Can we identify design features?

↓

Can we make detailed drawings of 2 contrasting vases/ pots?

↓

Can we investigate ways of shaping clay into pots? (thumb, coil, slab).

↓

Can we design a pot and identify how its surface will be decorated?

↓

Can we make our pot and apply decorations when 'leather hard'?

↓

Can we either glaze and fire or paint and varnish our dry pot?

↓

Can we evaluate our work, and link the stages of work in progress to our science?

Can we examine a range of design features of purses and bags?

↓

Can we identify materials and techniques used?

↓

Can we investigate techniques and materials for features, e.g. seams, fastening, etc.

↓

Can we investigate ideas for decoration?

↓

Can we use a newspaper to trial our ideas?

↓

Can we make the purse?

↓

Can we evaluate our work?

Can we locate 1) UK 2) England 3) Our region 4) Our County 5) Our local area and neighborhood, large city/ cities on maps (and a globe) of the UK?

↓

Can we use aerial and oblique photographs to identify and name key features of our area? Can we discuss land use?

↓

Can we use field study to investigate patterns of land use? Can we use ICT to show percentage/ proportions of land used for each purpose?

↓

Can we identify and explain one area of change in land use?

↓

Can we conduct a jobs survey to discover what jobs are available in the areas and where people go to work?

↓

Can we present our findings in charts and graphs?

↓

Can we identify one or more environmental issues in our area, suggest how it has arisen and what steps could be taken to improve it?

Discrete Subjects:
PE: U4 Gymnasium
      U1 Outdoor and
      Adventurous
Literacy   RE
Mathematics   ICT
Music U14 'Salt, Pepper, Vinegar'

Literacy Opportunity
Newspaper reports on environmental issues

Plan for: Citizenship, PSHE, Themes & Links, S&L

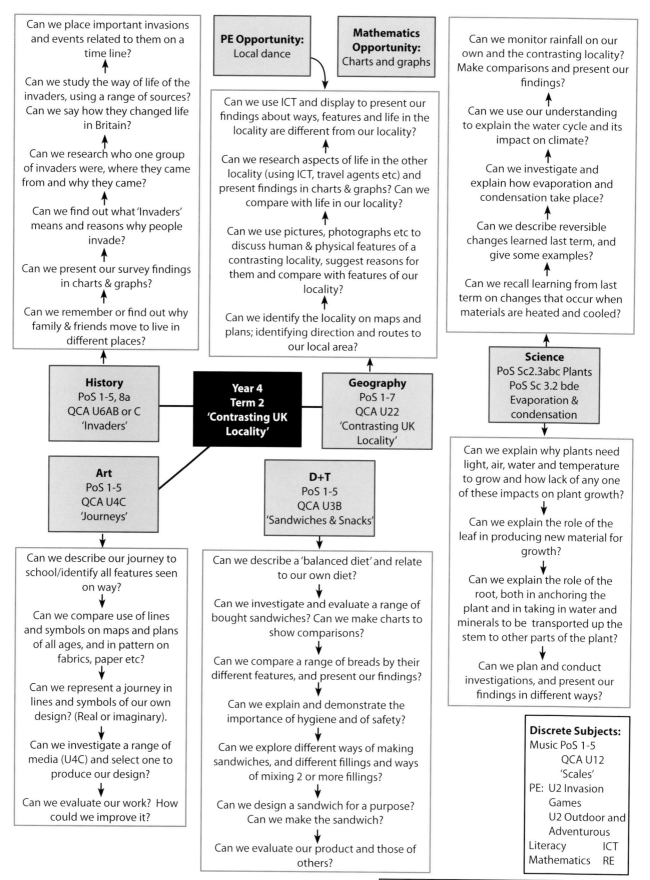

History
PoS 1-5, 8a
QCA U6AB or C
'Invaders'

Can we remember or find out why family & friends move to live in different places?

Can we present our survey findings in charts & graphs?

Can we find out what 'Invaders' means and reasons why people invade?

Can we research who one group of invaders were, where they came from and why they came?

Can we study the way of life of the invaders, using a range of sources? Can we say how they changed life in Britain?

Can we place important invasions and events related to them on a time line?

PE Opportunity:
Local dance

Mathematics Opportunity:
Charts and graphs

Can we identify the locality on maps and plans; identifying direction and routes to our local area?

Can we use pictures, photographs etc to discuss human & physical features of a contrasting locality, suggest reasons for them and compare with features of our locality?

Can we research aspects of life in the other locality (using ICT, travel agents etc) and present findings in charts & graphs? Can we compare with life in our locality?

Can we use ICT and display to present our findings about ways, features and life in the locality are different from our locality?

Year 4 Term 2 'Contrasting UK Locality'

Geography
PoS 1-7
QCA U22
'Contrasting UK Locality'

Can we monitor rainfall on our own and the contrasting locality? Make comparisons and present our findings?

Can we use our understanding to explain the water cycle and its impact on climate?

Can we investigate and explain how evaporation and condensation take place?

Can we describe reversible changes learned last term, and give some examples?

Can we recall learning from last term on changes that occur when materials are heated and cooled?

Science
PoS Sc2.3abc Plants
PoS Sc 3.2 bde
Evaporation & condensation

Art
PoS 1-5
QCA U4C
'Journeys'

Can we describe our journey to school/identify all features seen on way?

Can we compare use of lines and symbols on maps and plans of all ages, and in pattern on fabrics, paper etc?

Can we represent a journey in lines and symbols of our own design? (Real or imaginary).

Can we investigate a range of media (U4C) and select one to produce our design?

Can we evaluate our work? How could we improve it?

D+T
PoS 1-5
QCA U3B
'Sandwiches & Snacks'

Can we describe a 'balanced diet' and relate to our own diet?

Can we investigate and evaluate a range of bought sandwiches? Can we make charts to show comparisons?

Can we compare a range of breads by their different features, and present our findings?

Can we explain and demonstrate the importance of hygiene and of safety?

Can we explore different ways of making sandwiches, and different fillings and ways of mixing 2 or more fillings?

Can we design a sandwich for a purpose? Can we make the sandwich?

Can we evaluate our product and those of others?

Can we explain why plants need light, air, water and temperature to grow and how lack of any one of these impacts on plant growth?

Can we explain the role of the leaf in producing new material for growth?

Can we explain the role of the root, both in anchoring the plant and in taking in water and minerals to be transported up the stem to other parts of the plant?

Can we plan and conduct investigations, and present our findings in different ways?

Discrete Subjects:
Music PoS 1-5
　　QCA U12
　　'Scales'
PE: U2 Invasion Games
　　U2 Outdoor and Adventurous
Literacy　　ICT
Mathematics　　RE

Plan for: Citizenship, PSHE, Themes & Links, S&L

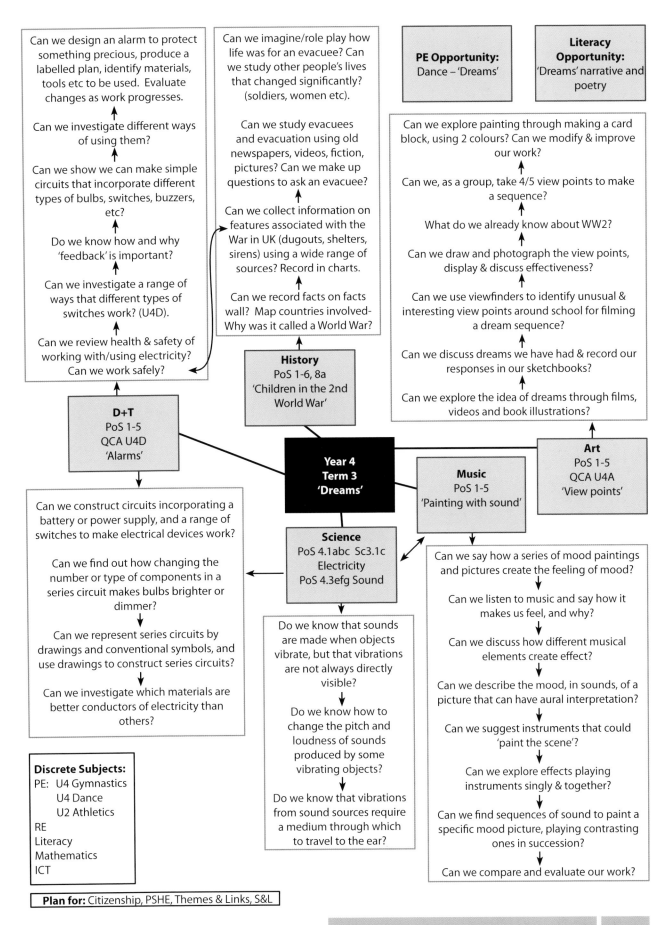

Can we design an alarm to protect something precious, produce a labelled plan, identify materials, tools etc to be used. Evaluate changes as work progresses.

↑

Can we investigate different ways of using them?

↑

Can we show we can make simple circuits that incorporate different types of bulbs, switches, buzzers, etc?

↑

Do we know how and why 'feedback' is important?

↑

Can we investigate a range of ways that different types of switches work? (U4D).

↑

Can we review health & safety of working with/using electricity? Can we work safely?

Can we imagine/role play how life was for an evacuee? Can we study other people's lives that changed significantly? (soldiers, women etc).

Can we study evacuees and evacuation using old newspapers, videos, fiction, pictures? Can we make up questions to ask an evacuee?

↑

Can we collect information on features associated with the War in UK (dugouts, shelters, sirens) using a wide range of sources? Record in charts.

↑

Can we record facts on facts wall? Map countries involved- Why was it called a World War?

PE Opportunity:
Dance – 'Dreams'

Literacy Opportunity:
'Dreams' narrative and poetry

Can we explore painting through making a card block, using 2 colours? Can we modify & improve our work?

↑

Can we, as a group, take 4/5 view points to make a sequence?

↑

What do we already know about WW2?

↑

Can we draw and photograph the view points, display & discuss effectiveness?

↑

Can we use viewfinders to identify unusual & interesting view points around school for filming a dream sequence?

↑

Can we discuss dreams we have had & record our responses in our sketchbooks?

↑

Can we explore the idea of dreams through films, videos and book illustrations?

History
PoS 1-6, 8a
'Children in the 2nd World War'

D+T
PoS 1-5
QCA U4D
'Alarms'

**Year 4
Term 3
'Dreams'**

Music
PoS 1-5
'Painting with sound'

Art
PoS 1-5
QCA U4A
'View points'

Can we construct circuits incorporating a battery or power supply, and a range of switches to make electrical devices work?

↓

Can we find out how changing the number or type of components in a series circuit makes bulbs brighter or dimmer?

↓

Can we represent series circuits by drawings and conventional symbols, and use drawings to construct series circuits?

↓

Can we investigate which materials are better conductors of electricity than others?

Science
PoS 4.1abc Sc3.1c
Electricity
PoS 4.3efg Sound

Do we know that sounds are made when objects vibrate, but that vibrations are not always directly visible?

↓

Do we know how to change the pitch and loudness of sounds produced by some vibrating objects?

↓

Do we know that vibrations from sound sources require a medium through which to travel to the ear?

Can we say how a series of mood paintings and pictures create the feeling of mood?

↓

Can we listen to music and say how it makes us feel, and why?

↓

Can we discuss how different musical elements create effect?

↓

Can we describe the mood, in sounds, of a picture that can have aural interpretation?

↓

Can we suggest instruments that could 'paint the scene'?

↓

Can we explore effects playing instruments singly & together?

↓

Can we find sequences of sound to paint a specific mood picture, playing contrasting ones in succession?

↓

Can we compare and evaluate our work?

Discrete Subjects:
PE: U4 Gymnastics
U4 Dance
U2 Athletics
RE
Literacy
Mathematics
ICT

Plan for: Citizenship, PSHE, Themes & Links, S&L

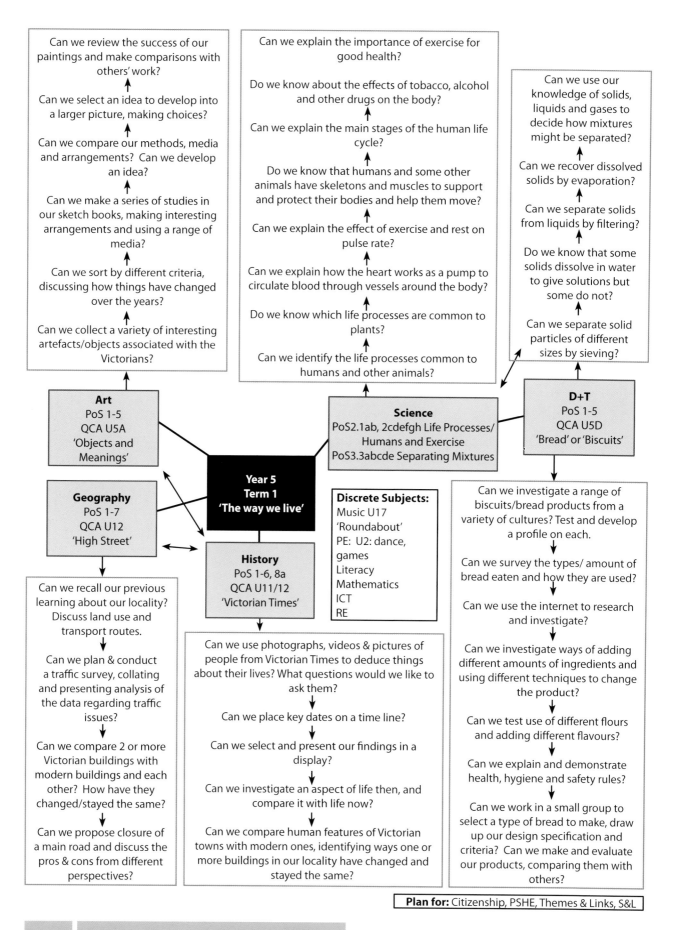

Can we review the success of our paintings and make comparisons with others' work?

↑

Can we select an idea to develop into a larger picture, making choices?

↑

Can we compare our methods, media and arrangements? Can we develop an idea?

↑

Can we make a series of studies in our sketch books, making interesting arrangements and using a range of media?

↑

Can we sort by different criteria, discussing how things have changed over the years?

↑

Can we collect a variety of interesting artefacts/objects associated with the Victorians?

Can we explain the importance of exercise for good health?

Do we know about the effects of tobacco, alcohol and other drugs on the body?

↑

Can we explain the main stages of the human life cycle?

↑

Do we know that humans and some other animals have skeletons and muscles to support and protect their bodies and help them move?

↑

Can we explain the effect of exercise and rest on pulse rate?

↑

Can we explain how the heart works as a pump to circulate blood through vessels around the body?

↑

Do we know which life processes are common to plants?

↑

Can we identify the life processes common to humans and other animals?

Can we use our knowledge of solids, liquids and gases to decide how mixtures might be separated?

↑

Can we recover dissolved solids by evaporation?

↑

Can we separate solids from liquids by filtering?

↑

Do we know that some solids dissolve in water to give solutions but some do not?

↑

Can we separate solid particles of different sizes by sieving?

Art
PoS 1-5
QCA U5A
'Objects and Meanings'

Science
PoS2.1ab, 2cdefgh Life Processes/ Humans and Exercise
PoS3.3abcde Separating Mixtures

D+T
PoS 1-5
QCA U5D
'Bread' or 'Biscuits'

Year 5 Term 1 'The way we live'

Geography
PoS 1-7
QCA U12
'High Street'

Discrete Subjects:
Music U17 'Roundabout'
PE: U2: dance, games
Literacy
Mathematics
ICT
RE

History
PoS 1-6, 8a
QCA U11/12
'Victorian Times'

Can we recall our previous learning about our locality? Discuss land use and transport routes.

↓

Can we plan & conduct a traffic survey, collating and presenting analysis of the data regarding traffic issues?

↓

Can we compare 2 or more Victorian buildings with modern buildings and each other? How have they changed/stayed the same?

↓

Can we propose closure of a main road and discuss the pros & cons from different perspectives?

Can we use photographs, videos & pictures of people from Victorian Times to deduce things about their lives? What questions would we like to ask them?

↓

Can we place key dates on a time line?

↓

Can we select and present our findings in a display?

↓

Can we investigate an aspect of life then, and compare it with life now?

↓

Can we compare human features of Victorian towns with modern ones, identifying ways one or more buildings in our locality have changed and stayed the same?

Can we investigate a range of biscuits/bread products from a variety of cultures? Test and develop a profile on each.

↓

Can we survey the types/ amount of bread eaten and how they are used?

↓

Can we use the internet to research and investigate?

↓

Can we investigate ways of adding different amounts of ingredients and using different techniques to change the product?

↓

Can we test use of different flours and adding different flavours?

↓

Can we explain and demonstrate health, hygiene and safety rules?

↓

Can we work in a small group to select a type of bread to make, draw up our design specification and criteria? Can we make and evaluate our products, comparing them with others?

Plan for: Citizenship, PSHE, Themes & Links, S&L

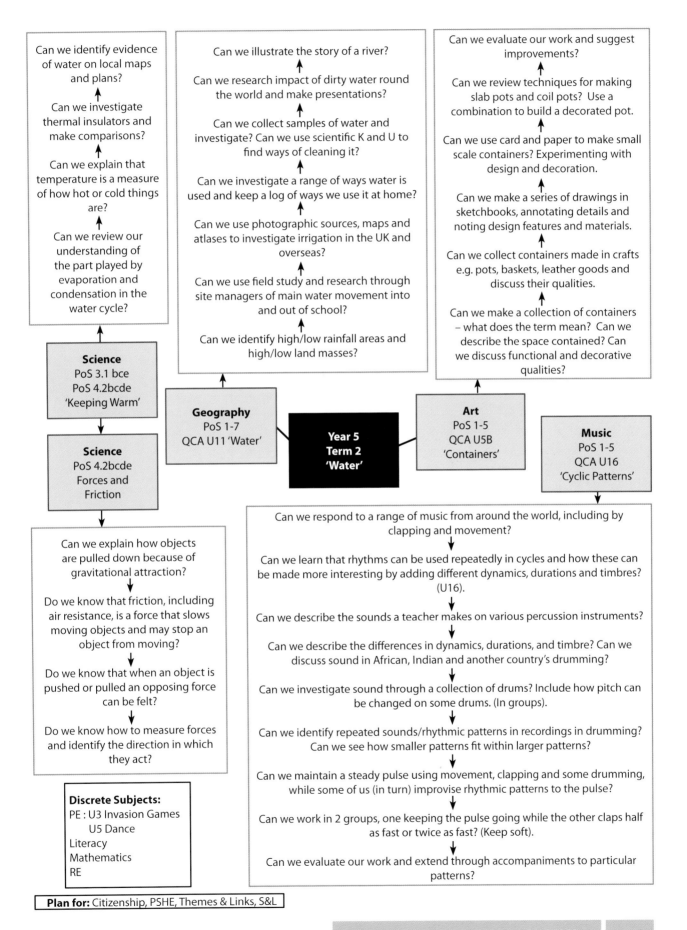

Can we identify evidence of water on local maps and plans?

↑

Can we investigate thermal insulators and make comparisons?

↑

Can we explain that temperature is a measure of how hot or cold things are?

↑

Can we review our understanding of the part played by evaporation and condensation in the water cycle?

Can we illustrate the story of a river?

↑

Can we research impact of dirty water round the world and make presentations?

↑

Can we collect samples of water and investigate? Can we use scientific K and U to find ways of cleaning it?

↑

Can we investigate a range of ways water is used and keep a log of ways we use it at home?

↑

Can we use photographic sources, maps and atlases to investigate irrigation in the UK and overseas?

↑

Can we use field study and research through site managers of main water movement into and out of school?

↑

Can we identify high/low rainfall areas and high/low land masses?

Can we evaluate our work and suggest improvements?

↑

Can we review techniques for making slab pots and coil pots? Use a combination to build a decorated pot.

↑

Can we use card and paper to make small scale containers? Experimenting with design and decoration.

↑

Can we make a series of drawings in sketchbooks, annotating details and noting design features and materials.

↑

Can we collect containers made in crafts e.g. pots, baskets, leather goods and discuss their qualities.

↑

Can we make a collection of containers – what does the term mean? Can we describe the space contained? Can we discuss functional and decorative qualities?

Science
PoS 3.1 bce
PoS 4.2bcde
'Keeping Warm'

Science
PoS 4.2bcde
Forces and Friction

Geography
PoS 1-7
QCA U11 'Water'

Year 5 Term 2 'Water'

Art
PoS 1-5
QCA U5B 'Containers'

Music
PoS 1-5
QCA U16 'Cyclic Patterns'

Can we explain how objects are pulled down because of gravitational attraction?

↓

Do we know that friction, including air resistance, is a force that slows moving objects and may stop an object from moving?

↓

Do we know that when an object is pushed or pulled an opposing force can be felt?

↓

Do we know how to measure forces and identify the direction in which they act?

Discrete Subjects:
PE : U3 Invasion Games
U5 Dance
Literacy
Mathematics
RE

Can we respond to a range of music from around the world, including by clapping and movement?

↓

Can we learn that rhythms can be used repeatedly in cycles and how these can be made more interesting by adding different dynamics, durations and timbres? (U16).

↓

Can we describe the sounds a teacher makes on various percussion instruments?

↓

Can we describe the differences in dynamics, durations, and timbre? Can we discuss sound in African, Indian and another country's drumming?

↓

Can we investigate sound through a collection of drums? Include how pitch can be changed on some drums. (In groups).

↓

Can we identify repeated sounds/rhythmic patterns in recordings in drumming? Can we see how smaller patterns fit within larger patterns?

↓

Can we maintain a steady pulse using movement, clapping and some drumming, while some of us (in turn) improvise rhythmic patterns to the pulse?

↓

Can we work in 2 groups, one keeping the pulse going while the other claps half as fast or twice as fast? (Keep soft).

↓

Can we evaluate our work and extend through accompaniments to particular patterns?

Plan for: Citizenship, PSHE, Themes & Links, S&L

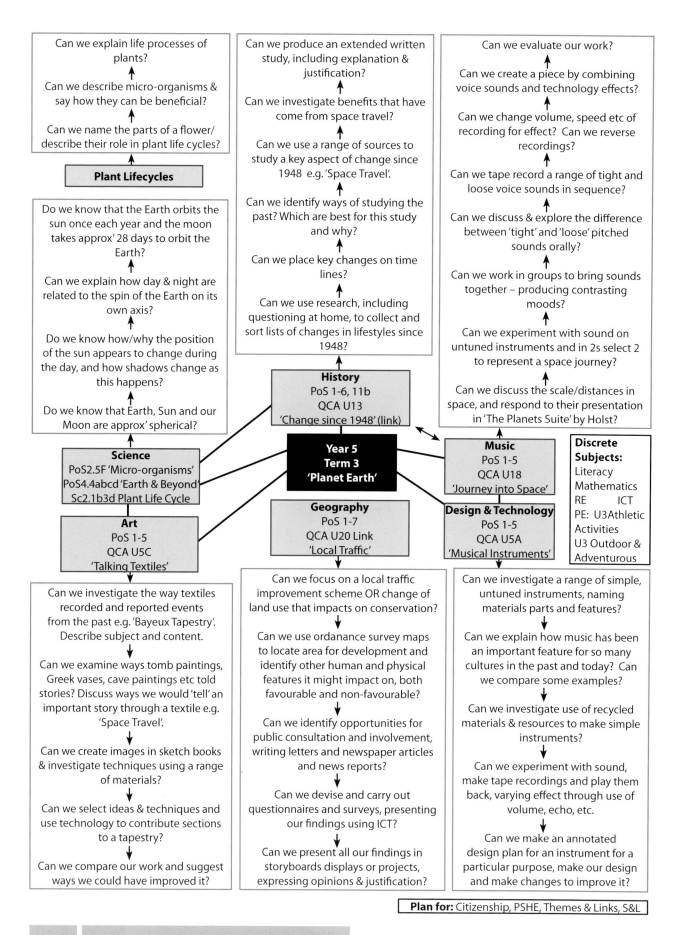

Can we explain life processes of plants?

↑

Can we describe micro-organisms & say how they can be beneficial?

↑

Can we name the parts of a flower/ describe their role in plant life cycles?

↑

Plant Lifecycles

↑

Do we know that the Earth orbits the sun once each year and the moon takes approx' 28 days to orbit the Earth?

↑

Can we explain how day & night are related to the spin of the Earth on its own axis?

↑

Do we know how/why the position of the sun appears to change during the day, and how shadows change as this happens?

↑

Do we know that Earth, Sun and our Moon are approx' spherical?

↑

Science
PoS2.5F 'Micro-organisms'
PoS4.4abcd 'Earth & Beyond'
Sc2.1b3d Plant Life Cycle

↓

Art
PoS 1-5
QCA U5C
'Talking Textiles'

↓

Can we investigate the way textiles recorded and reported events from the past e.g. 'Bayeux Tapestry'. Describe subject and content.

↓

Can we examine ways tomb paintings, Greek vases, cave paintings etc told stories? Discuss ways we would 'tell' an important story through a textile e.g. 'Space Travel'.

↓

Can we create images in sketch books & investigate techniques using a range of materials?

↓

Can we select ideas & techniques and use technology to contribute sections to a tapestry?

↓

Can we compare our work and suggest ways we could have improved it?

Can we produce an extended written study, including explanation & justification?

↑

Can we investigate benefits that have come from space travel?

↑

Can we use a range of sources to study a key aspect of change since 1948 e.g. 'Space Travel'.

↑

Can we identify ways of studying the past? Which are best for this study and why?

↑

Can we place key changes on time lines?

↑

Can we use research, including questioning at home, to collect and sort lists of changes in lifestyles since 1948?

↑

History
PoS 1-6, 11b
QCA U13
'Change since 1948' (link)

**Year 5
Term 3
'Planet Earth'**

Geography
PoS 1-7
QCA U20 Link
'Local Traffic'

↓

Can we focus on a local traffic improvement scheme OR change of land use that impacts on conservation?

↓

Can we use ordanance survey maps to locate area for development and identify other human and physical features it might impact on, both favourable and non-favourable?

↓

Can we identify opportunities for public consultation and involvement, writing letters and newspaper articles and news reports?

↓

Can we devise and carry out questionnaires and surveys, presenting our findings using ICT?

↓

Can we present all our findings in storyboards displays or projects, expressing opinions & justification?

Can we evaluate our work?

↑

Can we create a piece by combining voice sounds and technology effects?

↑

Can we change volume, speed etc of recording for effect? Can we reverse recordings?

↑

Can we tape record a range of tight and loose voice sounds in sequence?

↑

Can we discuss & explore the difference between 'tight' and 'loose' pitched sounds orally?

↑

Can we work in groups to bring sounds together – producing contrasting moods?

↑

Can we experiment with sound on untuned instruments and in 2s select 2 to represent a space journey?

↑

Can we discuss the scale/distances in space, and respond to their presentation in 'The Planets Suite' by Holst?

Music
PoS 1-5
QCA U18
'Journey into Space'

Discrete Subjects:
Literacy
Mathematics
RE   ICT
PE: U3Athletic Activities
U3 Outdoor & Adventurous

Design & Technology
PoS 1-5
QCA U5A
'Musical Instruments'

↓

Can we investigate a range of simple, untuned instruments, naming materials parts and features?

↓

Can we explain how music has been an important feature for so many cultures in the past and today? Can we compare some examples?

↓

Can we investigate use of recycled materials & resources to make simple instruments?

↓

Can we experiment with sound, make tape recordings and play them back, varying effect through use of volume, echo, etc.

↓

Can we make an annotated design plan for an instrument for a particular purpose, make our design and make changes to improve it?

Plan for: Citizenship, PSHE, Themes & Links, S&L

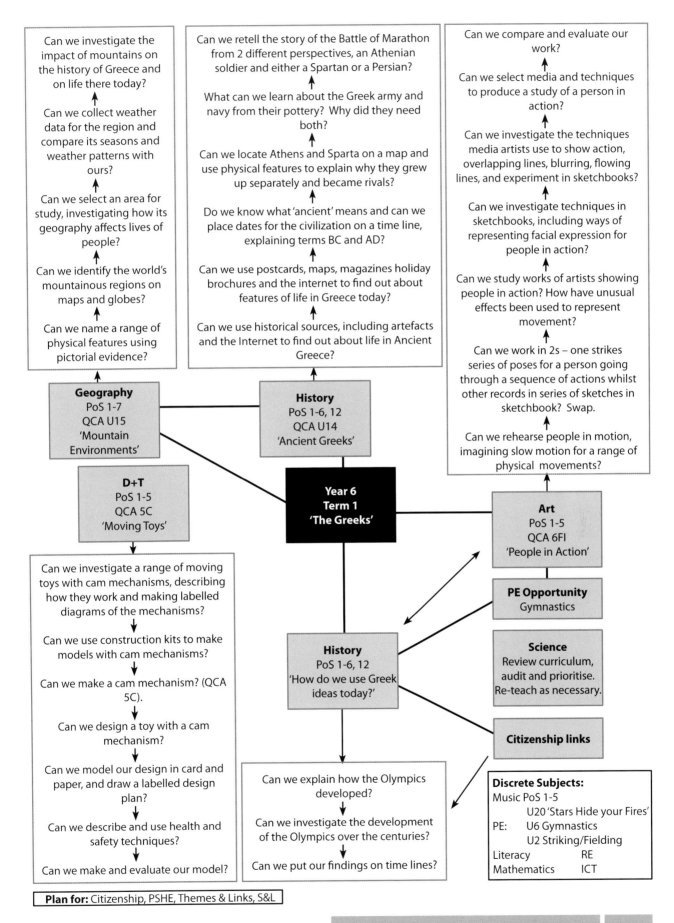

Can we investigate the impact of mountains on the history of Greece and on life there today?

↑

Can we collect weather data for the region and compare its seasons and weather patterns with ours?

↑

Can we select an area for study, investigating how its geography affects lives of people?

↑

Can we identify the world's mountainous regions on maps and globes?

↑

Can we name a range of physical features using pictorial evidence?

Can we retell the story of the Battle of Marathon from 2 different perspectives, an Athenian soldier and either a Spartan or a Persian?

↑

What can we learn about the Greek army and navy from their pottery? Why did they need both?

↑

Can we locate Athens and Sparta on a map and use physical features to explain why they grew up separately and became rivals?

↑

Do we know what 'ancient' means and can we place dates for the civilization on a time line, explaining terms BC and AD?

↑

Can we use postcards, maps, magazines holiday brochures and the internet to find out about features of life in Greece today?

↑

Can we use historical sources, including artefacts and the Internet to find out about life in Ancient Greece?

Can we compare and evaluate our work?

↑

Can we select media and techniques to produce a study of a person in action?

↑

Can we investigate the techniques media artists use to show action, overlapping lines, blurring, flowing lines, and experiment in sketchbooks?

↑

Can we investigate techniques in sketchbooks, including ways of representing facial expression for people in action?

↑

Can we study works of artists showing people in action? How have unusual effects been used to represent movement?

↑

Can we work in 2s – one strikes series of poses for a person going through a sequence of actions whilst other records in series of sketches in sketchbook? Swap.

↑

Can we rehearse people in motion, imagining slow motion for a range of physical movements?

Geography
PoS 1-7
QCA U15
'Mountain Environments'

History
PoS 1-6, 12
QCA U14
'Ancient Greeks'

**Year 6
Term 1
'The Greeks'**

Art
PoS 1-5
QCA 6FI
'People in Action'

D+T
PoS 1-5
QCA 5C
'Moving Toys'

PE Opportunity
Gymnastics

Can we investigate a range of moving toys with cam mechanisms, describing how they work and making labelled diagrams of the mechanisms?

↓

Can we use construction kits to make models with cam mechanisms?

↓

Can we make a cam mechanism? (QCA 5C).

↓

Can we design a toy with a cam mechanism?

↓

Can we model our design in card and paper, and draw a labelled design plan?

↓

Can we describe and use health and safety techniques?

↓

Can we make and evaluate our model?

History
PoS 1-6, 12
'How do we use Greek ideas today?'

Science
Review curriculum, audit and prioritise. Re-teach as necessary.

Citizenship links

Can we explain how the Olympics developed?

↓

Can we investigate the development of the Olympics over the centuries?

↓

Can we put our findings on time lines?

Discrete Subjects:
Music PoS 1-5
          U20 'Stars Hide your Fires'
PE: U6 Gymnastics
          U2 Striking/Fielding
Literacy   RE
Mathematics   ICT

Plan for: Citizenship, PSHE, Themes & Links, S&L

Can we select a topical phrase or issue and compose our own song?

↑

Can we make-up football chants and supporter songs in 2s?

↑

Can we explain how and why the most catchy phrases are often in the chorus?

↑

Can we analyse the structure of each of the songs?

↑

Can we compare 2 contrasting songs by John Lennon (Or another song writer from the 60's)? Can we discuss what messages he was giving out & why?

↑

Can we play a song from the 1940s, picking out and discussing key phrases? Can we improve?

↑

Can we play a song from the charts that we all know, recording and discussing key phrases?

↑

Music
PoS 1-5
QCA U19
'Songwriter'

Can we compare life in 1960s with life today, and compare how pop music was promoted with how it is today?

↑

Can we use a range of sources, including questioning adults about their memories of the 1960s?

↑

Can we study the life of one famous person from 1960s, e.g. John Lennon?

↑

Can we place key dates from 1960s on a time line?

↑

Can we investigate and name a range of famous people and events in 1960's?

↑

History
PoS 1-6, 13
QCA U20
'The life of a Famous Person'

Can we evaluate our work?

↑

Can we select a view, media and techniques to produce an urban portrayal?

↑

Can we study the works of Lowry & Hockney identifying techniques they use to give an industrial perspective?

↑

Can we use our viewfinders in 2 contrasting localities – urban & rural and make thumbnail sketches?

↑

Can we discuss different media & techniques for portraying views? Can we experiment in our sketchbook?

↑

Can we examine the works of 2 artists, one portraying rural views and one urban?

↑

Can we make thumbnail sketches of views around our school in our sketchbooks?

↑

Can we use viewfinders to select & focus on interesting views around our school?

↑

Art
PoS 1-5
QCA U6C
'A Sense of Place'

PE Opportunity:
Dance from 1960s

Literacy Opportunities:
Song lyrics

Year 6 Term 2 'The 1960s'

D+T
PoS 1-5
QCA U6D
'Controllable Vehicles'

Science
As in Term 1 plus:
Revise and practise test techniques

Can we investigate how a range of controllable vehicles work?

↓

Can we make labelled drawings to show how they are constructed and how they work?

↓

Can we review our knowledge of switches and how they work?

↓

Can we use construction kits to make controllable vehicles?

↓

Can we revise our knowledge of circuits and switches, designing and making our own circuits and switches?

↓

Can we use a range of tools safely and correctly?
Can we work in 2s to design & make a vehicle for a purpose selecting our own materials etc?

↓

Can we compare & evaluate our work?

Discrete Subjects:
PE: U3 Outdoor & Adventurous
     U4 Invasion Games
Literacy
Mathematics
ICT
RE

Plan for: Citizenship, PSHE, Themes & Links, S&L

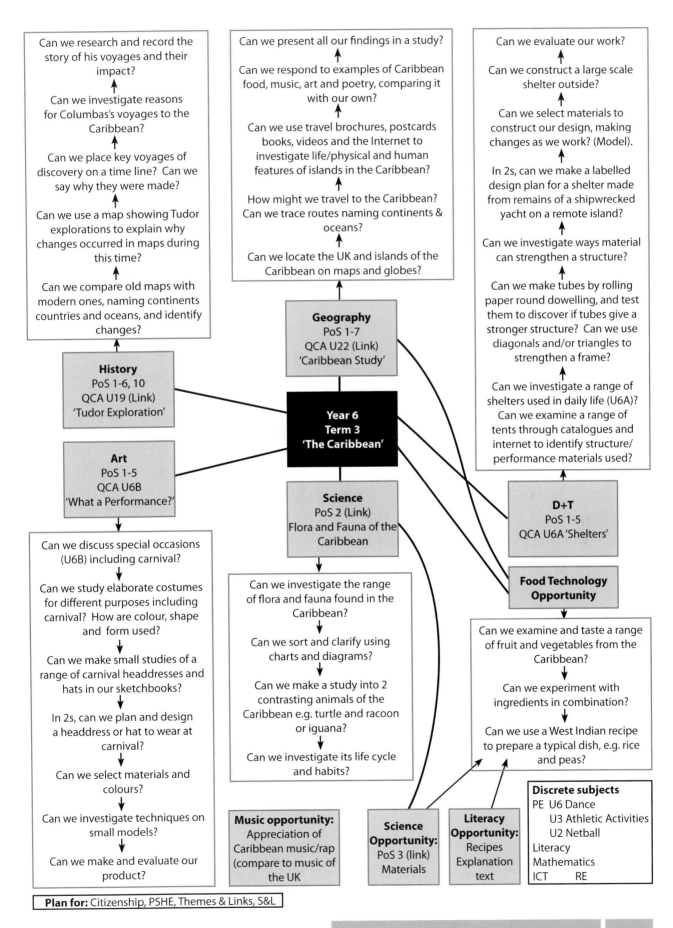

Can we research and record the story of his voyages and their impact?

↑

Can we investigate reasons for Columbas's voyages to the Caribbean?

↑

Can we place key voyages of discovery on a time line? Can we say why they were made?

↑

Can we use a map showing Tudor explorations to explain why changes occurred in maps during this time?

↑

Can we compare old maps with modern ones, naming continents countries and oceans, and identify changes?

History
PoS 1-6, 10
QCA U19 (Link)
'Tudor Exploration'

Art
PoS 1-5
QCA U6B
'What a Performance?'

Can we discuss special occasions (U6B) including carnival?

Can we study elaborate costumes for different purposes including carnival? How are colour, shape and form used?

Can we make small studies of a range of carnival headdresses and hats in our sketchbooks?

In 2s, can we plan and design a headdress or hat to wear at carnival?

Can we select materials and colours?

Can we investigate techniques on small models?

Can we make and evaluate our product?

Can we present all our findings in a study?

Can we respond to examples of Caribbean food, music, art and poetry, comparing it with our own?

↑

Can we use travel brochures, postcards books, videos and the Internet to investigate life/physical and human features of islands in the Caribbean?

↑

How might we travel to the Caribbean? Can we trace routes naming continents & oceans?

↑

Can we locate the UK and islands of the Caribbean on maps and globes?

Geography
PoS 1-7
QCA U22 (Link)
'Caribbean Study'

**Year 6
Term 3
'The Caribbean'**

Science
PoS 2 (Link)
Flora and Fauna of the Caribbean

Can we investigate the range of flora and fauna found in the Caribbean?

↓

Can we sort and clarify using charts and diagrams?

↓

Can we make a study into 2 contrasting animals of the Caribbean e.g. turtle and racoon or iguana?

↓

Can we investigate its life cycle and habits?

Can we evaluate our work?

↑

Can we construct a large scale shelter outside?

↑

Can we select materials to construct our design, making changes as we work? (Model).

↑

In 2s, can we make a labelled design plan for a shelter made from remains of a shipwrecked yacht on a remote island?

↑

Can we investigate ways material can strengthen a structure?

↑

Can we make tubes by rolling paper round dowelling, and test them to discover if tubes give a stronger structure? Can we use diagonals and/or triangles to strengthen a frame?

↑

Can we investigate a range of shelters used in daily life (U6A)? Can we examine a range of tents through catalogues and internet to identify structure/ performance materials used?

D+T
PoS 1-5
QCA U6A 'Shelters'

Food Technology Opportunity

Can we examine and taste a range of fruit and vegetables from the Caribbean?

↓

Can we experiment with ingredients in combination?

↓

Can we use a West Indian recipe to prepare a typical dish, e.g. rice and peas?

Music opportunity:
Appreciation of Caribbean music/rap (compare to music of the UK

Science Opportunity:
PoS 3 (link)
Materials

Literacy Opportunity:
Recipes
Explanation text

Discrete subjects
PE U6 Dance
    U3 Athletic Activities
    U2 Netball
Literacy
Mathematics
ICT   RE

Plan for: Citizenship, PSHE, Themes & Links, S&L

9 THE CREATIVE CURRICULUM CHALLENGES

WHAT ARE THE CREATIVE CURRICULUM CHALLENGES (CCCs)?

The Creative Curriculum Challenges and Mini-Challenges provide a model for thematic cross-curricular investigations that can either run throughout the term (for example for half a day a week or a fortnight) or as a blocked unit of one or two weeks at the end of a term.

Their purpose is to promote those skills suggested as being the highest priorities for citizens of the twenty-first century.

The short term challenges create exciting and challenging contexts for pupils to develop the valued core skills of a school through co-operative and collaborative learning.

WHAT MIGHT THE CORE (KEY) SKILLS INCLUDE?

Listed below are the core (key) skills that might be the recurring, transferable elements of a school's curriculum. Besides providing as many opportunities as possible for pupils to develop these skills across as many subjects and experiences as possible, schools should provide further opportunities that enable pupils to pursue in-depth study that requires them to consolidate and deploy these skills in order to achieve independence and confidence, and to make choices.

The following might represent the core skills pupils should be deploying:

1. The ability to talk confidently, using a sophisticated range of language structures and vocabulary to discuss, debate, explain, justify, describe and recount.

2. The ability to use ICT confidently for the full range of purposes, including processing, presenting, researching, analysing, computing, illustrating and communicating.

3. Physical and mental well being, good health and an active life style.

4. The ability to work and play with others, co-operating and collaborating, responding and communicating successfully.

5. The ability to work alone and with others to hypothesise, plan , investigate, record, analyse, conclude and re-hypothesise.

6. Reading skills that include:

» the ability to read at progressively more challenging levels

» the ability to synthesise out information from texts, to interpret information and to use and apply information.

» higher order reading comprehension skills including the ability to infer and deduce from text.

7. Writing skills that include:

» the four Basic Skills of Writing including the ability

to use accurate grammatical structures, a neat and accurate cursive style, accurate spelling both through basic sight vocabulary and phonic skills and the ability to construct and punctuate sentences accurately. (See: 'Write on Target' – the 'gold book', Chapter 8, Ros. Wilson, 2006)

» the ability to accurately apply the characteristics of the full range of text types and genre

» the ability to respond appropriately to a wide range of stimuli

» a higher level writing voice as achieved through the VCOP of Big Writing, (see 'Strategies for Immediate Impact on Writing Standards', 2003, and 'Write on Target', Chapters 3 and 8, 2006).

8. Be numerate and use and apply a high level of numeracy skills confidently and accurately in their work across the curriculum.

9. Be creative through music, art, dance, gymnastics, design and construction.

10. Confidently tackle and solve problems involving some or all of the core skills.

11. Confidently make decisions and choices without fear of risk taking.

12. Be creative learners who are inquisitive, determined and be able to work independently through self-motivation.

Not only should such challenges provide opportunities for integrated learning that provides clarity and coherence to the curriculum but furthermore they should place pupils in control of short term decisions such as:

» Where to start.

» How to make decisions.

» How to investigate and research.

» How to organise themselves and manage time.

» How to prioritise.

» How to delegate and share responsibilities.

» How to work with others to achieve a good outcome for the group.

» How to present and communicate outcomes effectively.

NB: Only the model for the third term of each year has been provided here. This is to encourage schools to use this as a model only and to design their own challenges that more closely reflect the needs of their pupils and the resources available within their community.

NB: The levelled key questions in the clouds are synthesised from the Hierarchy of Leaning Skills (Chapter 11).

YEAR 1 TERM 3 'AROUND OUR SCHOOL' CREATIVE CURRICULUM CHALLENGE

The Context:
The school's Governing Body is giving the school money to develop an oasis on the school field. They are inviting you to design models for this and the best will be selected to be built.

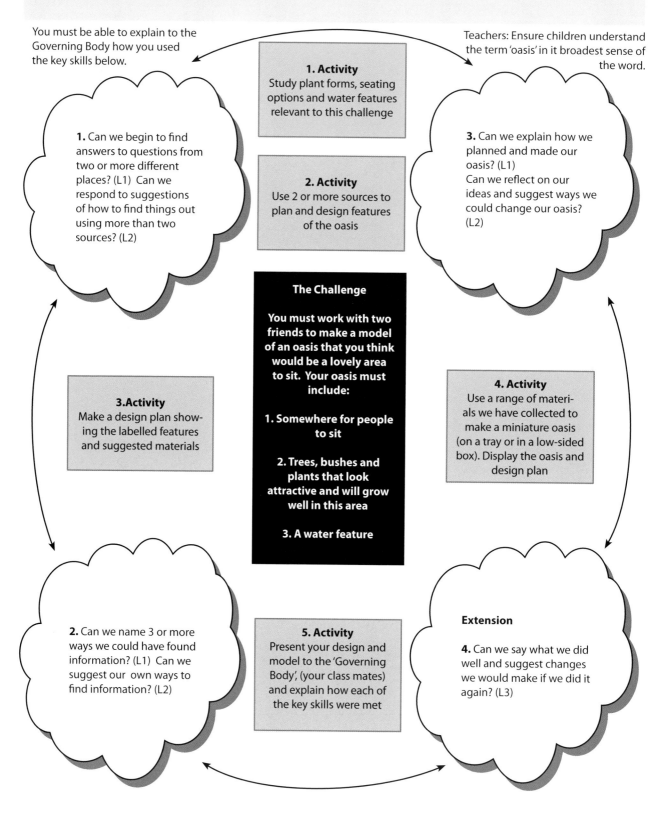

You must be able to explain to the Governing Body how you used the key skills below.

Teachers: Ensure children understand the term 'oasis' in it broadest sense of the word.

1. Activity
Study plant forms, seating options and water features relevant to this challenge

2. Activity
Use 2 or more sources to plan and design features of the oasis

1. Can we begin to find answers to questions from two or more different places? (L1) Can we respond to suggestions of how to find things out using more than two sources? (L2)

3. Can we explain how we planned and made our oasis? (L1)
Can we reflect on our ideas and suggest ways we could change our oasis? (L2)

The Challenge

You must work with two friends to make a model of an oasis that you think would be a lovely area to sit. Your oasis must include:

1. Somewhere for people to sit

2. Trees, bushes and plants that look attractive and will grow well in this area

3. A water feature

3.Activity
Make a design plan showing the labelled features and suggested materials

4. Activity
Use a range of materials we have collected to make a miniature oasis (on a tray or in a low-sided box). Display the oasis and design plan

2. Can we name 3 or more ways we could have found information? (L1) Can we suggest our own ways to find information? (L2)

5. Activity
Present your design and model to the 'Governing Body', (your class mates) and explain how each of the key skills were met

Extension

4. Can we say what we did well and suggest changes we would make if we did it again? (L3)

YEAR 2 TERM 3 'THE SEASIDE' CREATIVE CURRICULUM CHALLENGE

The Context:
Alton Towers is looking for an exciting and vibrant seaside town where they can build a second fun park. They are inviting 7, (8?) towns to send their promotional brochure or booklet by the first week of June. The Directors of Alton Towers will then select the best brochure or booklet and that will be the seaside town selected.

You must be able to explain to the Directors how you used the key skills below, to make your brochure or booklet

This could be delivered through a half day a week over the term, one day for fortnight, or a 2 week project to celebrate the theme. All other lessons would be planned using the school's usual short term plan

Activities
Choose material and ideas that will make your brochure/booklet about the 4 aspects in the Challenge Box, using all your skills to present your information in different ways

1. Can we select information from sources provided? (L2) Can we find answers to questions by using sources in ways that go beyond simple observations? (L3)

2. Can we respond to suggestions of how to find things out? (L2)

4. Can we reflect on ideas and make suggestions with help? (e.g. on improvements?) (L2) Can we say what we did well and begin to suggest ways we might change things next time? (L3)

3. Can we use information and observation to ask and respond to questions? (L2) Can we begin to choose the skills and sources to respond to questions? (L3)

The Challenge

You must work with a friend to make a brochure or booklet to inform tourists about your seaside town, and to attract them to it. You can use you work from other lessons. Your brochure or booklet must include:

1. A map to show where it is in the UK, and 2 transport routes to get there from our school

2. A simple map of the seaside town showing main tourist attractions, with pictures of the attractions either round it or referenced to it.

3. 3 examples of how the seaside town has changed since Victorian times, with illustrations.

4. Posters, reports and other work to encourage tourists to go there.

Activities
Present art work in different ways, using your writing, geography, art, music, D and T and ICT skills

5. Can we use ICT to help generate and communicate ideas in different forms? (L2) Can we use ICT to generate and organise and present ideas? (L3)

6. Provide simple explanations for why some changes happened as they did? (L3)

YEAR 3 TERM 3 'TUDOR TIMES' CREATIVE CURRICULUM CHALLENGE

The Context:
The local museum wants to create a Tudor street. Your group must research, design and make an authentic Tudor house to be placed on the street

You must show evidence of having used the key skills in your work. Be prepared to say what each group member contributed to the challenge.

1. Activity
Use a range of sources to research Tudor homes

2. Activity
Produce design plans for an exterior and an interior

3. Activity
Gather materials to construct a home

4. Activity
Prepare a group presentation on how the project was researched and completed

1. Can we find answers to our research questions in ways that go beyond simple observations? (L3) Can we produce structured work and make appropriate use of information? (L4

2. Can we discuss our work and explain our thinking? (L3) Can we begin to select and combine information from sources? (L4)

3. Can we say what we did well and begin to suggest ways we might change things next time? (L3) Can we evaluate our own work bearing in mind our objectives? (L4)

4. Can we offer reasons for some of our decisions? (L3) Can we explain reasons for our choices, (e.g. methodology) and for materials? (L4)

The Challenge

You must use open topped boxes assembled on their sides to create an authentic Tudor house. Inside each box you must create a Tudor room.

Your work must include:

1. Research into Tudor homes

2. A design plan with annotated features and suggested materials

3. A presentation to show key differences between homes then and now

4. An authentic Tudor interior

5. An authentic Tudor facade, (front outside)

YEAR 4 TERM 3 'DREAMS' CREATIVE CURRICULUM CHALLENGE

The Context:
Radio 2 are looking for new dramas to help children in their learning about aspects of history. The best examples will be selected and broadcast to the whole country, naming the producers. Your taped broadcast must be sent in by the last week of June.

You must be able to explain to the radio managers how you used the key skills below to make your broadcast.

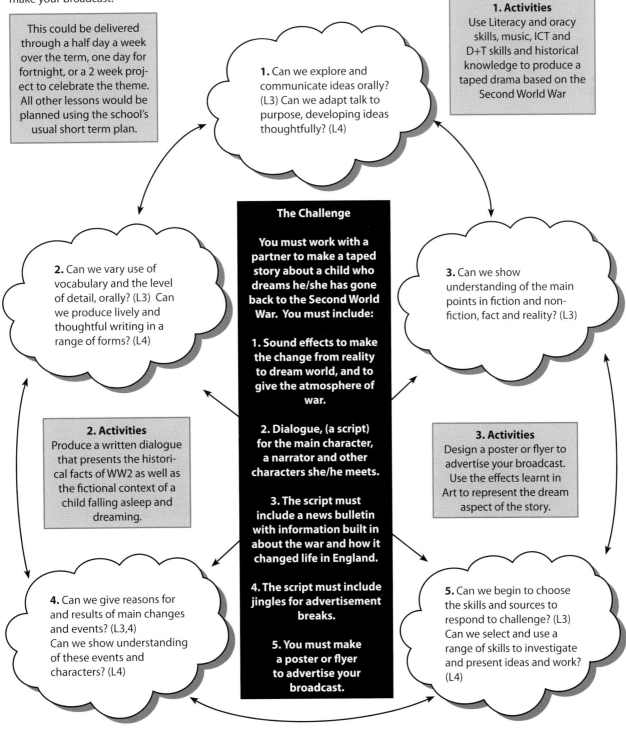

This could be delivered through a half day a week over the term, one day for fortnight, or a 2 week project to celebrate the theme. All other lessons would be planned using the school's usual short term plan.

**1. Can we explore and communicate ideas orally? (L3) Can we adapt talk to purpose, developing ideas thoughtfully? (L4)

1. Activities
Use Literacy and oracy skills, music, ICT and D+T skills and historical knowledge to produce a taped drama based on the Second World War

2. Can we vary use of vocabulary and the level of detail, orally? (L3) Can we produce lively and thoughtful writing in a range of forms? (L4)

The Challenge

You must work with a partner to make a taped story about a child who dreams he/she has gone back to the Second World War. You must include:

1. Sound effects to make the change from reality to dream world, and to give the atmosphere of war.

2. Dialogue, (a script) for the main character, a narrator and other characters she/he meets.

3. The script must include a news bulletin with information built in about the war and how it changed life in England.

4. The script must include jingles for advertisement breaks.

5. You must make a poster or flyer to advertise your broadcast.

3. Can we show understanding of the main points in fiction and non-fiction, fact and reality? (L3)

2. Activities
Produce a written dialogue that presents the historical facts of WW2 as well as the fictional context of a child falling asleep and dreaming.

3. Activities
Design a poster or flyer to advertise your broadcast. Use the effects learnt in Art to represent the dream aspect of the story.

4. Can we give reasons for and results of main changes and events? (L3,4) Can we show understanding of these events and characters? (L4)

5. Can we begin to choose the skills and sources to respond to challenge? (L3) Can we select and use a range of skills to investigate and present ideas and work? (L4)

YEAR 5 TERM 3 'PLANET EARTH' CREATIVE CURRICULUM CHALLENGE

The Context:
Moon Mission Control are interested in purchasing a newly designed lunar landing craft. They are inviting design plans and models, including clear evidence of how it will stand on the moon's surface.

You must present your design plan and model to Moon Mission Control, explaining how you used the key skills.

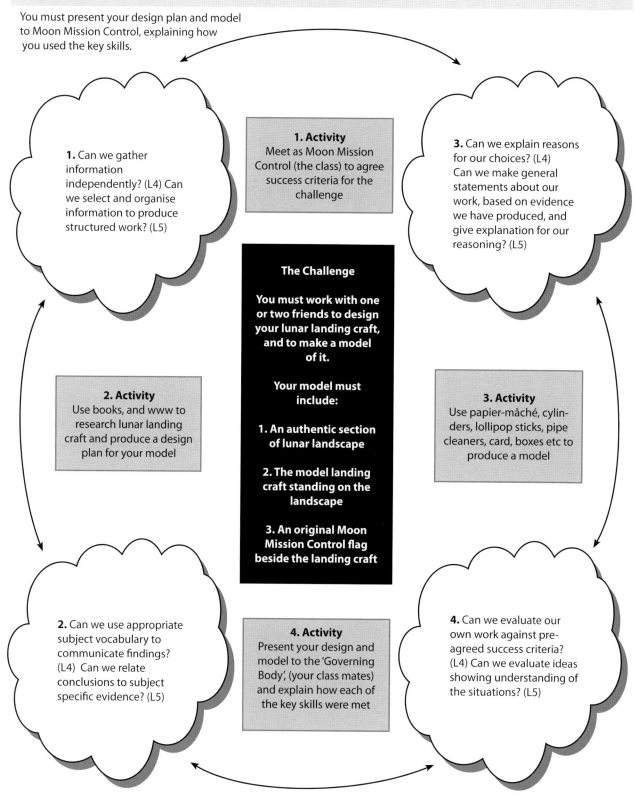

1. Can we gather information independently? (L4) Can we select and organise information to produce structured work? (L5)

1. Activity
Meet as Moon Mission Control (the class) to agree success criteria for the challenge

3. Can we explain reasons for our choices? (L4) Can we make general statements about our work, based on evidence we have produced, and give explanation for our reasoning? (L5)

The Challenge

You must work with one or two friends to design your lunar landing craft, and to make a model of it.

Your model must include:

1. An authentic section of lunar landscape

2. The model landing craft standing on the landscape

3. An original Moon Mission Control flag beside the landing craft

2. Activity
Use books, and www to research lunar landing craft and produce a design plan for your model

3. Activity
Use papier-mâché, cylinders, lollipop sticks, pipe cleaners, card, boxes etc to produce a model

2. Can we use appropriate subject vocabulary to communicate findings? (L4) Can we relate conclusions to subject specific evidence? (L5)

4. Activity
Present your design and model to the 'Governing Body', (your class mates) and explain how each of the key skills were met

4. Can we evaluate our own work against pre-agreed success criteria? (L4) Can we evaluate ideas showing understanding of the situations? (L5)

YEAR 6 TERM 3 'THE CARIBBEAN' CREATIVE CURRICULUM CHALLENGE

The Context:
'Happy _____ Holiday Tours Mall' will be located down the west wall of the hall (or down a wide corridor, or round the classroom walls), from the first week of June until the last week of term. The whole community will be invited to vote for the 'Travel Agent of the Year' award, having visited each kiosk in town

You must show evidence of having the key skills mapped within your group. Annotate your displays to evidence skills and who was the user of that skill

This could be delivered through a half day a week over the term, one day a fortnight, or a 3 week project to celebrate the theme. All other lessons would be planned using the school's usual short term plan.

1. Activities
Use travel brochures, post-cards, books, videos and the internet to investigate life on, and physical and human features of a Caribbean Island.

2. Activities
Use maps, globes and plans to locate islands within the Caribbean. Show routes from the UK to the Caribbean, and show land use on one island.

2. Can we locate ideas and information? (L4) Can we select essential points from a range of texts/sources? (L5)

1. Can we draw on our own knowledge and understanding to suggest questions for study? (L4) Can we draw on our own knowledge and understanding to select and use appropriate skills? (L5)

3. Can we organise findings/writing appropriately for purpose and reader? (L4) Can we produce varied and interesting writing in a range of forms for different readers? (L5)

The Challenge

You must open a kiosk representing your travel agency on the 'Happy_____ (School or community name) Holiday Tours Mall'.

Your branch is promoting a holiday to a Caribbean Island of your choice as a free prize to the first customer to correctly name the island.

You must include in your displays, leaflets etc:

1. Location maps
2. Island maps
3. Route/travel information
4. Seasonal weather information
5. Holiday attractions of different types
6. Ways of life for islanders
7. Cultural interests, art, music, dance and literature
8. Flora and Fauna

4. Activities
Use Art, Music and D+T skills to enrich your display

4. Can we begin to take account of the views and preferences of others? (L4)

3. Activities
Organise information and present in different ways to produce a lively and challenging 'kiosk'

6. Can we use ICT to combine different forms of information? (L4) Can we use ICT appropriately to organise, refine and present information in different forms and styles for specific purposes and audiences? (L5)

5. Can we select and combine ideas and information from sources? (L4) Can we identify sources of information most useful for different tasks? (L5)

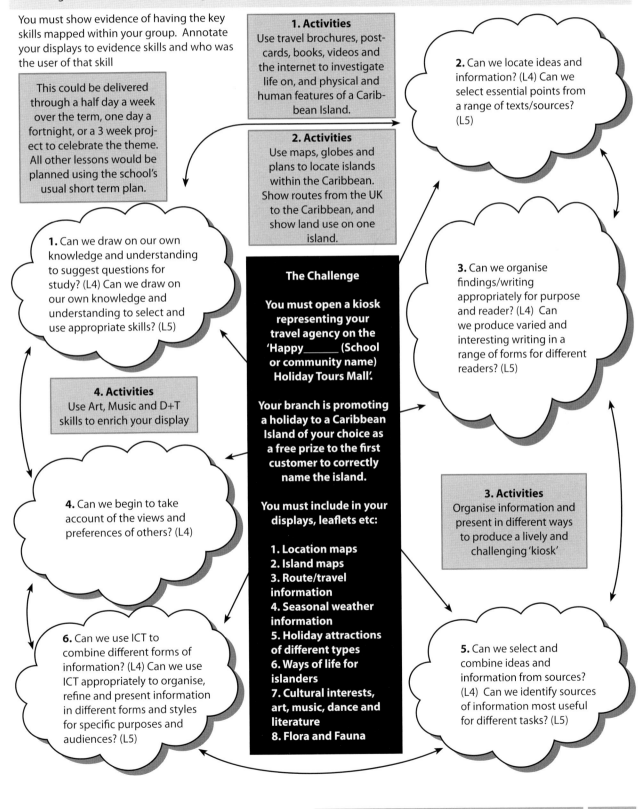

10 THE OPTIONAL MINI CHALLENEGES

THE MINI CHALLENGES (MCs): PROVIDE OPTIONAL ADDITIONAL INTEGRATED CREATIVE INVESTIGATIONS FOR EACH TERM.

THE TEACHER MAY CHOOSE TO USE JUST ONE, ANY TWO OR ALL THREE IN A TERM. S/HE MAY USE ALL THREE AT THE SAME TIME, ALLOWING GROUPS TO CHOOSE WHICH THEY PURSUE, OR ALL GROUPS MIGHT ROTATE ROUND ALL THREE ON A CAROUSEL.

YEAR 1 TERM 1

OPTIONAL MINI CHALLENGES

COULD BE DEVELOPED AS HALF-DAYS OF INTEGRATED STUDY THROUGHOUT THE TERM

1. Your challenge is to perform a musical and dramatic performance of a traditional tale. As a group:

» Choose a tale eg Red Riding Hood, Goldilocks and the Three Bears, Jack and the Beanstalk, read and enjoy it

» Try out different characters and musical effects to tell the story. You may want to record some of your work on a tape recorder

» Make a poster to advertise your performance

» Practise your performance

» Perform for your friends

2. Your challenge is to plan a musical accompaniment to your own gymnastic or dance sequence, to represent the importance of eating a healthy diet. Working as a group:

» Plan the sort of movement and sequence that could represent the effect of both a healthy and unhealthy diet

» Develop your sequence

» Plan and develop an improvised musical accompaniment to your sequence

» Practise performing your sequence and accompaniment together

» Perform for your friends

3. Your challenge is to make a booklet or display about your life so far. You should:

» Put a series of photographs of yourself from birth to now in chronological, (time) order

» Plan questions, (with your class) to ask at home

» Ask questions to find out key things about yourself at each of these ages

» Use ICT to record information you have found

» Arrange your photographs and information in a booklet or a display, making sure they look attractive. Write headings for each section

YEAR 1 TERM 2

OPTIONAL MINI CHALLENGES.......'HOMES LONG AGO'

COULD BE DEVELOPED AS HALF-DAYS OF INTEGRATED STUDY THROUGHOUT THE TERM

1. Your challenge is to produce a fabric collage on a piece of hessian, which is at least 66cm by 100cm. It should illustrate a typical Victorian living room.
In 2s or 3s:

» Collect a range of fabrics, textiles etc

» Plan your living room and identify good background fabrics to represent typical wall and floor coverings.

» Cover the hessian base with your selected backgrounds, using glue to attach. Test your glues first to make sure they do not spoil the effect.

» Make paper templates for furnishings, ornaments, pictures etc and arrange on the background.

» Select the best fabrics for each item. Cut out using the templates as a stencil and attach by glue

» Attach a border round the edge

2. Your challenge is to make a Valentine card for your mother or another adult you care about. Work on your own, but you should talk about your ideas with your friends:

» Study a range of Valentine Cards and decide, as a class, what the main features are

» Try out some ideas for making inset panels, (hearts, flowers, poems etc) using cut-out windows with fabrics, (satin, velvet etc) set in behind.

» Design your own card

» Make up your own verse to include in your design

» Make your card. How can you make the back of the inset look neat?

» (Spring Term before February 14th)

3. Your challenge is to make a shadow puppet show to retell one of the stories set in Victorian times that you are studying. In 2s or 3s:

» Investigate materials to make a screen, trialling the use of spotlights, angle poise, torches etc to produce the best shadows.

» Decide which characters need to be in your retell of the story

» Design and cut out each character, (using card) and attach to lollipop sticks

» Practise your retell until you are all good at doing the actions and voices

» Perform for your friends. [N.B a story such as 'The Tale of Two Bad Mice' by Beatrix Potter would be very good for this

YEAR 1 TERM 3

OPTIONAL MINI CHALLENGES……. 'AROUND OUR SCHOOL'

COULD BE DEVELOPED AS HALF-DAYS OF INTEGRATED STUDY THROUGHOUT THE TERM

1. Your challenge is to help develop a section of the garden area of the school grounds, or set of tubs outside the school. You might help your class to collect seedlings for flowering plants from home or from a garden centre or market. You will help to:

» Look after the seedlings as they grow into healthy plants

» Investigate how tall the different plants will grow and the conditions they need, (water, sunlight)

» Plan how you would arrange the plants to make the garden or tubs more attractive

» Plant your plants according to your plan

» Look after your plants over the following weeks

» Paint studies of flowers found in your garden

2. Your challenge is to make a pamphlet to be sent to tourists who want to visit your locality. Use the information you have collected through your geography lessons to make a six sided pamphlet that will make tourists want to come. Work with two friends. You must include:

» A title page that names the locality and has an attractive picture of one important building

» Maps and plans of the locality

» Three or more important features that tourists would enjoy

» A web site address for tourists to find our name (Have you explored this website to get ideas?)

NB. 6 sided pamphlet = 1 sheet A4 folded concertina-style into 3. Use both sides.

3. Your challenge is to visit a local building that has good surfaces for making further rubbings. This might be a church, museum or famous house. You must work with a friend to:

» Make 2 rubbings, (or more) of interesting surfaces

» Make 2 drawings of interesting objects.

» Make a plan of the building in its setting, over one of the rubbings

» Make notes about things you enjoy and things you don't.

» Join with 2 other friends to plan and present your findings to your class

» Use WWW, pamphlets and other sources to find out as much as you can before you go

YEAR 2 TERM 1

OPTIONAL MINI CHALLENGES...... 'OUR LOCALITY'

COULD BE DEVELOPED AS HALF-DAYS OF INTEGRATED STUDY THROUGHOUT THE TERM

1. Your challenge is to help to set up a Toy Museum.

» Work with your class to collect old toys from home and sort them by agreed criteria, (moving/non-moving, mechanical, dolls and animals, riding etc)

» Work with your class to plan the organisation and layout of the museum

» Work with friends to plan one display in the museum, (one of the sorted collections). Plan how they will be displayed so that all toys can be seen.

» Make labels for each toy saying who it belongs to and what it is. List materials it is made from and design features

» Make a sign to attract visitors to your display

» Visit a local toy museum if possible

2. Your challenge is to use some of the old toys or toy packaging no longer wanted from the Toy Museum, to create a sculpture or mobile for the entrance to the museum.

» Investigate assembling the toys in different ways.

» Experiment with different structures to give height, or depth (boxes, book or music stands, coat hangers etc)

» Investigate ways of fastening things together

» Assemble and secure your sculpture or mobile

3. Your challenge is to work with one friend to write a ghost story set in the school or a famous local building. Use your VCOP to make your story really scarey. You are going to record your story for a radio broadcast. You must:

» Experiment with technology and alternative spaces, (that could produce echoes) to produce echo and distorted sounds, (e.g. playing a cassette at reduced speed or in a heavy box)

» Experiment with musical instruments from two or more families to develop scarey background music and sound effects.

» Practise reading your story and playing the accompaniment or pre-recording the story and adding the accompaniment

» Record your performance. Can you improve it? Play it to an audience?

YEAR 2 TERM 2

OPTIONAL MINI CHALLENGES….. 'THE WORLD AROUND US'

COULD BE DEVELOPED AS HALF-DAYS OF INTEGRATED STUDY THROUGHOUT THE TERM

1. Your challenge is to produce a puppet show to tell all the story of either Florence Nightingale or the Great Fire of London. You must work with a group of friends to:

» Write the story as a play script, (dialogue)

» Try out reading different parts

» Make puppets to represent characters in the story

» Practise acting out the story through the puppets

» Perform for your friends

NB Your puppets can be made from:

» card and lollipop sticks

» a sock with felt features glued on

» a glove puppet made from a template

» other

2. Your challenge is to set up a weather station to measure temperature, wind speed and rainfall every school day. Working with your class you must help to:

» Keep up-to-date records for the weather each day

» Compare the weather each day with the weather in one contrasting UK and one overseas locality (using WWW)

» Record the 3 sets of information on a chart

» Decide whether the weather has been typical for the localities and compare how it would affect daily life

3. Your challenge is to help to produce a class book, display or PowerPoint presentation on caring for small pets. With 2 friends you must:

» Use WWW, books and other sources to research about the natural home of the pet you have chosen, (rabbit, guinea pig, gerbil, terrapin etc)

» Use similar range of sources to find out how the chosen animal should be cared for as a pet.

» Make a list of Do's and Don'ts

» Record and present your work through ICT, and assemble as part of a book, display or PowerPoint

» Share with your friends

» Is it possible to visit a pet hypermarket and talk to/ interview the vet or a member of staff about popular pets/pet care etc?

YEAR 2 TERM 3

OPTIONAL MINI CHALLENGES….. 'THE SEASIDE'

COULD BE DEVELOPED AS HALF-DAYS OF INTEGRATED STUDY THROUGHOUT THE TERM

1. Your challenge is to use collage techniques to illustrate a bathing scene, (at the beach) from times past. Work with two or three friends to:

» Collect a large number of coloured pages from old magazines

» Sort by dominant colour/ tones, (e.g. blues, greys, yellows, oranges, reds, greens etc)

» Plan a large-scale outline picture of one or two bathers and a bathing machine, (on a beach) on A3 or A1 paper, (sugar quality or back of wall paper sample)

» Tear and mix shapes of close tone to glue into appropriate areas, (about 2cm diameter). Use contrast tones where shapes meet. Completely cover the background first, perhaps with blues/greys for sky, dark blues/ greens/white for sea and yellow/ oranges for sand

2. Your challenge is to write your own song about the weather, and compose the music to accompany it. Work with three or four friends to:

» Discuss weather types and select one

» Agree the type of mood and atmosphere you would think of with this weather

» List as many words as you can about this weather, words for how it feels, for the way it looks, for the effect it has, for how we behave in it

» Make up one or more verses about the weather, using these words

» Investigate sounds associated with the type of weather and select those appropriate to compose a background

» Practise and perform your song

3. Your challenge is to study railways from the past, as these were the main way that people travelled to the seaside. Working with two or three friends you must:

» Use WWW, books, pictures and other sources to find out about the development of the railway during and since Victorian times

» Make drawings and notes of main developments and changes over time

» Find out how railways changed life, both in industry and leisure

» Present all your findings in a display

[It would be good to take children on a steam train or to a railway museum]

YEAR 3 TERM 1

OPTIONAL MINI CHALLENGES...... 'SETTLEMENT'

COULD BE DEVELOPED AS HALF-DAYS OF INTEGRATED STUDY THROUGHOUT THE TERM

1. Your challenge is to produce a model village on a large tray or board. You must work with two or three friends to:

» Finalise your map of a village of your own design from geography

» Include an area for growing each of 3 different crops of your choice and areas to keep at least 3 types of animals. It should also have buildings for weaving, the blacksmith, the miller, and an inn for travellers. It will need stables for horses, and a manor house for the Lord of the village

» Collect lollipop sticks, pipe cleaners, cardboard and cardboard boxes to construct your areas

» Use a range of fabrics, foils, crepe paper etc to produce effects

» Label the different places and their uses

2. Your challenge is to make a chant or rap to make the world know how great your class or school is. You must work with one or two friends to:

» Investigate clap and drum rhythms as a development from your music lessons

» Make up at least eight sentences and phrases to celebrate the good things about your class or school

» Arrange the lines in sequence, fitting them to a clapped or beaten rhythm

» Practise as a chant or rap

» Perform for your friends

3. Your challenge is to produce a design for a stained glass window for the manor house in your village. Working with two or three friends your must:

» Use WWW, books and photographs to research stained glass windows and heraldry of wealthy families. What is a family crest?

» Try out design ideas for a stained glass window that represents life in the village. It should have 4 panels

» The top panel should be your own design for the family crest

» The other 3 panels should each show one aspect of life in simple outline. It may be constructed through use of coloured foils or cellophane panels behind cut out shapes in black paper or card

YEAR 3 TERM 2

OPTIONAL MINI CHALLENGES….. 'ANIMAL KINGDOM'

COULD BE DEVELOPED AS HALF-DAYS OF INTEGRATED STUDY THROUGHOUT THE TERM

1. Your challenge is to prepare a website or electronic folder to introduce your class and school to your twin school. You must work with friends to:

» Write a 'pen portrait' about yourself, giving your age, gender, a brief description, likes, dislikes, hobbies etc

» Include a digital photograph of yourself

» In 3s, select an aspect of your school or of lessons that you particularly like. Describe it and include photographs

» This is an opportunity to share this information in reality through an on-line community using a product such as 'MyLO' (My Learning Online)

2. Your challenge is to design a quiz based on the habitat and habits of one species of wild animal. You must work in 2s or 3s to:

» Use WWW, books, videos and photographs to gather information about your chosen animal

» Make up questions about the habitat and habits of your animal. Include both easy and hard questions

» Decide how to present your questionnaire, (as a class) – Database? Electronic? Word processed?

» Decide how people will find the answers

» Exchange questionnaires with other groups in the class

» Collate and present the results

3. Your challenge is to investigate either a species of animal or a natural feature of Earth that is under threat, (ice caps, rainforest, drought area or similar). You must plan a campaign to raise public awareness about your study.
Work with 2 friends to:

» Use WWW, books, videos, magazines and photographs to find out about the threat

» Produce a 6 sided pamphlet explaining what the threat is. Include maps and charts.

» Make a poster to get your message round quickly and easily

NB. 6 sided pamphlet = 1 sheet A4 folded concertina-style into 3. Use both sides.

YEAR 3 TERM 3

OPTIONAL MINI CHALLENGES….. 'TUDOR TIMES'

COULD BE DEVELOPED AS HALF-DAYS OF INTEGRATED STUDY THROUGHOUT THE TERM

1. Your challenge is to study one famous explorer from Tudor Times. (NB Tudor Explorers are studied as a theme in Year 6). Working with 2 friends you must:

» Use WWW, books, video and photographs to find out about your explorer

» Make maps to show the journey or journeys he made

» Make a model of his main form of transport

» Write a letter from the explorer to Queen Elizabeth 1 telling her about his journey, things he has found and things he has seen

2. Your challenge is to make a fridge magnet in the form of a cameo. You must work with a friend, but make one each. You must:

» Make a flat-backed dome-shaped circular or oval base, (about 3cm diameter) using plaster, papier-mâché or a modelling media. Allow to set.

» Study a range of cameos or photographs of cameos and identify the features: pastel backgrounds, white relief head sometimes in profile.

» Practise profile portraits of your friend using an OHP shining onto A1 paper to throw a relief

» Reduce by grid system or by eye until down to size of base

» Use a template to draw onto base. Then wax to resist

» Paint background and varnish

» Rinse in hot water. Glue on magnet

3. Your challenge is to make the bottom of shoe boxes into the façade, (front) of a Tudor House. You will help your class to assemble a Tudor street using the houses. You must work with one or two friends to:

» Study features of Tudor house fronts; windows, doors, the projecting upper floor, beams and roof.

» Investigate ways of constructing the projection and giving the effects of windows, wood beams etc

» Construct your house, discussing and making improvements

» Discuss ways of making the cobble effect for a street on a table or cupboard top

» Arrange the houses along the street, almost touching

YEAR 4 TERM 1

OPTIONAL MINI CHALLENGES...... 'CHANGE'

COULD BE DEVELOPED AS HALF-DAYS OF INTEGRATED STUDY THROUGHOUT THE TERM

1. Your challenge is to set up an employment agency as a class. Research how jobs are advertised and what information is given to applicants and required from applicants.
Work with a friend to:

» Research, using WWW, newspapers and field study, how jobs are advertised

» Create 2 jobs needing applicants in your school. They need not be real or serious. Write an advertisement for the jobs, and an application form.

» As a class, develop questions to ask applicants for jobs

» Work with another group to be interviewers and interviewees

2. Your challenge is to make a money box to store your change in. Work with one or two friends to share ideas but each make your own. You must:

» Study a range of money boxes and identify main features

» Come up with an original idea as to what the appearance of your money box might represent, (An animal? A coin? A face or figure? A vehicle etc)

» Select a cardboard box, tube, cone etc most suited to your design

» Investigate strengthening methods and use to reinforce the sides and bottom

» Create your design, including 3 dimensional features, using card if possible

» Paint and varnish exterior

» Make the opening slot to the lid or upper side

3. Your challenge is to find out about the history of fireworks, and different celebrations that they are used for. Work with one or two friends to:

» Use WWW, books and other sources to research the history of fireworks

» Make a display of information and pictures of use of fireworks for a range of celebrations around the world

» Find out the full story of why we have Bonfire Night, and make up a playlet to tell the story. Act it for your friends.

» Make a poster advertising health and safety procedures for handling fireworks

YEAR 4 TERM 2

OPTIONAL MINI CHALLENGES...... 'CONTRASTING UK LOCALITY'

COULD BE DEVELOPED AS HALF-DAYS OF INTEGRATED STUDY THROUGHOUT THE TERM

1. Your challenge is to research the type of nautical craft one group of invaders used to come to Britain. Work with one friend to:

» Use WWW, books, photographs etc to find out all you can about the boats used by your invaders

» Make sketches and drawings of the boats

» Draw a design plan. Label the parts and note materials to be used

» Gather materials and construct the boat

» Display with a card explaining who used it and when

2. Your challenge is to find the cost of a trip to the locality you are studying for your group. You must work with three or four friends to:

» Use the WWW and/or travel agents/brochures to find the cost of travel by at least 2 routes, 2 different types of accommodation for the number in your group and insurance for the trip

» Use the WWW and/or catalogues to purchase a new outfit to travel in and suitable clothing for the climate and activities you might take part in, and for a new suitcase for each to take

» Find the minimum and maximum cost for the group trip

3. Your challenge is to plan and take part in a class celebration of the locality you are studying. As a group, you will study and produce one of the following:

» A typical snack or part of a meal from the locality

» A dance from the locality

» A poem or reading from a poet or author from the locality, (may be about the locality)

» A large map of the locality, with small pictures of main tourist features attached in the right places

» A poster to persuade tourists to visit the locality

YEAR 4 TERM 3

OPTIONAL MINI CHALLENGES….. 'DREAMS'

COULD BE DEVELOPED AS HALF-DAYS OF INTEGRATED STUDY THROUGHOUT THE TERM

1. Your challenge is to produce a painting or sculpture that reflects the mood of your music from music lessons. You must:

» Investigate ways of using the materials available to produce an effect

» Discuss your ideas and investigations with friends

» Select one approach and use it to investigate mood and atmosphere

» Produce your piece

» Explain your choices and decisions to your friends, and say how you might improve it

2. Your challenge is to produce a drumming sequence and dance that expresses mood. You must work in a group to:

» Investigate a range of drums, including some where the pitch can change. Link your findings to your science lessons

» Explore a range of dance moves, thinking about change in speed, shape and height to reflect mood

» Experiment with drummed sequences to reflect and stimulate the dance

» Practise and perform a sequence

3. Your challenge is to produce the front page of a newspaper published during the Second World War. Working as a group you must:

» Study some newspapers from the time, advertisements and other common features, using the WWW and/or field study in a local museum

» Research an important event in the war and write a newspaper report for it

» Illustrate the report

» Write at least 2 other front page articles about fictitious but possible local events of that day

» Include at least one advertisement in the style of the time

» Publish your work on a sheet of A1

YEAR 5 TERM 1

OPTIONAL MINI CHALLENGES…. 'THE WAY WE LIVE'

COULD BE DEVELOPED AS HALF-DAYS OF INTEGRATED STUDY THROUGHOUT THE TERM

1. Your challenge is to redesign the road system around your school to create a vehicle-free zone, so that parents and children can meet, chat, and walk to and from school safely. Working with 2 or 3 others you must:

- » Study some designs for pedestrian precincts through the WWW, books or magazines

- » Decide which road/s to close and how traffic will be diverted. Make a map to show changed routes

- » Design your pedestrian area. It must include: trees, tubs, seats and a picnic table

- » Make a model of your pedestrian area on board or a tray. Label the features

2. Your challenge is to make a Victorian sampler. You must work on your own but discuss your ideas and progress with your friends.

- » Study a range of Victorian samplers and identify the most common features

- » Learn and practise at least 3 stitches to use in your sampler

- » Design your sampler on squared paper, working on the scale to be used

- » Transfer your design onto binca or a similar fabric

- » Work your design onto your sampler using complementary colours

3. Your challenge is to produce an interior of a Victorian room. You will work in a group of three who will join with three other groups. The four rooms will be assembled into a doll's house.

As a large group you must:

- » Research Victorian interiors and dolls' houses through WWW, books, pictures and real dolls' houses

- » Agree which room each small group will do: lounge, dining room, bedroom or kitchen

As a small group you must:

- » Use research to design your room and select fabrics, wallpaper samples etc

- » Wall paper and carpet your room in character

- » Make your furniture using matchboxes, small boxes, pots, card etc

- » Make model pictures and ornaments

YEAR 5 TERM 2

OPTIONAL MINI CHALLENGES…. .'WATER'

COULD BE DEVELOPED AS HALF-DAYS OF INTEGRATED STUDY THROUGHOUT THE TERM

1. Your challenge is to design and make an umbrella. You must work with one friend to:

» Use WWW, catalogues and actual umbrellas to study designs and patterns

» Investigate ways umbrellas open and close, relating the mechanisms to your science studies on friction

» Make a paper parasol that opens and closes, to put in a drink as decoration

» Design an umbrella and select materials and media to make it. It does not have to close

» Make your umbrella. Find a way to display it with the rest of the classes

» (Ceiling? Along a shelf? Mobiles?)

2. Your challenge is to produce a display, web page or booklet on life and conditions beside a world famous river or canal, (Amazon, Nile, Rhine, Thames, Venice, Panama Canal etc). You must work with one or two friends to:

» Use WWW, books and tourist brochures to research the river/ canal you have chosen

» Share out jobs and agree the standards to be achieved

» Produce at least one of each of the following:

  » Report on a historical aspect
  » Report on life there today
  » Information on location, climate, population etc
  » Maps
  » Picture of key features

» Combine your work to make your display, webpage or booklet look attractive.

3. Your challenge is to design a water feature for the entrance to your school. The best feature may be used in the entrance hall, (an electronic pump will be purchased). The class must agree success criteria to be used in judging, as a panel, each feature. You must work in 2s or 3s to:

» Use WWW, catalogues and field study in a garden centre to study a range of designs for water features

» Select at least 3 containers, tubes, lengths of guttering or sectioned drainpipe, pots, etc

» Investigate ways of assembling at least 3 of your selected items, using a watering can or jug to test water flow

» Investigate ways of fixing your items so that the feature can be moved safely

» Demonstrate your feature to the 'panel', explaining what you did and improvements you made

YEAR 5 TERM 3

OPTIONAL MINI CHALLENGES….. 'PLANET EARTH'

COULD BE DEVELOPED AS HALF-DAYS OF INTEGRATED STUDY THROUGHOUT THE TERM

1. Your challenge is to design a sundial to track the path of the sun as the Earth turns. Working with one friend you must:

» Discover how and when sundials were used in the past

» Use WWW, photographs, catalogues and/or field study at a Garden Centre to study the design of a range of sundials, making labelled drawings

» Identify a setting in the school grounds for a sundial

» Design the face of the sundial, the shadow maker and the pedestal, in a labelled drawing, identifying materials to be used.

» Collect your materials

» Make your sundial

» Test it outdoors on a sunny day

2. Your challenge is to devise and use a class questionnaire to discover how 'green' your school and community are. You must work with one or two friends to:

» Help to devise the questionnaire in a way that will let you find out how 'green' aware an organisation is and what practices they use

» Use WWW to investigate aspects of recycling and conservation in local organisations

» Identify key departments/ functions in school, (kitchens, caretaking, ICT suite, administration etc) and local businesses/departments, (shop, health centre, nursery etc) and allocate to class groups

» Use a questionnaire to investigate your key focus's approach to conservation

» Prepare a report, including graphs and charts

» Contribute your report to a class display or presentation

3. Your challenge is to investigate an aspect of space or work associated with space. You must work with one or two friends to:

» Use WWW, books and magazines to gather information for a space study. This could focus on a planet or solar system, an aspect of the development of space travel from your history studies, science fiction in literature or film, horoscopes/astrology, astronomy etc)

» Present your findings in picture, chart and written forms, through a PowerPoint presentation

» Present your PowerPoint to your class, (and the school?)

YEAR 6 TERM 1

OPTIONAL MINI CHALLENGES….. 'THE GREEKS'

COULD BE DEVELOPED AS HALF-DAYS OF INTEGRATED STUDY THROUGHOUT THE TERM UNLIKE MINI CHALLENGES IN PREVIOUS YEARS, THESE MAY BE PREPARED BY 3 SEPARATE Y6 GROUPS WITHIN THE SAME TIME FRAME

1. Your challenge is to plan for a major Olympic athletic event to be held in your locality in 2008. You must:

» Work out how many competitors there would be in a race if every competing country entered 2 competitions

» Work out how long the event would take and plan the sequence so that no runner has to run twice in close succession. There will be heats for all competitors, quarter finals for 2 fastest from each heat, semi-finals for 2 fastest from each quarter and finals. There will be 5 minutes between each heat, 15 minutes between ¼ finals, 30 minutes between semi-finals and 1 hour before the final

» Find a hotel or hotels near the motorway to accommodate all the competitors. How much will this cost?

» Prepare an information brochure for the competitors

2. Your challenge is to plan for a major Olympic athletic event to be held in your locality in 2008. You must:

» Select a stadium large enough to host the event and find out how much the hire for the day will be.

» Draw up a guest list of important people to invite

» Find out how much it will cost to accommodate the guests in a good hotel near the event

» Ask Group 1 how much accommodating the athletics is going to cost

» Find out how many people can be seated in the stadium

» Now add all your expenses and calculate how much you need to charge each spectator in order to cover your costs

» Prepare an advert to advertise the event in the newspaper

3. Your challenge is to plan the entertainment for a major Olympic athletic event to be held in your locality in 2008. You must:

» Investigate the range of entertainment often available at major events

» Plan a programme for before and after the event

» Investigate local bands, organisations, etcetera who might perform

» Draft a team of cheer leaders (can be imaginary) to support the event. Plan their dance sequence and chant.

» Design a costume for the cheer leaders. Make a 2D mock up on a cardboard cut-out figure, using fabrics of choice

» Design official male and female outfits for Team GB for the event. Make 2D mock-ups on cardboard cut-out figures, using fabrics of choice.

YEAR 6 TERM 2

OPTIONAL MINI CHALLENGE….. 'THE 1960S'

COULD BE DEVELOPED AS HALF-DAYS OF INTEGRATED STUDY THROUGHOUT THE TERM

As a class:

Can you divide the life of John Lennon, (or a similar icon of the 1960s) into four or six aspects? Allocate an aspect to each of four groups. As a group you must:

» Research more deeply into John's life in your aspect

» Identify two or three key events you wish to cover

» Write a play script for a scene from 'The John Lennon Show' that enacts these events

» Build opportunities into your scene for at least 2 of The Beatles' songs. Network with the other groups to make sure they are not using them

» Rehearse a mini-performance of your scene

» Perform with the other 3 scenes in an agreed sequence. Perform for the school?

YEAR 6 TERM 3

OPTIONAL MINI CHALLENGES….. 'THE CARIBBEAN'

COULD BE DEVELOPED AS HALF-DAYS OF INTEGRATED STUDY THROUGHOUT THE TERM

Instead of conventional mini challenges we suggest that the whole of the theme could be studied as independent challenges in groups. Each group could be given an aspect of each area of study to research and achieve an outcome. They could then work through an integrated approach to complete their studies, and feed back to the class.

Each group might therefore:

» Investigate and construct a different type of shelter

» Plan and cost a holiday to the Caribbean

» Investigate an aspect of West Indian culture and make examples e.g. food, music, dance, costume for carnival

» Investigate the history of slavery in the West Indies, and how it was brought to an end

» Make a study of 2 contrasting animals found in the West Indies

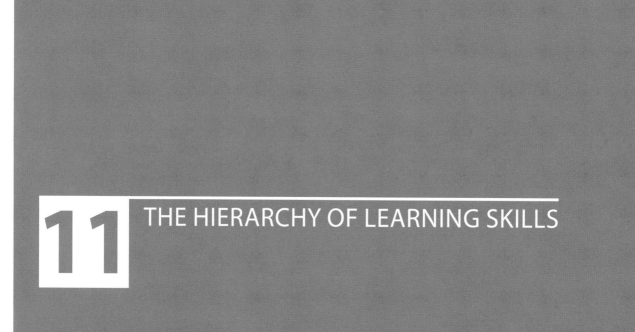

11 THE HIERARCHY OF LEARNING SKILLS

WHAT IS 'THE HIERARCHY OF LEARNING SKILLS'?

The Hierarchy of Learning Skills provide an assessment scale for the generic skills of the whole curriculum. They have been synthesized out of the Level Descriptions for every subject of the National Curriculum. This hierarchy is a generic scale for assessing the development of transferable skills across the curriculum.

It is recommended that the hierarchy be used to inform planning through identifying and tracking which key skills could be learned, consolidated or applied and thus assessed through a particular theme's subject opportunities.

It is further recommended that assessment be through ongoing observational records (similar to best Foundation Stage practice) through ticking, highlighting or a traffic light system to show levels of understanding.

The numbering system is to make referencing on planning more manageble - it does **not** denote a hierarchy of skills within a level and pupils will frequently achieve skills randomly within levels and across levels whilst still working towards some previous skills.

LEVEL 1 - THE HIERARCHY OF LEARNING SKILLS (ROS WILSON)

No	Skill	Unit	Year	Term
1	Begin to provide some detail to extend ideas or events, (orally)			
2	Identify aspects they like, (e.g. in stories, poems, videos, productions)			
3	Know and recount episodes from stories, (fact and fiction)			
4	Begin to find answers to questions from appropriate sources of information			
5	Recognise features			
6	Express views on things they find attractive or unattractive			
7	Use resources provided and own observations, to respond to questions			
8	Discuss their work			
9	Communicate findings in simple ways			
10	Use ICT to communicate ideas, (text and symbols)			
11	Show awareness that information exists in a variety of forms, (e.g. can name at least 3, such as books, videos, INTERNET, magazines, people)			

LEVEL 2 - THE HIERARCHY OF LEARNING SKILLS (ROS WILSON)

No	Skill	Unit	Year	Term
1	Include relevant detail in ideas or events, (orally)			
2	Develop and extend ideas orally			
3	Express opinions about major events or ideas in stories, poems and non-fiction			
4	Discuss work using appropriate language			
5	Begin to identify some different ways things are represented			
6	Respond to suggestions of how to find things out			
7	Select information from sources provided			
8	Use information and observation to ask and respond to questions			
9	Ask and respond to, 'What would happen if…..?'			
10	Make comparisons between things they can observe			
11	Describe their observations			
12	Reflect on ideas and make suggestions, with help, (e.g. on improvements)			
13	Use ICT to help them generate and communicate ideas in different forms			
14	Suggest ways to find information			

LEVEL 3 - THE HIERARCHY OF LEARNING SKILLS (ROS WILSON)

No	Skill	Unit	Year	Term
1	Explore and communicate ideas orally			
2	Vary the use of vocabulary and the level of detail, orally			
3	Show understanding of the main points in fiction and non-fiction, reality and creation.			
4	Express preferences in text, including non-fiction			
5	Use main features of different forms, and purposes for writing, appropriately to present ideas and understanding			
6	Begin to adapt writing for different audiences and purposes			
7	Begin to give reasons for and results of main changes and events			
8	Identify different ways in which things are represented			
9	Find answers to questions by using sources in ways that go beyond the simple observations			
10	Describe and compare features			
11	Offer reasons for some of their observations and judgements			
12	Begin to choose the skills and sources to respond to questions			
13	Discuss their work and begin to explain their thinking			
14	Make simple predictions			
15	Provide simple explanations for why things happened as they did			
16	Say what they found out, orally and in writing			
17	Make realistic suggestions for how intentions might be achieved			
18	Draw on their knowledge and understanding to help generate ideas and suggest further ideas if asked			
19	Say what they did well and begin to suggest ways they might change things next time			
20	Use ICT to generate, amend, organise and present ideas			
21	Describe their own use of ICT, and its use in the wider world			

LEVEL 4 - THE HIERARCHY OF LEARNING SKILLS (ROS WILSON)

No	Skill	Unit	Year	Term
1	Adapt their talk to purpose, developing ideas thoughtfully			
2	Describe events and convey opinions			
3	Recognise and describe features and how things can change			
4	Ask questions responsive to the ideas and views of others			
5	Show understanding of themes, events and characters			
6	Locate and use ideas and information			
7	Begin to use inference and deduction			
8	Refer to text when expressing views			
9	Produce lively and thoughtful writing in a range of forms			
10	Sustain/develop ideas in different ways			
11	Organise writing appropriately for purpose and reader			
12	Produce structured work, making appropriate use of information			
13	Give reasons for, and results of significant events and changes			
14	Begin to select and combine information from sources			
15	Draw on own knowledge and understanding to suggest questions for study			
16	Gather information independently			
17	Select and use a range of skills to investigate			
18	Use appropriate subject vocabulary to communicate findings			
19	Explain reasons for their choices e.g. methodology and/or materials			
20	Search for patterns when trying ideas			
21	Identify and interpret patterns or trends			
22	Make predictions			
23	Make choices between alternatives			
24	Draw conclusions			
25	Begin to take account of the views and preferences of others			
26	Evaluate their own work, bearing in mind their objectives			
27	Use ICT to combine different forms of information			
28	Show awareness of audience			

LEVEL 5 - THE HIERARCHY OF LEARNING SKILLS (ROS WILSON)

No	Skill	Unit	Year	Term
1	Vary expressions and vocabulary orally			
2	Ask questions to develop ideas			
3	Make contributions that take account of others' views			
4	Select essential points from a range of texts			
5	Use inference and deduction where and when appropriate			
6	Identify and describe key characters, themes and features			
7	Select sentences and phrases containing relevant information to support views			
8	Retrieve and collate information from a range of sources			
9	Produce varied and interesting vocabulary in a range of forms for different readers			
10	Use more formal styles in writing when appropriate			
11	Describe and make links between relevant reasons for and results of events and change			
12	Know that some events, people and changes have been represented in different ways			
13	Begin to evaluate sources of information			
14	Identify sources of information most useful for different tasks			
15	Select and organise information to produce structured work			
16	Identify, describe and begin to offer explanations for patterns			
17	Draw on knowledge and understanding to select and use appropriate skills			
18	Reach plausible conclusions and present findings			
19	Make general statements about their own work, based on evidence they have produced and give explanations for their reasoning			
20	Make appropriate predictions based on subject specific knowledge and understanding			
21	Offer explanations for differences in outcomes of investigations			
22	Draw conclusions consistent with the evidence			
23	Relate conclusions to the subject specific evidence			
24	Generate ideas that draw upon external sources			
25	Clarify their own ideas through discussion			
26	Evaluate ideas showing understanding of the situations			
27	Use ICT appropriately to organise, refine and present information in different forms and styles for purposes and audiences			

12 TAKING THE ISSUES INTO PLANNING – REMODELLING THE TEACHING OF TEXT TYPES FOR COHERENCE

This chapter suggests a revised approach to the teaching and development of the text types within the literacy elements of the Primary National Strategies (PNS) through exemplification in two of the termly maps.

HOW MIGHT WE REVISE THE DELIVERY OF THE LITERACY STRATEGY?

The teaching of characteristics of the text types in a focused and managed sequence is one of the strengths of the literacy strategy within the PNS. However, one of the flaws is that the setting of a national schedule for their teaching has meant they are frequently taught in isolation with little regard to giving them coherence through purpose linked to cross-curricular themes.

As schools restructure their curriculum, they should reconsider their literacy plans and identify the key features to be taught and the most relevant sequence for their delivery in relation to the remainder of the curriculum.

The elements of the English curriculum that certainly should be retained are:

1. Speaking and Listening, (planned as an ongoing unit as described in Chapter 5, 'The Importance of Talk'.

2. Drama and role play (planned as an ongoing opportunity in the Foundation Stage and Year 1, and as a termly or half termly focus related to themes throughout Years 2 to 6.

3. Debate taught as a focused blocked unit related to themes throughout Key Stage 2.

4. Reading skills taught as an ongoing unit throughout the entire primary phase and encompassing both decoding skills and comprehension skills, and group reading.

5. Writing skills = basic skills taught throughout Key Stage 1 and as weekly ten minute opportunities throughout Key Stage 2 (see 'Strategies for Immediate Impact on Writing Standards' 2003 and 'Write on Target' 2006).

6. Writing skills = pro-active teaching of 'voice' through VCOP (see 'Strategies for Immediate Impact on Writing Standards' 2003 and 'Write on Target' 2006).

7. The characteristics of Text Types, taught as blocked units linked to relevant themes for using and applying for purpose.

8. Appreciation and composition of poetry.

9. A love of literature.

10. Associated literacy skills including use of text types of all varieties and use of dictionaries, thesauruses, encyclopaedia and other reference books.

11. Library skills.

12. Performance and presentation skills.

Use of ICT and associated media should be embedded within all the above.

HOW CAN WE MAKE THE BLOCKED UNITS WORK ALONGSIDE OUR THEMATIC CURRICULUM?

The revised literacy aspect of the PNS was available in the autumn of 2006. It enables the teaching of skills over longer periods of time, allowing for a dedicated period of review and refreshment prior to the introduction of the next layer of teaching. Furthermore, teachers and schools may now allocate the teaching of skills to best opportunities for purposeful acquisition and application which may reflect the thematic links of their curriculum.

The following is a model for the linking of text types and other blocked opportunities to the exemplar Long Term Plan provided for Key Stage 2 in Chapter 7 of this publication.

Some thematic titles have been adapted for increased focus and opportunities for creativity.

The writer does not support the focused teaching of the range of text types at Key Stage 1. She believes that young children should be allowed to develop a love of literature and application of literacy skills without too many rigid dictates and rules. The processes of learning to read and write fluently are sufficient imposition for children up to the age of six. From six to seven the range of purposes for reading and writing will broaden and may now including narrative, report writing (local and personal news), recount genre (traditional and loved tales), verse and simple explanations and information text, but without the imposition of rigid rules.

This model is purely exemplification and should be adapted and altered to work for a school's own curriculum.

To interpret this model the reader should lay it alongside the model Long Term Curriculum Plan.

NB A FURTHER MODEL FOR ALLOCATION FOR KEY STAGE 2 IS PROVIDED IN APPENDIX 1

THE MODEL ALLOCATION OF BLOCKED ENGLISH SKILLS ACROSS KEY STAGE 2

Term and Theme	English Skills
Y3 Term 1 **'Settlement'**	1. Newspaper reports (T) (for a newspaper of the times reporting the invasions from both perspectives). 2. Instructions (T) = how to build a shelter? 3. Myths and Legends. 4. Local tales. 5. Works of local poets and authors.
Y3 Term 2 **'Animal Kingdoms'**	1. Reports = (information). 2. Discursive (T) (should we protect the environment or do we need the fuels and space for housing?) 3. Explanation (T) = environmental theme 4. Animal themes in stories and poetry.
Y3 Term 3 **'Tudor Times'** **See CCM**	1. Persuasive text (T) (from wife of Henry VIII? To improve the lot of ordinary people who lived in Tudor Times?) 2. Reports = why people undertook voyages of discovery. 3. Recount = Tudor tales 4. Dialogue = (T) play scripts 5. Instructional = how to … (Tudor dance? Recipe ? Game?) 6. Role Play Tudor villagers, townships and mansions.
Y4 Term 1 **'Change'**	1. Persuasive text (resist an imagined negative change within the local area). 2. Discursive (T) = plan a debate. on the same issue or a different one. 3. Reports (T)= including newspaper reports on proposed changes. 4. Debate = should we build a chicken farm on the school playing field? 5. Narrative = Relevant literature and poetry.
Y4 Term 2 **'Contrasting UK Locality'**	1. Reports (information text) for tourist pamphlets (geography link) and on ancient civilisation (history link). 3. Questionnaires (T) = re families choice of destinations and modes of travel 4. Explanation (T) = choices of destinations and modes of travel 5. Fables and traditional tales (T) linked to locality.
Y4 Term 3 **'Dreams'** **see CCM**	1. Narrative and poetry on 'dream' theme. 2. Recount (T) = stories from the war 3. Stories and poems (T) set in the second world war. 4. Dialogue = developed from role play of life of an evacuee. 5. Literature on theme of Second World War.
Y5 Term 1 **'The Way We Live'**	1. Instructional text (T) = Victorian and contemporary recipes? 2. Debate: Role of Healthy Diets and Exercise? 3. Dialogue (T) = developed from debate plus life in Victorian times 4. Report = ways of life…. 5. Narrative and poetry from the times

Term and Theme	English Skills
Y5 Term 2 'Water'	1. Persuasive text (T) = conservation issues. 2. Discursive text (T) to prepare a debate on why we need to protect rivers and water tables / why our valley (or a known valley) should NOT be flooded to make a new reservoir. 3. Newspaper reports = pollution / preservation 4. Explanation = how pollution damages rivers ? 5. Myths and legends with a water theme. 6. Debate: the flooding of the valley.
Y5 Term 3 'Planet Earth'	1. Reports = the impact of travel / forms of travel / changes over time 2. Recount = science fiction 4. Questionnaires (T) 5. Instructional text = how to ….(Build a space ship? Make a model solar system? Use a named ICT programme?) 6. Produce a presentation or publication. 7. Role play and debate local reactions to key issues. 8. Associated literature and poetry (T).
Y6 Term 1 'The Greeks'	Use all text types (through Big Writing?) to:_produce a detailed study of life in Greece from ancient times to the present, including the development of the Olympics (key focus every 4 years). Myths and Legends as a stimulus for reading and writing.
Y6 Term 2 'Books'	Use all text types (through Big Writing?) to: produce a study of a contemporary or historical 'hero' of the pupils' choice (Beatles? Beckham? Boudica?) Show accurate knowledge and use of characteristics of all text types. Use life / work of character as stimulus to read and interrogate text. Explain and illustrate own preferences in literature of all types.
Y6 Term 3 'The Caribbean'	Produce an in-depth study on an aspect of life in the Caribbean of your choice, eg tourism, music, cookery, geography, pirates, invasion and settlement etc. Use all text types in your presentation. West Indian literature, poetry and song.

T = TAUGHT

NB A second model is provided in Appendix 1

MODEL FOR THE ALLOCATION OF TEXT TYPES

Key Stage 1 = range of purposes for reading and writing taught without the rigidity of focusing specifically on characteristics of text types. Range to include: narrative, poetry, recount, reports and simple explanations.

Text Types	Year 3 Term 1 'Settlement'	Year 3 Term 2 'Animal Kingdom	Year 3 Term 3 'Tudors'	Year 4 Term 1 'Change'	Year 4 Term 2 'Resorts'	Year 4 Term 3 'Light / Sound'	Year 5 Term 1 'Way We Live'	Year 5 Term 2 'Water'	Year5 Term 3 'Planet Earth'
Fiction	√ local tales	√		√	√	√ taught	√		√
Myths / Legends	√				√ taught	√		√	
Poetry	√	√		√		√ taught	√		√ taught
Recount			√			√ taught	√		√
Report	√ taught	√	√	√ taught	√		√	√	√
Instruct	√ taught		√				√ taught		√
Explain		√ taught				√ taught		√	
Persuade			√ taught	√				√ taught	
Discuss		√ taught		√ taught				√ taught	√
Dialogue			√ taught			√	√ taught		
Question-naire					√ taught				√ taught

NB A second model is provided in Appeandx 1

Year 6 will rotate through all text types, one a week. This will be in the 'Big Writing' session if schools are using this approach (see 'Strategies for Immediate Impact on Writing Standards' 2003 and 'Write on Target' 2006). If the teacher identifies, through this process, weaknesses in a particular text type they will be addressed in a literacy session.

In the last two months before the May tests, Year 6 might write 3 different text types each week; one long one in Big Writing, one long one in a second subject for this subject's purpose and a third, short piece in a third subject for that subject's purpose. Pupils should then compare the quality of their work as they moved accross text types.

In most terms five text types have been identified as having particular relevance to the theme, however usually only two at most have been identified for in-depth teaching, one per half term. The others would be used on alternate weeks in the 'Big Writing' session, interspersed by all other text types.

NB The teaching, review and analysis take place in the literacy sessions whereas the writing takes place in the once a week writing session (Big Writing). The above is a model for how this might look:

13 TAKING THE ISSUES INTO PLANNING – ADAPTING THE CCMS

This chapter provides models for how the medium term plans might be adapted to increase the coherence of the thematic links without losing the rigour of good teaching.

The writer has chosen to take Year 2 Term 3 and Year 5 Term 3 for exemplification purposes.

The models given are only exemplification and are intended to illustrate how adaptation of existing QCA Unit Plans through reduction, change of content focus and emphasis of core skills through creative learning opportunities can produce a truly creative curriculum without a radical rewrite of the whole curriculum.

How might we adapt the Creative Curriculum Maps?

The following are the steps in the process that a school might go through in adapting the Creative Curriculum Maps. Again, Years 2, Term 3 and 5, Term 3 have been chosen for exemplification purposes.

YEAR 2 TERM 3 'THE SEASIDE'

Step 1:

Examine the appropriate Medium Term Map and determine what your school's priorities are.

Might any subject planned:

1. Not actually run this term without jeopardising the overall coherence and rigour of the subject?

2. Be modified this term without jeopardising the overall coherence and rigour of the subject? (Bear in mind all are already modified from QCA with reduced content)

3. Have a change of focus for greater coherence and increased opportunities for cross-curricular links?

Might other subjects be planned to complement this map? (Refer to the lozenges at foot of map).

The adapted maps follow. Prior to each there is a short summary of the process that was undertaken to produce the adapted maps.

1. Decisions

2. Revised medium term objectives

The medium term objectives would be transferred on to the school's medium term planning format and either attached to the map or displayed on facing pages in a ring binder. The list of objectives for each subject might be included as a summarising overview as given below.

Chapter 14 explains the interpretation of medium term

objectives in the short term planning.
(Exemplar planning is for an imaginary school located in a West Yorkshire industrial area.)

Year 2 Term 3 – 'The Seaside'

Decisions:

1. All Units as planned on map contribute well and are coherent.

2. No further modification needed.

3. Art to be refocused and become collage.

4. Art and D&T to run for half a term each.

5. Geography and history to run for half a term each (in that order).

6. Literacy to provide opportunity to:

» Write and address postcards
» Write reports for history, 'Changes to a resort over time'
» Write reports for science, eg 'The impact of chocolate on a healthy diet.'
» Write reports for Literacy, 'A holiday or journey I enjoyed'
» Write a simple dialogue (group work)
» Write verses for class rain song
» Read seaside stories / poems

7. Mathematics to provide opportunity to:

» Produce a chart to show common features for three / four or six holiday locations
» Produce a chart to show features associated with a seaside holiday
» Make a graph to show numbers of children who have visited popular seaside locations around our coasts
» Use measures in distances to the three / four or six localities and times of travel using different methods of transport
» Use measures in designing and constructing a vehicle
» Use measures in distances and speed changes for vehicles in science / D&T

8. ICT to provide opportunity to:

» Research into three / four / six seaside locations
» Research into changes over time of one of those locations
» Use of XXXXX programme in composition for music
» Present information in graphs (mathematics link)

NB A SECOND MODEL FOR ALL OF KS2 IS PROVIDED IN APPENDIX 1

9. PSHCE to provide opportunity to:

» Investigate care of the coastal features – erosion and pollution

» Examine the role of leisure activities – WHY do we go on holiday?

10. S&L planned activities to:

» Conduct a debate on 'Should we travel by train or car to our resort?'

» Discuss and agree why main changes have happened in the targeted seaside resort

» Create verses for a rain song (group verses to class song)

Final Decision:

Refocus map to centre round a dramatic production entitled 'xxxxxx (name the resort) then and now, either for radio show or assembly presentation.

All research is for the purpose of making an informed production.

Rename the Unit, *'Name a regional resort e.g. Scarborough'*

-

YEAR 2 TERM 3 – 'THE SEASIDE THEN AND NOW' ADAPTED MAP

To make up a role play about a small group of children travelling back in time from a seaside resort now to the same resort in Edwardian times. Objective: To show knowledge of ways resorts changed during the 20th century.
H.A: To script the play. L.A: Peer support – mixed ability groups

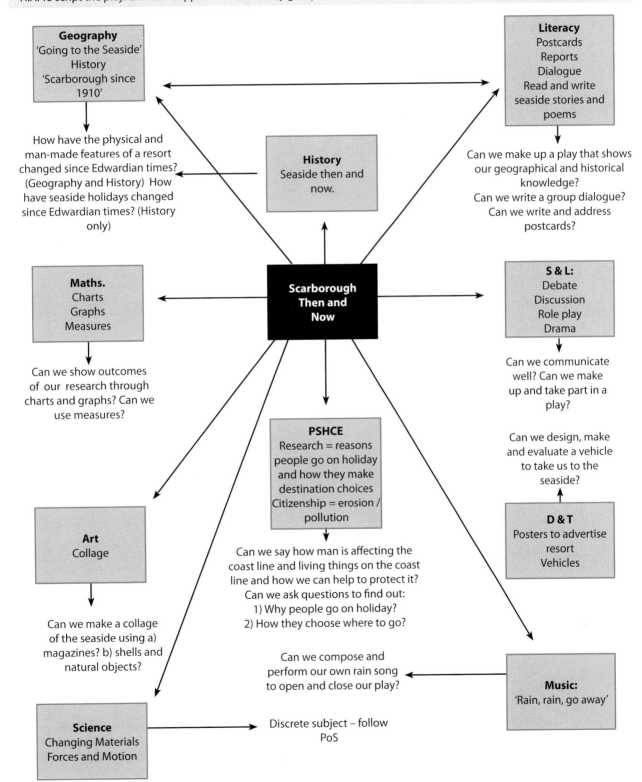

Geography
'Going to the Seaside'
History
'Scarborough since 1910'

How have the physical and man-made features of a resort changed since Edwardian times? (Geography and History) How have seaside holidays changed since Edwardian times? (History only)

History
Seaside then and now.

Literacy
Postcards
Reports
Dialogue
Read and write seaside stories and poems

Can we make up a play that shows our geographical and historical knowledge?
Can we write a group dialogue?
Can we write and address postcards?

Maths.
Charts
Graphs
Measures

Can we show outcomes of our research through charts and graphs? Can we use measures?

Scarborough Then and Now

S & L:
Debate
Discussion
Role play
Drama

Can we communicate well? Can we make up and take part in a play?

Can we design, make and evaluate a vehicle to take us to the seaside?

Art
Collage

Can we make a collage of the seaside using a) magazines? b) shells and natural objects?

PSHCE
Research = reasons people go on holiday and how they make destination choices
Citizenship = erosion / pollution

Can we say how man is affecting the coast line and living things on the coast line and how we can help to protect it?
Can we ask questions to find out:
1) Why people go on holiday?
2) How they choose where to go?

D & T
Posters to advertise resort
Vehicles

Can we compose and perform our own rain song to open and close our play?

Music:
'Rain, rain, go away'

Science
Changing Materials
Forces and Motion

Discrete subject – follow PoS

Year 5 Term 3: 'Planet Earth'

Step 1:

Examine the appropriate Medium Term Map and determine what your school's priorities are.

Might any subject planned:

1. Not actually run this term without jeopardising the overall coherence and rigour of the subject?

2. Be modified this term without jeopardising the overall coherence and rigour of the subject? (Bear in mind all are already modified from QCA with reduced content)

3. Have a change of focus for greater coherence and increased opportunities for cross-curricular links?

Might other subjects be planned to complement this map? (Refer to the lozenges at foot of map.)

Decisions:

1. Focus adapted to move into context of space flight but main subject foci broadly retained and all core skills and processes retained with exception of D & T.

2. D & T to be refocused to 'publishing'. (Consider where else in the Key Stage 2 curriculum the skills exemplified in the unit 'Musical Instruments' might now be addressed).

3. History and geography to run for half term each in that order.

4. Music and D & T to run for half term each in that order.

5. Geography and citizenship:

» To research possible areas for a small space station using maps and plans of the district, including ordnance survey maps and the web

» To identify physical and human features where it might have either a favourable or unfavourable impact

» To identify opportunities for public consultation and involvement, writing letters to persons such as the M.P., the editor of the local paper, the Green Party etc.

» To write newspaper articles and news reports arguing both for and against, and letters to the newspaper producing examples of discursive (balanced argument), reports and other information texts.

» To discuss how re-designation of a rural area affects the lives of residents for both better and worse

» To devise and carry out a survey using own questionnaires with known and trusted people within and out of school

» To present the outcomes of survey using ICT to make charts and graphs

» To plan and design a magazine or other publication to promote the building of the space station using ICT

» To retell (recount) stories from science fiction in literature and video

6. Design and Technology (second half term):

» To study magazines, pamphlets, news bulletins etc promoting a particular product, area or similar. (Hotels? Leisure centres? Conference centres? Resorts, airports and space centres on the web?) Identify the main features in language, illustration and layout. Evaluate and compare different models.

» To design the layout and illustrations required to produce a publication promoting the building of a small space station in our region.

» To produce articles, items, illustrations, maps and plans in appropriate sizes to achieve the layout

» To publish the outcomes using ICT

7. History (first half term):

» To select own focus for research into one or more developments in space flight during the 20th Century using books, magazines , video and the www

» To research a pending major development in own region or elsewhere that is to have a major impact on the environment eg a new runway or airport, a new motorway or major road, a new shopping complex or estate

» To solicit and study different points of view towards the development of a space station and use this to speculate on different attitudes to developments in space travel on all levels: a) physical geography of localities b) man made features c) lifestyles in the locality d) ethical issues

» To identify ways space travel over the 20th century contributed to major scientific and medical developments today

» To publish all information in articles for the rationale of your publication using ICT

8. Art (second half term):

» To study ways that tapestry and textiles were used to report events in history using books, museums and the www

» To select and design an aspect of the story of the development of space travel in the 20th century for a group contribution to a class tapestry or banner.

» To investigate materials and methods

» To be able to allocate responsibilities

» To execute contributions, reviewing work and making changes as necessary

» To assemble the tapestry or banners, complete and display

9. Music (first half term):

» To discuss scale / distances in space (mathematics link) and respond to their representation in 'The Planets' Suite' by Holst.

» To experiment with sound on un-tuned instruments and make selections that might represent a space journey.

» To work in groups to bring sounds together, producing contrasting effects and moods.

» To discuss the difference between 'tight' and 'loose' voice sounds.

» To tape record a range of 'tight' and 'loose' voice sounds in sequence and be able to identify which are which.

» To experiment changes in volume, speed etc of the recording for effect. Can we reverse recordings?

» To create a piece by combining voice sounds and technological effects.

» To evaluate the work.

10. Mathematics:

» To investigate a range of ways of presenting data in graphs and charts through ICT

» To select and use two methods to present the outcomes of the questionnaires

» To use co-ordinates to three decimal places in reading maps and charts

» To use scale to interpret and produce maps and charts

11. Literacy:

» To analyse the characteristics of newspaper / magazine reports, items in promotional pamphlets and questionnaires, (include balanced argument, report and information text) across the term.

» To produce writing in all the targeted text types for the publication.

» To use ICT

» To use debate to inform writing of dialogue.

» To discuss ways of questioning and use knowledge to construct a questionnaire in order to conduct research.

» To read space stories and poems (write and retell in the genre?).

12. Speaking and Listening:

» To discuss questionnaires and the skill of questioning, including closed and open questions. Make up examples.

» To discuss and rehearse communication and questioning skills for a range of audiences including close friends, family, neighbours, teachers and strangers

» To discuss putting different points of view and the language of debate (link to the discursive writing/ balanced argument)

» To plan and prepare, in groups, a debate taking opposing sides for the construction of a space station in the locality. Consider how re-designation of land impacts on the lives of residents.

» To discuss outcomes of all above work and make summarising statements

Final Decision:

Refocus map to centre round publishing a pamphlet or magazine to market the building of a space station in the region.

All research is for the purpose of making an informed publication.

Rename the Unit, '*Space Flight in the 20th Century*'

YEAR 5 TERM 3 – 'SPACE FLIGHT IN THE 20TH CENTURY' ADAPTED MAP

To design and make a magazine or information booklet on developments in space flight throughout the 20th Century.
To design a power point presentation to market the publication.
Mixed ability groupings.

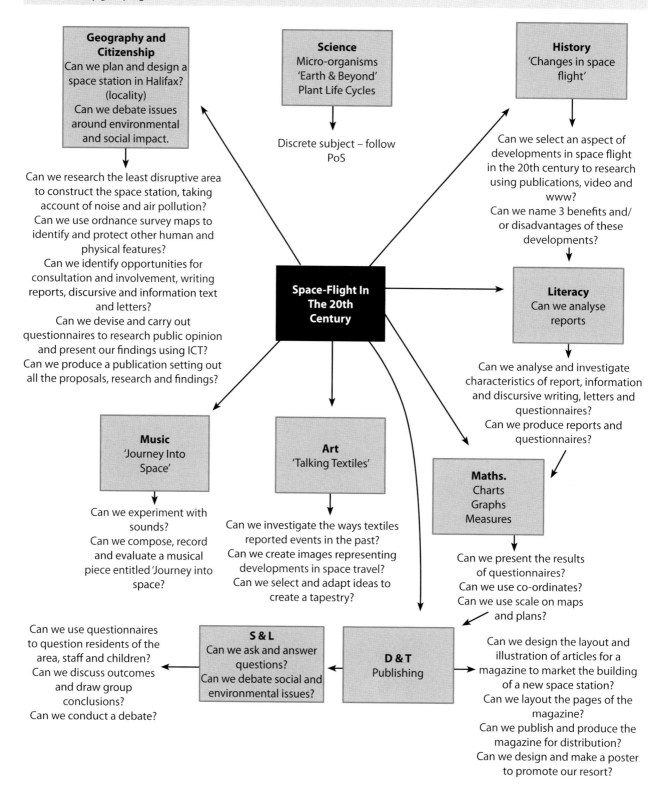

Geography and Citizenship
Can we plan and design a space station in Halifax? (locality)
Can we debate issues around environmental and social impact.

Can we research the least disruptive area to construct the space station, taking account of noise and air pollution?
Can we use ordnance survey maps to identify and protect other human and physical features?
Can we identify opportunities for consultation and involvement, writing reports, discursive and information text and letters?
Can we devise and carry out questionnaires to research public opinion and present our findings using ICT?
Can we produce a publication setting out all the proposals, research and findings?

Science
Micro-organisms
'Earth & Beyond'
Plant Life Cycles

Discrete subject – follow PoS

History
'Changes in space flight'

Can we select an aspect of developments in space flight in the 20th century to research using publications, video and www?
Can we name 3 benefits and/or disadvantages of these developments?

Space-Flight In The 20th Century

Literacy
Can we analyse reports

Can we analyse and investigate characteristics of report, information and discursive writing, letters and questionnaires?
Can we produce reports and questionnaires?

Music
'Journey Into Space'

Can we experiment with sounds?
Can we compose, record and evaluate a musical piece entitled 'Journey into space?

Art
'Talking Textiles'

Can we investigate the ways textiles reported events in the past?
Can we create images representing developments in space travel?
Can we select and adapt ideas to create a tapestry?

Maths.
Charts
Graphs
Measures

Can we present the results of questionnaires?
Can we use co-ordinates?
Can we use scale on maps and plans?

Can we use questionnaires to question residents of the area, staff and children?
Can we discuss outcomes and draw group conclusions?
Can we conduct a debate?

S & L
Can we ask and answer questions?
Can we debate social and environmental issues?

D & T
Publishing

Can we design the layout and illustration of articles for a magazine to market the building of a new space station?
Can we layout the pages of the magazine?
Can we publish and produce the magazine for distribution?
Can we design and make a poster to promote our resort?

14 TAKING THE MEDIUM TERM INTO THE SHORT TERM

What are Medium Term Objectives?

Medium Term Objectives are usually broad objectives that are to be achieved by the end of the Unit, half term or term. Key broad objectives steer assessment of the unit. However they also play an important role in the scaffolding of the unit and in ensuring that all who are to teach the unit provide the appropriate learning experiences in the short term in order to achieve the process and to protect the integrity of the subject.

The Year 2 Term 3 medium term planning model provided in the previous chapter has one shared objective for both history and geography.

'How have the physical and man-made features of a seaside changed since Edwardian times?'

This objective is a useful one to steer the learning of both subjects towards longer term assessment. If a child can answer that key question, providing relevant detail to show knowledge and understanding, then a large amount of learning must have taken place.

However, the key objective as it stands does not give a precise enough framework or scaffold to ensure the necessary study and learning will take place and that the process of the subject will be guaranteed.

It would be perfectly possible to teach pupils a standard answer to that question. For example:

"There are far more buildings, cars and people. The people are dressed very differently for the beach and they spend a lot of their time at attractions and amusements. The coast has been worn away by the sea and the weather so that some buildings have disappeared, and the fish stocks are becoming scarce because of over fishing."

This is the way that much of learning took place until the mid-20th century and beyond in some schools. It provides answers for examination questions and quiz shows and can lead to impressive qualifications in some quarters. Learning by rote in this way, however, does not educate the child for the needs of the 21st century. It by-passes the SKILLS and processes of the subject, that is - the 'AT1' described in Chapter 7 (Creative Curriculum Long Term Plan) or the ability to 'behave like a historian' or 'behave like a geographer'.

To enable effective formative assessment that tells the teacher precisely what the pupil knows or is able to do, the medium term objective needs to be broken down into very precise small steps that also ensure the process. The following is one way this might be done in the Year 2 Term 3 Medium Term Plan:

Medium Term (key question)	Specific (short term) Objectives
1. GEOGRAPHY: 'How have the physical and man-made features of a seaside resort changed since Edwardian times?'	**1.** Can we name one or more English seaside resorts that we have each visited? **2.** Can we find the resorts on maps? **3.** Can we use photographs and videos to name common features of seaside resorts? **4.** Can we say which features are man made and which are natural? **5.** Can we compare photographs (and film?) of Scarborough (named regional resort) in Edwardian times with ones of today to say how places have changed? **6.** Can we name three (adjust for ability level) or more physical (natural) and three human features that have changed and say how they have changed? **7.** (Extension) Can we explain why changes have taken place?
2. HISTORY: 'How have the physical and man-made features of a seaside resort changed since Edwardian times?'	**1.** Can we use photographs, videos and the www to investigate how the seaside was in Edwardian times? **2.** Can we compare buildings, pastimes, clothing and other aspects of a seaside holiday in Edwardian times with those seen today? **3.** Can we give three, (five? more?) ways holidays in Edwardian times would have been different from today? **4.** (Extension) Can we explain why changes have taken place

NB The model given for geography above creates a scaffold that actually provides the appropriate short term objectives for the seven weeks of short term planning. The model given for history creates a scaffold that actually provides the appropriate short term objectives to steer each one of two week short term plans for the unit.

The medium term objectives in the Year 5 Term 3 plan are more specific and already embody more of the process. Some may be used directly as written or with small modifications in the short term, others may benefit from amplification to enable accurate and productive assessment in order to inform the next steps for each child.

Geography	
1. Can we research the least disruptive area to construct the space station, taking account of noise and air pollution?	» Can we read an ordnance survey map? » Can we select a potential site for a space station? » Can we give reasons why we chose that site? » Can we debate issues around the positive and negative impact on a particular site?
2. Can we use ordnance survey maps to identify and protect other human and physical features?	» Can we show 2 other sites on ordinance survey maps and say why we rejected them? » Can we give geographical and human reasons for and against consideration of these sites?
3. Can we identify opportunities for consultation and involvement, writing articles, news reports and letters?	» Can we make a list of people and organisations that should be consulted? » Can we write information texts, (discursive text, reports and letters) for different purposes and audiences? (NB Each of these text types could be separated into an individual objective in the short term)
4. Can we devise and carry out questionnaires to research public opinion and present our findings using ICT?	» Can we investigate, trial questions and make up questionnaires to research public opinion? » Can we publish our questionnaires? » Can we use our questionnaires to seek opinions of family, neighbours and friends? » Can we collate and publish the outcomes and use them to draw conclusions?
5. Can we produce a publication setting out all the proposals, research and findings?	» Can we investigate pamphlets and magazine articles? » Can we design a pamphlet or article with 2 or more sides, using photographs, reports, charts, maps and other forms of communication?
History	
1. Can we research developments in space flight during the 20th Century?	» Can we use at least three different sources to identify the main stages of development in space exploration in the last century? » Can we present our findings in report form, information text or a poster using text, diagrams, pictures and other methods?
2. Can we use a range of sources?	» Can we name our sources in a bibliography? » Can we say which parts of our publication is from each source?
3. Can we name 3 benefits and/or disadvantages of these developments?	» Can we research ways exploration of space has contributed to life today and publish our findings in a different form? » Can we name at least three ways space flight has benefitted/disadvantaged man?

The short term objectives should then be the teaching focus for a lesson or a week.

c1 CASE STUDY 1

LINTHWAITE CLOUGH JIN SCHOOL, LINTHWAITE, NEAR
HUDDERSFIELD, WEST YORKSHIRE

Linthwaite Clough JIN School is a school of 300 children, located five miles from the former woollen industry town of Huddersfield in West Yorkshire. It is one of two schools serving a small community that straddles the Manchester Road, a busy road that runs from Huddersfield over the Pennines to Rochdale and Manchester. The road is lined with narrow terrace housing in dark, granite Yorkshire stone and there are several old mills that have been closed for many years and are now mainly used by small industry. The second school is higher up the hill, close to the parish church, and is a Church of England denominational school.

For the past four years Linthwaite Clough has built weekly opportunities for the creative curriculum into its planning. The whole school reorganises vertically, usually by Key Stage but sometimes from Year R to Year 6, for half or full day cross-curricular investigations and learning opportunities that are self- selected and pursued through an integrated approach to the curriculum. All adults in the school are trained and regarded as Teaching Practitioners for the delivery of aspects of the curriculum appropriate to their skills, thus leading to reduced group sizes and increased opportunities for pupil choice.

Linthwaite Clough JIN School was inspected in the second week of the academic year 2005 to 2006. Because the inspection regime had been restructured HMI shadowed the team. Both OFSTED inspectors and HMI observed 'CCLs' in process. As HMI left the school he commented, 'This is a wonderful school, I would put my child in it.'

The head teachers, Gail Newton and Jane Browning, have provided the following case study.

A CREATIVE ORIENTATION TO LEARNING

CCL - Confident Creative Learning

At Linthwaite Clough Junior, Infant and Early Years School we believe that a child's education should be a continuous and seamless progression. This continuity needs to be planned and reviewed, as are other aspects of school life, if it is to be successful.

We believe that high levels of involvement and self-esteem are necessary for all learners and that the continuous curriculum is the ideal vehicle to deliver this. It should provide opportunities for questioning, exploration and thinking – learning! Therefore the continuous curriculum is a vital part of learning in the Early Years, Key Stage 1 and Key Stage 2.

Our school vision is held and owned by the whole school community. As creative thinkers and responsive listeners our vision has led to the development of sessions in which the compartmentalization of the curriculum is challenged and the nurturing of life long learning skills becomes a key feature. It extends the principles and effective practice in the Curriculum Guidance for the Foundation Stage. These sessions have been named, Confident Creative Learning.

The school's VISION is:

'To create confident learners with a personal vision and a developing appreciation of life'.

1. Why did we feel it necessary to review the arrangements for curriculum access in KS1?

'High quality early childhood education can have a significant long term effect on children's learning, can lead to gains in educational achievement throughout schooling'

K Sylva (EPPE Project 2007)

As practitioners we were questioning the perceived compartmentalization of learning and imposed initiatives which we felt were having a negative effect on the children learning to be learners, whereas in the Foundation Stage principles and practices were supporting child development.

Children are:

» encouraged to take responsibility for themselves,

» able to make their own choices and decisions,

» supported by interested and sensitive adults, who value and were able to extend their thinking.

Our school vision is 'To create confident learners with a personal vision and a developing appreciation of life'. During discussions, concerns were expressed not only about accessing the curriculum from the Foundation Stage into KS1 but also the extent to which children experience continuity within the curriculum from the Foundation Stage to KS2.

Comments from teachers included:

'I don't feel that children are as excited about learning now that the curriculum is more compartmentalised and imposed, even though we have tried to keep our child centred approach alive!!!!'.

KS1 practitioner

'Spontaneity has lessened, teaching and learning is becoming blander. Education has always included 'missed opportunities' but this could become more the case'.

KS1 practitioner

My feelings are that we need to consider the KS2 learning opportunities, and continuity throughout the Foundation stage, KS1 and KS2, not just FS to KS1.'

KS2 practitioner

We then explored the extent to which the important skills developed in the Foundation Stage (e.g. independence, responsibility, creative thinking) were valued and promoted as the children moved into KS1/2. As a school we decided that we wanted to address this issue and began to explore ways of implementing a more 'continuous curriculum'. The result was to focus on 'Confident Creative Learning' sessions throughout the school which have been introduced to give children opportunities to develop their own ideas, and follow extended cross curricular learning.

CCL – What does it look like?

CCL sessions in KS1 are 30% of the teaching time, in KS2 Y3/4 are 30% and Y5/6 are 20%.

In our setting, CCL in KS1 means 3 classes of Y1 & Y2 children ~ 75 in all ~ working in 5 learning bases, with a minimum of 6 practitioners. CCL sessions are full morning or afternoon sessions to allow for sustained, extended learning opportunities. Practitioners are deployed on the Practitioner Focused Activities with at least 1 practitioner supporting child-initiated activities, negotiated opportunities and observations. Planning for CCL is taken from medium-term plans, and includes all areas of the curriculum, often in cross curricular contexts. Assessment opportunities are identified in the planning for individuals, groups and cohorts. Methods of assessment include observations, by outcome, practitioner comment-sheets and presentations.

The available activities have clearly identified cross-curricular learning objectives which are communicated to the children. They can be accessed in different learning bases both indoors and outdoors, within - and occasionally outside - the school environment. The differentiated activities are within the continuous provision and by the child, although practitioner focused or negotiated.

Within CCL sessions there is the expectation that children will continue to develop dispositions to work independently, cooperatively and collaboratively, to challenge themselves and on occasions to negotiate their self-chosen activity. They are given time and space for individual interests to be expanded on, and therefore involvement in their own learning to be maximised.

The CCL sessions are designed to promote - as it says - Confident Creative Learners.

'CCL stands for Confident Creative Learning. There is a sheet which tells us the choice of activities. You can choose an activity then write where you are going on the board then go. When you have done an activity there is a tick sheet, you find

your name then find the number of the activity you have done. It is really fun because you get to walk around school sensibly and choose an activity that you want to do. There is art, geography, literacy, science, DT and negotiate. Which is if you want to do something that is not on the list, but first you have to tell the teacher what you want to do and why. It is fun but hard and that is why we learn a lot from CCL.'

Quote by Charley and Olivia Y5

2. Would a creative orientation to learning in Key Stage 1 and 2 build on the strengths of Foundation Stage practice?

The initial observations of Confident Creative Learning (CCL) sessions in KS1 indicated a significant decrease in children's involvement levels compared to those evidenced throughout the Foundation Stage. This raised questions about how children learn most effectively in Key Stage 1 and led us to review our current practice, including our approaches to planning and assessment. Ways of encouraging children to be more involved in the learning process became a particular focus for reflection..

The impact over a short period of time was clear with regard to how involved the children were in the opportunities offered through CCL sessions (and also other subject based teaching). We are currently looking at the impact of the Creative Orientation to the Curriculum on all learning sessions not just in CCL.

Involvement Levels when observations were completed in KS1 Literacy, Numeracy and PESS (Physical Education and School Sports) sessions indicated similar involvement levels as in CCL. This will require further evidence but we feel that this creative approach is impacting positively on the learning opportunities across the whole curriculum.

Following the success of Confident Creative Learning (CCL) sessions in Key Stage 1, they were introduced into Key Stage 2 to promote opportunities for children to take more responsibility for their own learning and self-challenge.

Initially children found it extremely challenging to make choices about their learning using educational criteria, decisions were more often made according to peer group influences and their own levels of self confidence.

As the children began to be engaged in more in-depth discussions about learning and their role in the process, their levels of involvement became significantly increased. Children gained confidence, self-esteem and an appreciation of their educational needs, as reflected in their comments below:

'In CCL we have opportunities to do a variety of activities. I've only just come to this school and at first I was amazed because we didn't have anything at all like it at my old school and now its just ace'.

Joshua

'CCL is interesting because we get given the responsibility with what we do, where we do it, who with, but we have to show we can be responsible pupils. There's a lot more to CCL than you might think!!'.

Conor

'In CCL we get opportunities to make choices. Its always fun, we can negotiate to work on different things and work to our own timetables'.

Jordan

'In CCL we can work in different areas of the school. We make the choice but the teachers trust us to be responsible and sensible. Sometimes I choose all easier options but sometimes I challenge myself. Its good'.

Liam

Practitioners in Key Stage 2 were also excited by these sessions, and welcomed the opportunities they presented for engaging more deeply with the children and their learning.

The following are comments from practitioners:

'The fact that children have a choice of activity has increased ownership and involvement'.

'It's stimulating to work with a child on an activity of his/her choice - much less coercion required!! After initial input the child is responsible to a much greater extent for his/her behaviour, work and learning'.

3. How can we share our thinking with the whole school community?

The whole school community has been involved in the development of a more creative orientation to learning through the introduction of Confident Creative Learning sessions. The children have been the best advocates of this style of working and have 'spread the word' for us! This we feel is the most significant way of sharing initiatives with the whole school community. We have included references to Confident Creative Learning in Children's Record of Achievements and parents/carers have in turn, commented in response, for example:

'In CCL, Rachael shows that she can take responsibility for her own learning. She recognises the opportunities that are

available and makes good use of them'.

'Through CCL Ashley is developing more self-confidence when making choices and shows that he can use the time constructively to develop his interests within the curriculum'.

'Isabel particularly enjoys CCL sessions and often chooses to work in friendship groups. During these sessions she has particularly enjoyed the science activities, looking at plant reproduction and conducting her own research using books, videos and the Internet to find out about Jamaica'.

(Extracts from individual written Records of Achievement)

'CCL is also one of his favourite subjects, we know this as he talks about it at home quite a lot. He also gets very excited on the day you are doing CCL, and talks about it non stop in the car on the way to school'.

(Parent comment in response to written Record of Achievement)

Practitioners visiting from other schools and settings have also given us positive feedback, for example:

'The way in which creative independent learning is incorporated into the wider curriculum'.

'The experience of a totally different way of delivering the curriculum and children's approach to independent work and learning'.

'It has inspired me to try out a CCL approach within the Y1 classes'.

Feedback from School Contact Officers' on their monitoring visits has identified the 'excellent ethos and opportunities for children to become confident creative learners' and their reports have included these comments:

'Children taught the building blocks to allow creativity to flourish'.

'A very positive experience thoroughly enjoyed by the children. High levels of involvement: all were on task at all times in all activities. All could describe precisely what they had chosen to do and why. A superb environment in which to develop essential life skills'.

'Now create a balance of life and subject skills in all areas, whilst maintaining the very positive influence CCL sessions have on the pupils' attitudes, confidence and ability to be creative'.

References have been made in the Head teachers report to Governors and although there are no guarantees in this world, governors were convinced that this approach would have significant impact on pupil achievement including their attitudes to learning, confidence and belief in themselves.

"CCL (Confident Creative Learning) Sessions have continued to be a major initiative in school. This is where different activities meeting key skills objectives happen in a session and discrete subject teaching is used when appropriate. Following practitioner and pupil evaluations the sessions have been further developed to include extended CCL sessions. These have significantly increased the opportunities on offer to pupils and maximised the use of the whole school teaching environment. A further significant development in this area was the introduction of whole school CCL sessions.

CCL is…

when we work sensibly and are being trustworthy
Olivia

a chance to do gardening
Mark

something we should carry on all day without any breaks, just a short one at lunchtime! We can do Maths adventures next CCL.
Kieran

having fun
Ben

everyone co-operating
Holly

cool. There are more activities and you can work with more people – adults and children
Aidan

making choices then working wherever the activity is sensibly with children older and younger
Laurin

giving the teachers chance to do activities they really enjoy like Mrs Weavill likes music and Mrs Kershaw likes PE and Yoga
Rebecca"

Extract from Annual Governors' Report to Parents (2005)

The Governors are very interested in the involvement of other settings in this approach to the curriculum and are kept informed of ways in which we have been disseminating our experiences to date!

CASE STUDY 1 APPENDIX A - PUPIL OBSERVATIONS BY PRACTITIONERS FOR ASSESSMENT AND EVALUATION PURPOSES:

Observation 1:

Erin KS 1/2 - YR1 Sketch 2.11.05

"Erin was observed during a literacy session. She listened attentively to the input on Farmer Duck, answering questions and offering opinions confidently during the group discussion. The follow up task, 'To Write a Character's Profile', was set and as Erin left the carpet area she was heard saying to a friend, "There's more about the farmer so I'll choose him......I like writing."
Initially she worked from the practitioner model but quite quickly began to extend this. Her thought process became evident as she discussed her ideas about the character's address with another child, "I want it to be a hill not a road. How about.........Blackpool Hill....... No, it's a wiggly road with lots of bends.........How about Wiggly Hill!"
When it came to the character description she extended it further using bullet points, "So you can separate the sentences." Again she talked through her ideas quietly to herself as she wrote.
In discussion after she had finished she expanded one of her ideas more fully. She had written, "He is horubul bicose he ses go and do this go and do that." She explained to me, "No one should speak to any one like that, not people or ducks." When asked why, "Because it's not kind at all and it makes you feel bad inside."

On task 50 minutes Involvement Level 5"

Observation 2:

KS 1/2 - YR 2 Sketch 2.11.05

"Matthew and Adam were observed during a literacy session. After the initial input they were observed talking to each other and after a few moments they approached the practitioner and Adam asked confidently, "Can we work on there? It's easier if we do it on the white board if we make a mistake." Matthew added, "Because we do sometimes!" It was quickly agreed that the work must also be recorded by taking a photograph for their extended writing book and they began to make a list of the characters attribute's.
They worked cooperatively and collaboratively throughout, taking turns to each write a sentence and then handing the pen to each other when they had finished. Adam wrote more complex sentences but it was Matthew who reminded him, "Don't forget the full stop at the end!" At one point Adam stood back to look at his work saying, "Oops! I put capital letters in the middle!" and he self corrected rubbing them out with his finger and replacing with lower case letters.

On task 15 minutes   Involvement Level 4.5"

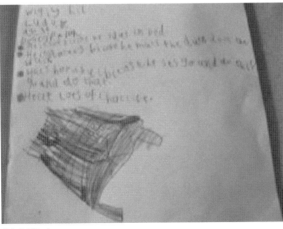

Erin's Work

Mathew & Adam Talking

CASE STUDY 1 APPENDIX B - EXAMPLES OF PLANNING FOR C.C.L.S FROM LINTHWAITE CLOUGH JIN SCHOOL:

KEY STAGE 1 CCL OVERVIEW   YR 2 TERM 1   (WEEK 4 AND 5)

Curriculum areas	Focused Activities in 3A	Focused Activities in 3BT	Focused Activities in 3D	Other locations
Science	Wet Sand: Homes for nocturnal animals. *To use the senses to identify objects in the dark. PF Ass Sheet 4			
ICT	Can I make a label to show that text comes in different sizes, colours and styles? Can I enter and correct letters?	Can I make a label to show that text comes in different sizes, colours and styles? Can I enter and correct letters?	Can I make a label to show that text comes in different sizes, colours and styles? Can I enter and correct letters?	
ICT Suite:	Dazzle: In response to the abstract work of Kandinsky can I create a picture using the shape, line and fill tool? PF			
Art	Paint Can I work collaboratively to paint a picture? (Children supported by children in KS2)		Can I create a collage using the shapes, colours and textures in response to the work of Kandinsky? (Self serve) - Opps. To develop language of shape. Can I identify ways in which artists represent themselves in art?PF Ass Sheet 4	
DT		* Can I do a running stitch through a range of materials? PF Ass Sheet 4 Can I make a moving vehicle using mobilo?		
Geography				
History				
Music				
PHSCE	Child Initiated and observations: CD Working cooperatively and imaginatively with the wild animals (in 3BT) SEN support/Negotiate – LM AH			OUTSIDE Can I plant some bulbs to improve the environment? PF (Welly Walks)
Literacy	Mark-making Small books Non fiction stimulus about animal homes	Role Play 'In Disguise' (Speaking & listening) Water – Imaginary world	Role Play 'The Opticians' (Speaking and listening) Mark making – variety of paper and mark making equipment	
Numeracy		*Can I make a row of houses and number the houses in the street? PF Ass sheet 4	Dry sand – stretchy socks (measuring)	

Input (see short term planning) – ICT Dazzle- using the line, shape and fill tool (Obj 4 & 5)

KEY STAGE 1 CCL OVERVIEW YR 2 TERM 1 (WEEK12AND13)

Curriculum areas	Focused Activities in 3A	Focused Activities in 3BT	Focused Activities in 3D	Other locations
Science		* Electricity Can I make a complete circuit using a battery, wire and bulb PF Ass Sheet 4	Light and dark Can I create a shadow puppet show? Can I make the shadow change size	
ICT Class based	Word processing Can I complete the sentence selecting the appropriate word from the word bank?	Word processing Can I complete the sentence selecting the appropriate word from the word bank?	Word processing Can I complete the sentence selecting the appropriate word from the word bank?	
ICT Suite	*PF – Black cat – Can I say how the information was collected? Can I input the information into a graph package? Can I find answers to simple questions by looking at a pictogram? Can I understand that graphing programs have limitations?			Access sheet to monitor uptake
Art	*Experiment with and use drawing media and techniques when considering self portraits (leading into self portraits in weeks ahead) PF - annotations on back of work Ass Sheet 4		Free paint – self serve – ready mix	
DT	Can I construct a model with moving parts from the diagrams? DACTA	Malleable - playdough	*Can I use my design to make a puppet using the running stitch technique? PF (wed only) Construction kit LEGO	
Geography	World Jigsaw. Small books for mark-making.	Wild Animals –supported by books on Africa Arctic animals in the water tray	PF Sheet 4. Visit to local supermarket and looking at land use on the way Ass Sheet 4	
History				
Music				
PHSCE	Child Initiated/Negotiate: HN SEN AH (Mon/Thurs)	SEN - LM based in 3D		Can I go on a welly walk and look at the seasonal changes that have occurred? PF (Mon/Thurs only)
Literacy	Mark-making Books writing own books including index and contents page.	Reading interviews WK 13 – CD Literacy games to support word level work in key stage 1	Handwriting patterns- on white boards Sieving coins in dry sand and sorting into real and nonsense words	
Numeracy	Maths game			

Input : ICT in 3A at 10.15 – QCA 1B objective 5 (Interactive Whiteboard), QCA 1E/2E Objective 6,7,8,9 - Graphs

CASE STUDY 2

PARKINSON LANE COMMUNITY PRIMARY SCHOOL,
CALDERDALE, WEST YORKSHIRE

Parkinson Lane Community Primary School occupies a fine old Victorian building set amid tightly packed Yorkshire stone terraced housing near the centre of Halifax in West Yorkshire. It serves a community of mixed ethnicity with the majority of pupils coming from families of Pakistani origin. There are just under 500 pupils on roll and the school falls within the lowest 10% for socio-economic and deprivation indicators within the country. The current Head teacher, Mr.Gulfarez Ahmed, has led the school since 2001.

The following case study has been provided by the Chair of Governors with the approval and support of the Head teacher and the Governing Body.

A STORY ABOUT CREATIVITY AND THE CURRICULUM

"How can we help children to write more creatively?" I asked my partner recently. I did not expect the sort of answer I got.

"Most stories follow a pattern: setting, initiating action, conflict and finally resolution. Get them to analyse well-known stories in these terms. Then encourage them to improvise orally or to write using this framework."

With help I managed to turn Cinderella into Parts 1 and 2 using these components. Apparently, good stories involve more than one cycle of the framework! I then started to think about how everyone at our school (Parkinson Lane Community Primary School in Halifax) has been using cycles of a framework like this to make our learning community more creative.

Like most good stories, there are settings that you can too easily learn to live with. Like most good stories things happen, or things are said, or ideas are had, or questions are asked. In a big or bureaucratic or highly controlled non-learning organisation there is a reaction that is far from initiating and the risk of conflict is avoided at all costs. Creative and confident leadership is essential for creative and confident learning. The innovative leadership of the head teacher of Parkinson Lane, with the support of his talented staff and the Governing Body, has enabled exciting things to happen both within the National Curriculum and across the wider curriculum. We believe learning, for children, staff, parents or governors, means taking risks. Often we get into situations where a Fairy Godmother would really have her work cut out. We have a 'Ball' though, and usually new learning cycles are sent spinning.

Once upon a time many of the British Asian children (making up 97-100% of pupils on roll) seemed to lack confidence, seemed to be confused about their cultural identity and about where they belonged. Our Head knew about a great Heera Dancing Group in Wolverhampton. He asked if they would like to come and stay in Halifax and do some work with every year group. They agreed and in no time at all boys and girls could be seen doing graceful dance steps as they played in the local streets. Performances were given to parents. Some asked if they could make Asian style costumes for the further performances and, over sewing machines in the staff room, the nucleus of a PTA was formed.

However, some complained that boys and girls dancing together was wrong! As a learning community we debated the difference between culture and religion. We debated what made behaviour acceptable or unacceptable.

Meanwhile, another cycle had been taking place. Once upon a time, our school had stopped doing trips. Because our staff volunteered to run a Summer Club for the first week of their holiday, we needed a climactic finale for the varied programme. Our Head offered a field on his farm as a campsite. This lead to some conflict, parental visits to the farm and, after parental consents had been secured, a lot of emotional phone calls to the farm on that first wonderful night under 'canvas'. Everyone agreed the Summer Club had been a great success. It became possible to talk about other trips involving a night away.

Meanwhile, just when we had reached a resolution of the differences over dancing and our dance troupe had completed a tour of local schools, someone said, "This is doing so much for the children's self-confidence. Why don't we do an international tour?"

There is a careful, rational, considered, risk-averse response to madness like this. It is very different from the usual creative one of a learning community like ours. The conflicts that followed are too numerous to mention, although had the Head actually been arrested for having the audacity to suggest that our children should dance under the glass pyramid of the Louvre in Paris (as we were told only 3 esteemed artists had ever done previously) I dare say it would have spun another interesting learning cycle. Our translator stepped in as fairy godmother on this occasion. We became the fourth to perform in that hallowed space, and a CD-ROM of that wonderful tour is available from the school.

Summer Club: 'Camping'

Cultural Indentity: 'Dancing'

But while this might be excellent and enjoyable, and it really was, how do we know that taking these risks and working through these conflicts is not at the expense of National Curriculum learning, or our inclusion objectives? Nervous governors have been reassured by the way creativity has also made assessment and tracking a strong feature of our school.

We were uncomfortable with assessment being a mystical art practised by shaman-like figures on innocents. We try to work together on assessment and tracking, agreeing together where we are (and why) and where we need to get to. Surprises have their place, but not in assessment. Let's look at what this means for the children (though one could do the same for staff, parents or governors). Every child in Key Stage 1 or 2 in our school would be able tell you what level they are achieving in the basic skills and what their targets are. Children in Key Stage 2 fill in the same report form on their progress as their teachers do, ticking the boxes on how hard the child has tried in different subjects (very revealing!) and writing the general comment. There is usually much consensus. Here are some examples:

CHILD:

When we go to trips no-one wants to be in his group because he asks so much questions he puzzles you.

TEACHER:

A--- likes to find out and investigate new ideas, asking probing questions and trying to find solutions himself.

CHILD:

Z---- always pays attention although sometimes goes off into her imaginary world. She is in the girls' football team which has developed her team work. She can get stroppy at times. Otherwise she's OK.

TEACHER:

Z--- likes to pay attention to detail and organises her work well. She is creative and also enjoys all sporting activities. She has been a member of the football team.

CHILD:

A--- is a very sensible boy. His favourite lesson is maths and design technology. He could sometimes get distracted from his mates or someone that sits next to him.

TEACHER:

[A---] particularly enjoys carrying out investigative tasks and can explain his findings clearly. He has had a settled year although on occasions he can act without thinking which can get him into trouble.

Of course, there are plenty of 'ugly stepsister-like' comments that assessment is really about high level targets and education politics. We are subject to the same disciplines as other schools but assessment data also plays a part in another creative approach to curriculum development.

Our teaching staff is grouped into 3 curriculum development teams that support the Subject Coordinators. Every year for every subject, and for areas like our work with gifted and talented children, they work on a hypothesis. For example the hypothesis the school is exploring for history this year is:

"Development of drama techniques encourages a wider, deeper understanding of historical enquiry."

This stimulates illuminating uses of the tracking data. One analysis, for example, showed that taking part in the dancing, taking part in 'Breakfast Club', after school and Summer Clubs and having parents that get involved in school life all accelerated the termly progress of children.

Work to explore the hypotheses is another way to make sure we never get too comfortable with the status quo! There is always something to initiate development and stop the 'setting' setting solid!

This brings me conveniently to the third framework element: conflict! Earlier this year the situation looked pretty desperate for the painted Iceni warriors of class 4A. A phalanx of highly disciplined cardboard-armoured Roman soldiers from 4S was bearing down on them in tight formation. Fusillades of bean bags were having no effect on an impenetrable wall and roof of shields. Suddenly a large carthorse wheeled into the playground with a regal Queen Boudicca up in the seat next to the kindly owner of the massive but gentle Boris. This battle was lost for the Romans but as our year 4 children will now tell you with passion, the Romans got their revenge later!

So how does this whole story fit the framework? I suppose the setting has been the use of a framework to aid creativity. My initiating action was to apply this framework to the developing curriculum at Parkinson Lane CP School in Halifax. I suppose the conflict involved my fear, that of others in our school and that of imagined readers, of risking the many targets that must be met, the budgets that must be managed and the school's reputation, so painstakingly built, so easily destroyed. Fortunately for all, the vision of the head teacher led us forward. So what is the resolution to this story? Are there readers out there picturing the way this image of the school as a creative learning community fits their vision for their school like some magic slipper? I do hope so.

Peter Smith
Chair of Governors
Parkinson Lane CP School
Halifax

June 2006

Attack by the Roman soldiers

Boudicca rescues the Iceni warriors

a1 APPENDIX 1

ADAPTED MAPS FOR KEY STAGE 2 AND THE ALLOCATION OF TEXT TYPES

The following is a model of the previously provided curriculum (chapter 8) further adapted for thematic links with the units for teaching the text types in literacy. It provides exemplar planning for the three terms of years 3 to 5.

This model has re-organised the recommended units in order to enable thematic links to be made and the text types to be taught, used and applied within credible contexts.

A map is provided at the opening of the Model that maps the taught literacy units across the three years of planned themes provided, plus identifies opportunities for visits to other text types taught in previous terms through the Big Writing session. This practice ensures all text types are kept on the 'front burner' and not left forgotten two or three terms ago.

All models are exemplar and for guidance only.

Key Stage 1 = range of purposes for reading and writing taught without the rigidity of focusing specifically on characteristics of text types. Range to include: narrative, poetry, recount, reports and simple explanations.

Text Types	Year 3 Term 1 'Settle-ment'	Year 3 Term 2 'Animal Kingdom'	Year 3 Term 3 'Tudors'	Year 4 Term 1 'Change'	Year 4 Term 2 'Named Locality'	Year 4 Term 3 'Broad-casting War'	Year 5 Term 1 'The Victorians'	Year 5 Term 2 'Water'	Year5 Term 3 'Planet Earth'
Fiction	√ local tales	√		√		√	√	√	√
Myths / Legends	√				√ taught	√		√	√
Poetry	√	√		√		√	√ taught	√	√ taught
Recount			√			√ taught	√		√
Report	√ taught	√	√	√ taught	√		√	√ taught	√
Instruct	√ taught		√		√ taught		√ taught		√
Explain		√ taught			√ taught		√ taught	√	
Persuade			√ taught	√				√ taught	
Discuss		√ taught		√ taught			√	√ taught	√
Dialogue			√ taught			√ taught			√
Question-naire	√ taught			√		√ taught			√ taught

Year 6 will rotate through all text types, one a week. This will be in the 'Big Writing' session if schools are using this approach (see 'Strategies for Immediate Impact on Writing Standards' 2003 and 'Write on Target' 2006). If the teacher identifies, through this process, weaknesses in a particular text type they will be addressed in a literacy session.

In the Spring Term they could write 3 texts per week: 1) One text type for purpose in Big Writing 2) A second text type for purpose in another subject 3) A third text type as a short piece in a third subject. Misunderstandings would be addressed in literacy sessions.

The models that follow assume four literacy sessions a week and one Big Writing. (See 'Strategies for Immediate Impact on Writing Standards' 2003 and 'Write on Target' 2006) As the forty-five minutes of actual writing in the Big Write session (thirty minutes in Year 1) is usually for another subject's purpose it counts as forty-five minutes of that subject for that week and releases another forty-five minutes elsewhere in the week for further creativity.

In most terms between 4 and 8 text types have been identified as having particular relevance to the theme, however only two, or three at most, have been identified for in-depth teaching. The others would be used on alternate weeks in the 'Big Writing' session, interspersed by all other text types the pupils have met previously.

Fiction, myths, legends and poetry are planned as an ongoing (continuous) unit running accross most themes. Teaching would be built in when the need is identified.

NB The teaching, review and analysis take place in the literacy sessions whereas the writing takes place in the once a week writing session (Big Writing). The following is a model for how this might look:

Can we:
Find out which places our families have moved to and from, and place the locations on maps?
Use questionnaires to find out why family members relocated and collate our reasons using a simple data base?
Conduct research into peoples who relocated between other countries and the UK on a large scale in the past?
(NOT Invaders, maybe a locally represented group to promote questionnaires eg West Indian, Polish or Pakistan community)
Locate major relocations in the past on a time line?
Study one main group? How did they contribute to change in their new locality?
Contribute information in a range of ways for a display?

Can we:
Say what early settlers in the UK needed and why they came here?
Find countries of origin and locations of settlement on maps?
Record reasons for changes of locality in our families on a data base and place the locations they moved from / to on maps?
Investigate origins of place names and endings?
Use maps to find clues to some names of early settlements?
Investigate the origins and development of one local village with historical roots?
Identify symbols on maps and plans?
Create a fictional village on a plan, using standard symbols?

History
'Settlement'

ENGLISH
Can we:
Write and use questionnaires?
Write reports and information texts for history and geography?
Read and write stories and poems (include myths & legends) about relocation?
Make advertising materials for our named resort?
Write to instruct?

Geography
'Village Settlers'

Science
'Materials'
'Light and Sight'

Art
'Settlers'

**Year 3
Term 1
'Settlement'**

Can we:
Compare everyday materials and sort by their properties?
Mix everyday materials and observe changes?
Separate solid particles by sieving?
Describe and group rocks and soils on the basis of their characteristics?
Can we identify the differences between solids, liquids and gases?

Explain that light travels from a source?
Explain how shadows are formed?
Explain that light is reflected from some sources and name ways this is used by humans in their communities?
Explain in simple terms how the eye works?
Write reports and instructions?

P.E.
Games,
Country dance

Can we:
Investigate use of pattern in the homes, artefacts or clothing on one group of settlers?
Compare patterns of different times and cultures?
Make multiple copies of simple shapes and place on grids to make patterns using rotation and symmetry?
Make a 2nd shape and locate on the grid, describing its relationship with the first in terms of size and shape?
Use the 2 shapes to make different patterns?
Explore pattern through ICT?
Use stencils and print blocks to produce repeat patterns?
Compare a range of our patterns and express likes and dislikes?

PSHCE
Responsibilities of living in a community.
Living and working together.
Respect for communities that we move into.

**Mathematics
Opportunity:**
Shape and Space / Symmetry

Discrete:
Music
R.E.
Mathematics

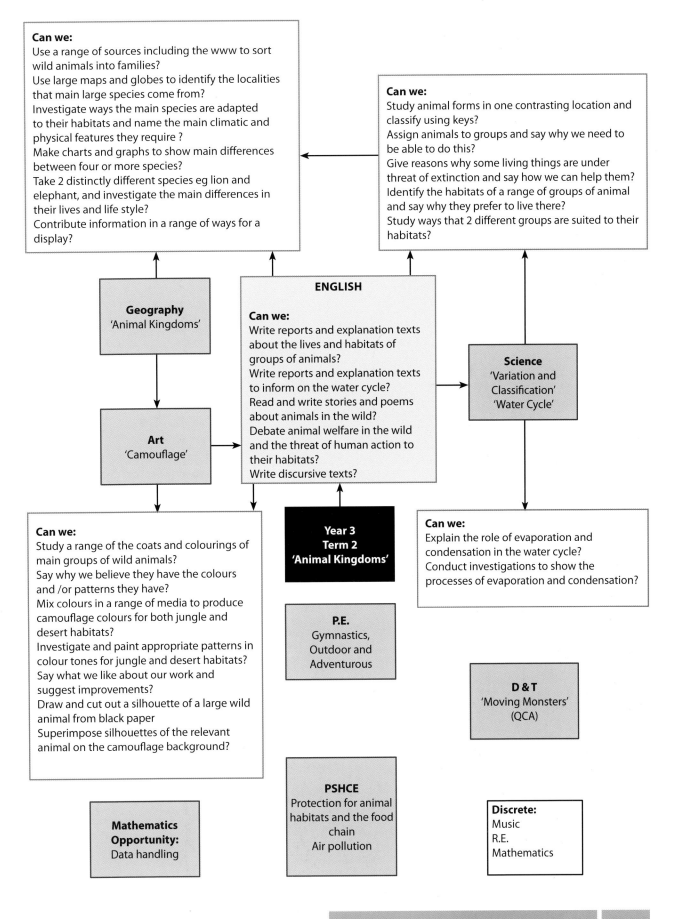

Can we:
Use a range of sources including the www to sort wild animals into families?
Use large maps and globes to identify the localities that main large species come from?
Investigate ways the main species are adapted to their habitats and name the main climatic and physical features they require ?
Make charts and graphs to show main differences between four or more species?
Take 2 distinctly different species eg lion and elephant, and investigate the main differences in their lives and life style?
Contribute information in a range of ways for a display?

Can we:
Study animal forms in one contrasting location and classify using keys?
Assign animals to groups and say why we need to be able to do this?
Give reasons why some living things are under threat of extinction and say how we can help them?
Identify the habitats of a range of groups of animal and say why they prefer to live there?
Study ways that 2 different groups are suited to their habitats?

Geography
'Animal Kingdoms'

ENGLISH

Can we:
Write reports and explanation texts about the lives and habitats of groups of animals?
Write reports and explanation texts to inform on the water cycle?
Read and write stories and poems about animals in the wild?
Debate animal welfare in the wild and the threat of human action to their habitats?
Write discursive texts?

Science
'Variation and Classification'
'Water Cycle'

Art
'Camouflage'

Can we:
Study a range of the coats and colourings of main groups of wild animals?
Say why we believe they have the colours and /or patterns they have?
Mix colours in a range of media to produce camouflage colours for both jungle and desert habitats?
Investigate and paint appropriate patterns in colour tones for jungle and desert habitats?
Say what we like about our work and suggest improvements?
Draw and cut out a silhouette of a large wild animal from black paper
Superimpose silhouettes of the relevant animal on the camouflage background?

**Year 3
Term 2
'Animal Kingdoms'**

Can we:
Explain the role of evaporation and condensation in the water cycle?
Conduct investigations to show the processes of evaporation and condensation?

P.E.
Gymnastics,
Outdoor and
Adventurous

D & T
'Moving Monsters'
(QCA)

**Mathematics
Opportunity:**
Data handling

PSHCE
Protection for animal habitats and the food chain
Air pollution

Discrete:
Music
R.E.
Mathematics

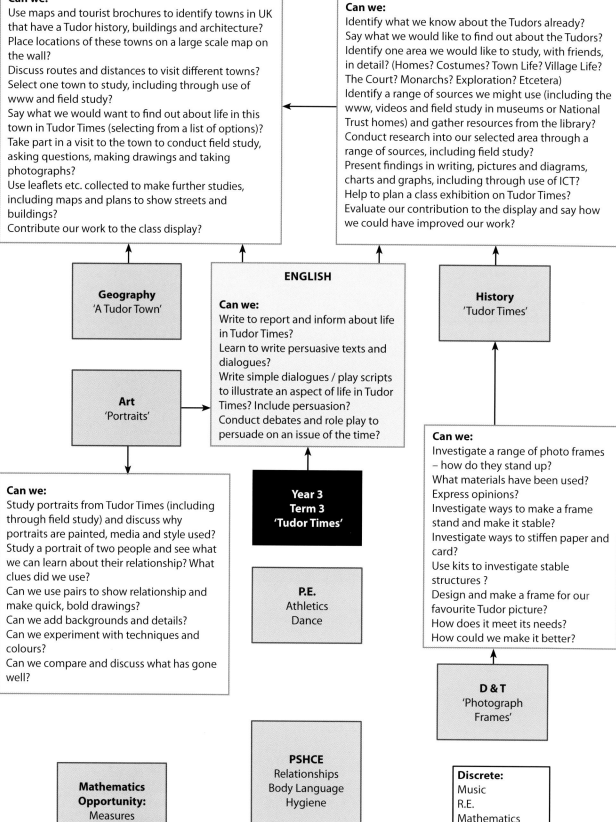

Can we:
Use maps and tourist brochures to identify towns in UK that have a Tudor history, buildings and architecture?
Place locations of these towns on a large scale map on the wall?
Discuss routes and distances to visit different towns?
Select one town to study, including through use of www and field study?
Say what we would want to find out about life in this town in Tudor Times (selecting from a list of options)?
Take part in a visit to the town to conduct field study, asking questions, making drawings and taking photographs?
Use leaflets etc. collected to make further studies, including maps and plans to show streets and buildings?
Contribute our work to the class display?

Can we:
Identify what we know about the Tudors already?
Say what we would like to find out about the Tudors?
Identify one area we would like to study, with friends, in detail? (Homes? Costumes? Town Life? Village Life? The Court? Monarchs? Exploration? Etcetera)
Identify a range of sources we might use (including the www, videos and field study in museums or National Trust homes) and gather resources from the library?
Conduct research into our selected area through a range of sources, including field study?
Present findings in writing, pictures and diagrams, charts and graphs, including through use of ICT?
Help to plan a class exhibition on Tudor Times?
Evaluate our contribution to the display and say how we could have improved our work?

Geography
'A Tudor Town'

ENGLISH

Can we:
Write to report and inform about life in Tudor Times?
Learn to write persuasive texts and dialogues?
Write simple dialogues / play scripts to illustrate an aspect of life in Tudor Times? Include persuasion?
Conduct debates and role play to persuade on an issue of the time?

History
'Tudor Times'

Art
'Portraits'

Can we:
Study portraits from Tudor Times (including through field study) and discuss why portraits are painted, media and style used?
Study a portrait of two people and see what we can learn about their relationship? What clues did we use?
Can we use pairs to show relationship and make quick, bold drawings?
Can we add backgrounds and details?
Can we experiment with techniques and colours?
Can we compare and discuss what has gone well?

**Year 3
Term 3
'Tudor Times'**

Can we:
Investigate a range of photo frames – how do they stand up?
What materials have been used? Express opinions?
Investigate ways to make a frame stand and make it stable?
Investigate ways to stiffen paper and card?
Use kits to investigate stable structures ?
Design and make a frame for our favourite Tudor picture?
How does it meet its needs?
How could we make it better?

P.E.
Athletics
Dance

D & T
'Photograph Frames'

Mathematics Opportunity:
Measures

PSHCE
Relationships
Body Language
Hygiene

Discrete:
Music
R.E.
Mathematics

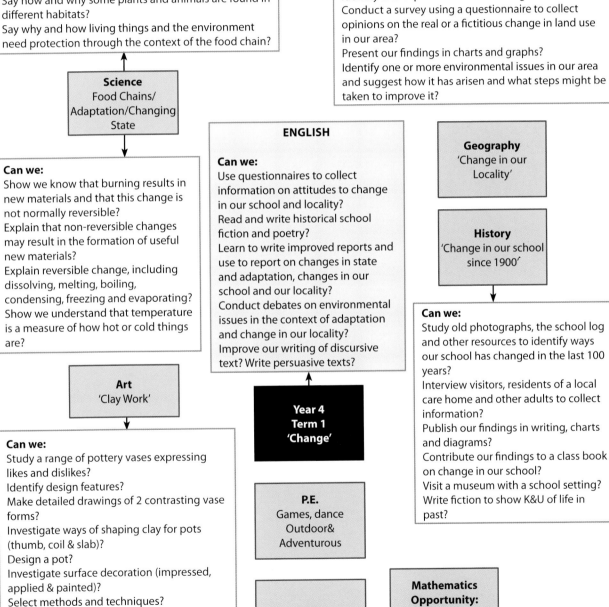

Can we:
Show we understand that micro-organisms are living things and are often too small to be seen and that they can be beneficial?
Explain that nearly all food chains start with a green plant?
Illustrate feeding relationships in habitats thro' the food chain?
Identify ways animals and plants in 2 different habitats are adapted to their environment?
Say how and why some plants and animals are found in different habitats?
Say why and how living things and the environment need protection through the context of the food chain?

Can we:
Locate the UK, England, our county, our locality and our neighbourhood on maps of different scales?
Use aerial and oblique photographs to identify and name key features of our area (Year 2 link)?
Use field study in our area to investigate patterns of land use?
Use ICT to show percentages / proportions of land use for different purposes eg housing / roads / schools / parks etc?
Identify and explain one area of change in land?
Conduct a survey using a questionnaire to collect opinions on the real or a fictitious change in land use in our area?
Present our findings in charts and graphs?
Identify one or more environmental issues in our area and suggest how it has arisen and what steps might be taken to improve it?

Science
Food Chains/
Adaptation/Changing
State

ENGLISH

Can we:
Use questionnaires to collect information on attitudes to change in our school and locality?
Read and write historical school fiction and poetry?
Learn to write improved reports and use to report on changes in state and adaptation, changes in our school and our locality?
Conduct debates on environmental issues in the context of adaptation and change in our locality?
Improve our writing of discursive text? Write persuasive texts?

Geography
'Change in our Locality'

History
'Change in our school since 1900'

Can we:
Show we know that burning results in new materials and that this change is not normally reversible?
Explain that non-reversible changes may result in the formation of useful new materials?
Explain reversible change, including dissolving, melting, boiling, condensing, freezing and evaporating?
Show we understand that temperature is a measure of how hot or cold things are?

Can we:
Study old photographs, the school log and other resources to identify ways our school has changed in the last 100 years?
Interview visitors, residents of a local care home and other adults to collect information?
Publish our findings in writing, charts and diagrams?
Contribute our findings to a class book on change in our school?
Visit a museum with a school setting?
Write fiction to show K&U of life in past?

Art
'Clay Work'

**Year 4
Term 1
'Change'**

Can we:
Study a range of pottery vases expressing likes and dislikes?
Identify design features?
Make detailed drawings of 2 contrasting vase forms?
Investigate ways of shaping clay for pots (thumb, coil & slab)?
Design a pot?
Investigate surface decoration (impressed, applied & painted)?
Select methods and techniques?
Make a pot and decorate when 'leather hard'?
Glaze and fire or paint and varnish our dried pot?
Evaluate our work and say how it might be improved?
Link the changes in state to our science?

P.E.
Games, dance
Outdoor&
Adventurous

PSHCE
School Rules
Bullying
Healthy diet in school

Mathematics Opportunity:
Data handling /
measures

Discrete:
Music
R.E.
Mathematics

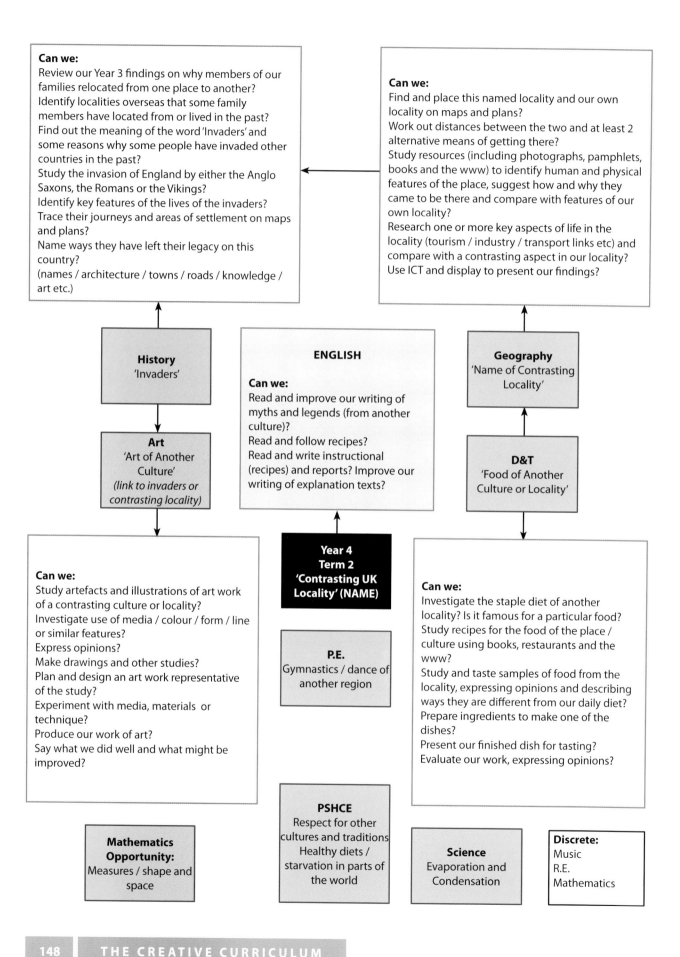

Can we:
Review our Year 3 findings on why members of our families relocated from one place to another?
Identify localities overseas that some family members have located from or lived in the past?
Find out the meaning of the word 'Invaders' and some reasons why some people have invaded other countries in the past?
Study the invasion of England by either the Anglo Saxons, the Romans or the Vikings?
Identify key features of the lives of the invaders?
Trace their journeys and areas of settlement on maps and plans?
Name ways they have left their legacy on this country?
(names / architecture / towns / roads / knowledge / art etc.)

Can we:
Find and place this named locality and our own locality on maps and plans?
Work out distances between the two and at least 2 alternative means of getting there?
Study resources (including photographs, pamphlets, books and the www) to identify human and physical features of the place, suggest how and why they came to be there and compare with features of our own locality?
Research one or more key aspects of life in the locality (tourism / industry / transport links etc) and compare with a contrasting aspect in our locality?
Use ICT and display to present our findings?

History
'Invaders'

ENGLISH

Can we:
Read and improve our writing of myths and legends (from another culture)?
Read and follow recipes?
Read and write instructional (recipes) and reports? Improve our writing of explanation texts?

Geography
'Name of Contrasting Locality'

Art
'Art of Another Culture'
(link to invaders or contrasting locality)

D&T
'Food of Another Culture or Locality'

**Year 4
Term 2
'Contrasting UK
Locality' (NAME)**

Can we:
Study artefacts and illustrations of art work of a contrasting culture or locality?
Investigate use of media / colour / form / line or similar features?
Express opinions?
Make drawings and other studies?
Plan and design an art work representative of the study?
Experiment with media, materials or technique?
Produce our work of art?
Say what we did well and what might be improved?

P.E.
Gymnastics / dance of another region

Can we:
Investigate the staple diet of another locality? Is it famous for a particular food?
Study recipes for the food of the place / culture using books, restaurants and the www?
Study and taste samples of food from the locality, expressing opinions and describing ways they are different from our daily diet?
Prepare ingredients to make one of the dishes?
Present our finished dish for tasting?
Evaluate our work, expressing opinions?

**Mathematics
Opportunity:**
Measures / shape and space

PSHCE
Respect for other cultures and traditions
Healthy diets / starvation in parts of the world

Science
Evaporation and Condensation

Discrete:
Music
R.E.
Mathematics

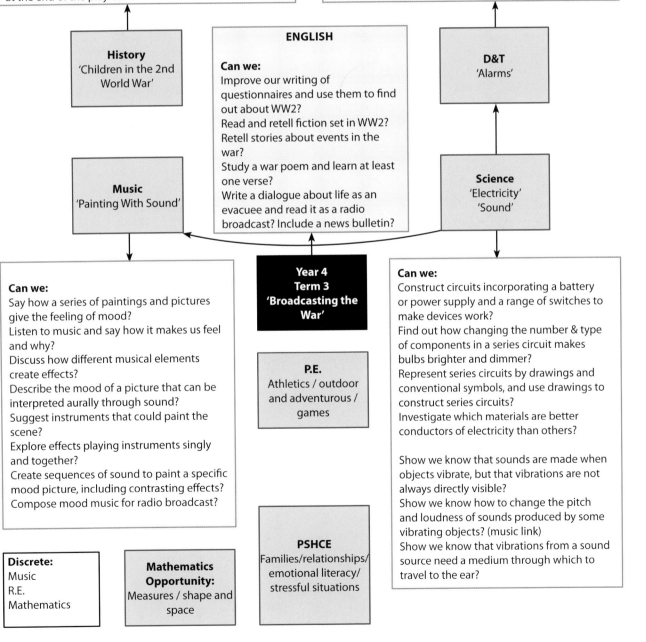

Can we:
Research facts about the second world war using a range of sources including the www? (Potential field visit eg Eden Camp in Yorkshire)
Collect and examine artifacts from the war? (Gas masks, ration books, black out curtains, uniforms etc)
Make drawings and diagrams of artifacts and other features? (Dug outs, shelters, sirens etc)
Contribute to a class display?
Study the lives of evacuees and issues around evacuation, using old newspapers, videos, fiction, pictures, using questionnaires and interviews (if possible)?
Perform a playlet (include mood music) as a radio broadcast to show our knowledge of the lives of children evacuated in World War 2? Can we add a news broadcast at the end of the playlet?

Can we:
Name a range of uses for alarms and sirens?
Review H&S of working with electricity?
Investigate a range of alarms and sirens, making links with history and science?
Investigate a range of ways that different types of switches work? (QCA Unit 4D)
Show we know how and why 'feedback' is important?
Show we can make simple circuits that incorporate different types of bulbs, switches, buzzers etcetera and explain how they work?
Design an alarm to protect something special, producing a labelled plan and identifying materials, tools etcetera to be used?
Make our alarm, evaluating our work as it progresses? Use our alarm in a broadcast?

History
'Children in the 2nd World War'

ENGLISH

Can we:
Improve our writing of questionnaires and use them to find out about WW2?
Read and retell fiction set in WW2?
Retell stories about events in the war?
Study a war poem and learn at least one verse?
Write a dialogue about life as an evacuee and read it as a radio broadcast? Include a news bulletin?

D&T
'Alarms'

Music
'Painting With Sound'

Science
'Electricity'
'Sound'

**Year 4
Term 3
'Broadcasting the War'**

Can we:
Say how a series of paintings and pictures give the feeling of mood?
Listen to music and say how it makes us feel and why?
Discuss how different musical elements create effects?
Describe the mood of a picture that can be interpreted aurally through sound?
Suggest instruments that could paint the scene?
Explore effects playing instruments singly and together?
Create sequences of sound to paint a specific mood picture, including contrasting effects?
Compose mood music for radio broadcast?

P.E.
Athletics / outdoor and adventurous / games

Can we:
Construct circuits incorporating a battery or power supply and a range of switches to make devices work?
Find out how changing the number & type of components in a series circuit makes bulbs brighter and dimmer?
Represent series circuits by drawings and conventional symbols, and use drawings to construct series circuits?
Investigate which materials are better conductors of electricity than others?

Show we know that sounds are made when objects vibrate, but that vibrations are not always directly visible?
Show we know how to change the pitch and loudness of sounds produced by some vibrating objects? (music link)
Show we know that vibrations from a sound source need a medium through which to travel to the ear?

Discrete:
Music
R.E.
Mathematics

Mathematics Opportunity:
Measures / shape and space

PSHCE
Families/relationships/ emotional literacy/ stressful situations

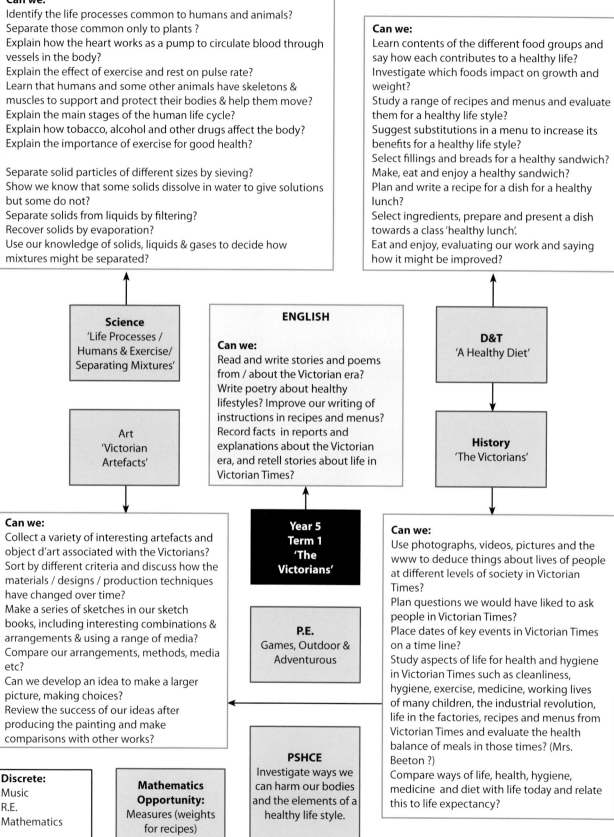

Can we:
Identify the life processes common to humans and animals?
Separate those common only to plants ?
Explain how the heart works as a pump to circulate blood through vessels in the body?
Explain the effect of exercise and rest on pulse rate?
Learn that humans and some other animals have skeletons & muscles to support and protect their bodies & help them move?
Explain the main stages of the human life cycle?
Explain how tobacco, alcohol and other drugs affect the body?
Explain the importance of exercise for good health?

Separate solid particles of different sizes by sieving?
Show we know that some solids dissolve in water to give solutions but some do not?
Separate solids from liquids by filtering?
Recover solids by evaporation?
Use our knowledge of solids, liquids & gases to decide how mixtures might be separated?

Can we:
Learn contents of the different food groups and say how each contributes to a healthy life?
Investigate which foods impact on growth and weight?
Study a range of recipes and menus and evaluate them for a healthy life style?
Suggest substitutions in a menu to increase its benefits for a healthy life style?
Select fillings and breads for a healthy sandwich?
Make, eat and enjoy a healthy sandwich?
Plan and write a recipe for a dish for a healthy lunch?
Select ingredients, prepare and present a dish towards a class 'healthy lunch'.
Eat and enjoy, evaluating our work and saying how it might be improved?

Science
'Life Processes / Humans & Exercise/ Separating Mixtures'

ENGLISH

Can we:
Read and write stories and poems from / about the Victorian era?
Write poetry about healthy lifestyles? Improve our writing of instructions in recipes and menus?
Record facts in reports and explanations about the Victorian era, and retell stories about life in Victorian Times?

D&T
'A Healthy Diet'

Art
'Victorian Artefacts'

History
'The Victorians'

Can we:
Collect a variety of interesting artefacts and object d'art associated with the Victorians?
Sort by different criteria and discuss how the materials / designs / production techniques have changed over time?
Make a series of sketches in our sketch books, including interesting combinations & arrangements & using a range of media?
Compare our arrangements, methods, media etc?
Can we develop an idea to make a larger picture, making choices?
Review the success of our ideas after producing the painting and make comparisons with other works?

**Year 5
Term 1
'The
Victorians'**

P.E.
Games, Outdoor & Adventurous

Can we:
Use photographs, videos, pictures and the www to deduce things about lives of people at different levels of society in Victorian Times?
Plan questions we would have liked to ask people in Victorian Times?
Place dates of key events in Victorian Times on a time line?
Study aspects of life for health and hygiene in Victorian Times such as cleanliness, hygiene, exercise, medicine, working lives of many children, the industrial revolution, life in the factories, recipes and menus from Victorian Times and evaluate the health balance of meals in those times? (Mrs. Beeton ?)
Compare ways of life, health, hygiene, medicine and diet with life today and relate this to life expectancy?

Discrete:
Music
R.E.
Mathematics

Mathematics Opportunity:
Measures (weights for recipes)

PSHCE
Investigate ways we can harm our bodies and the elements of a healthy life style.

Can we:
Review our prior learning about evaporation, condensation and the water cycle?
Explain that temperature is a measure of how hot or cold things are?
Investigate thermal insulators and make comparisons?
Identify evidence of water on local maps and plans?
Identify high and low rainfall areas?
Use field study to measure rainfall in our school's locality?
Use the media, including the www, to study national rainfall patterns over time?
Use field study and the help of the site manager to research and map water movement through our school?
Investigate a range of ways water is used domestically and keep a log of water use at home?
Collect samples of water from different sources and investigate?
Use scientific K&U to clean some natural water samples?
Illustrate the story of a river?
Identify the world's major rivers using atlases, globes and the www?

Can we:
Explain how objects are pulled down because of gravitational attraction?
Do we know that friction, including air resistance, is a force that slows moving objects and may stop an object from moving?
Do we know that when an object is pushed or pulled an opposing force can be felt?
Do we know how to measure forces and identify the direction in which they act?

Review our K&U of the water cycle and purification of water?
Test water samples and compare taste of drinking water from different sources, including homes and school?
Present findings using ICT?
Filter and sieve water samples from natural sources?

Geography
'Water'

ENGLISH

Can we:
Read and write stories and poems with a water theme, including myths and legends?
Learn part or all of a poem?
Improve our writing to persuade & report on water pollution issues and / or the creation of water based sports opportunities in the locality?
Improve our writing to debate (discursive) issues to do with conservation and the ecology?
Take part in discussions and debates?

Science
'Forces and Friction'
'Water'

PSHCE
Discuss water pollution and man's impact on the environment.
Leisure activities & the role of leisure in our lives.

Art
'Water'

**Year 5
Term 2
'Water'**

Can we:
Investigate use of water colours for effect?
Study a range of water colour paintings and/or paintings with a water theme, discussing light and dark / reflections etcetera?
Study a range of other pictorial and photographic sources on a water theme, discussing light / reflections / effects?
Investigate creation of effects?
Plan and produce a painting?
Evaluate our work and say how it might be improved?

Investigate use of wax resist with water colours or other liquid media? (Eg Inks)
Study a range of photographic sources for underwater pictures (the sea)?
Use thick white wax to plan an underwater scene?
Investigate use of colour washes to create underwater effects?
Colour wash our underwater scenes?
Evaluate our work?

P.E.
Games, Outdoor & Adventurous (water based?)
Gymnastics

Discrete:
Music
R.E.
History – life of a famous person?
(Link to construction of bridges? Canals? Railways?)
Mathematics

Mathematics Opportunity:
Measures / data handling

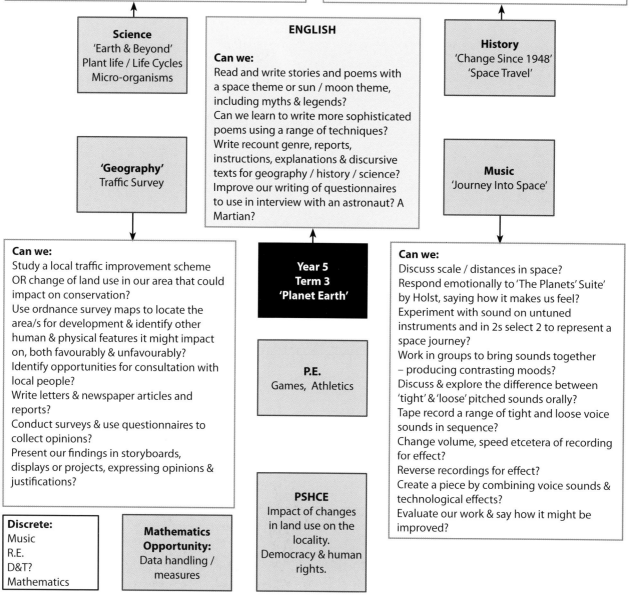

Can we:
Show we know that the Earth, sun and moon are approximately spherical?
Show knowledge of how & why the position of the sun appears to change during the day & how shadows change as this happens?
Explain how day & night are related to the spin of the Earth on its own axis?
Show we know that the Earth orbits the sun once each year & the moon takes approximately 28 days to orbit the Earth?

Name the parts of a flowering plant?
Describe the role of each part in a plant's life cycle?
Explain the life processes common to all plants?

Describe micro-organisms & say how they can be beneficial?

Can we:
Use questionnaires to find out major changes family, friends and persons chosen by the school (retirement home? Visitor?) have seen in key aspects of life since 1948? (Transport? Communications? Household appliances? Entertainment? Work? Leisure? Homes? Schools? Etcetera..)
Collate and present our findings using ICT?
In groups, select an aspect of change and conduct research using a range of sources including the www and field study (museum?) if possible?
Make sketches, take photographs and produce reports, instructions, explanations etcetera?
Produce a group display of changes we have identified?

Study, in depth, developments in space travel during the 20th Century using a range of sources including video and the www?
Make a class frieze of the main events in space travel?

Science
'Earth & Beyond'
Plant life / Life Cycles
Micro-organisms

ENGLISH

Can we:
Read and write stories and poems with a space theme or sun / moon theme, including myths & legends?
Can we learn to write more sophisticated poems using a range of techniques?
Write recount genre, reports, instructions, explanations & discursive texts for geography / history / science?
Improve our writing of questionnaires to use in interview with an astronaut? A Martian?

History
'Change Since 1948'
'Space Travel'

'Geography'
Traffic Survey

Music
'Journey Into Space'

**Year 5
Term 3
'Planet Earth'**

Can we:
Study a local traffic improvement scheme OR change of land use in our area that could impact on conservation?
Use ordnance survey maps to locate the area/s for development & identify other human & physical features it might impact on, both favourably & unfavourably?
Identify opportunities for consultation with local people?
Write letters & newspaper articles and reports?
Conduct surveys & use questionnaires to collect opinions?
Present our findings in storyboards, displays or projects, expressing opinions & justifications?

P.E.
Games, Athletics

Can we:
Discuss scale / distances in space?
Respond emotionally to 'The Planets' Suite' by Holst, saying how it makes us feel?
Experiment with sound on untuned instruments and in 2s select 2 to represent a space journey?
Work in groups to bring sounds together – producing contrasting moods?
Discuss & explore the difference between 'tight' & 'loose' pitched sounds orally?
Tape record a range of tight and loose voice sounds in sequence?
Change volume, speed etcetera of recording for effect?
Reverse recordings for effect?
Create a piece by combining voice sounds & technological effects?
Evaluate our work & say how it might be improved?

Discrete:
Music
R.E.
D&T?
Mathematics

Mathematics Opportunity:
Data handling / measures

PSHCE
Impact of changes in land use on the locality.
Democracy & human rights.

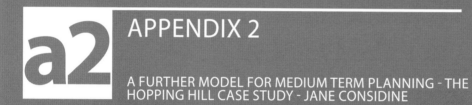

APPENDIX 2

A FURTHER MODEL FOR MEDIUM TERM PLANNING - THE
HOPPING HILL CASE STUDY - JANE CONSIDINE

THE CONNECTED CURRICULUM FRAMEWORK

The Connected Curriculum framework is a design model that integrates the National Curriculum, core skills and relevant experiences so that there is a cohesive approach to teaching and learning. This framework provides a structure to

- » support the curriculum redesign process
- » ensure that the National Curriculum is covered but there is a 'focusing on' the core transferable skills of learning
- » address current needs i.e. having the curriculum rooted in 'Every Child Matters'
- » discover the connections between subjects that will mutually enhance the learning and teaching across the whole curriculum
- » allow the school's uniqueness and individuality to be reflected as well as to ensure continuity and progression across all subjects
- » build innovation and creativity into the curriculum, knowing the core fundamentals have been addressed and tracked across the whole school

GUIDING PRINCIPLES

The Connected Curriculum framework reflects the need to layer in current agenda as well as to tailor-make a curriculum that is relevant to the pupils in the school. A modern curriculum cannot remain static and must be responsive to changes in society. For many teachers, even though this is a principle they agree with, without a flexible framework through which to embed these adjustments and adaptations the danger is that there are barriers to response to innovation.

This Connected Curriculum design model is built around five guiding principles.

1. National Curriculum - "Content and process entitlement"

The National Curriculum programmes of study need to be embedded. The content dimensions of the programmes of study can be adapted as long as access to the process of the subject is retained. Those programmes of study that can be linked together should be linked together so as to maximise on opportunities for pupils to make meaningful connections between different subjects.

2. Skills – "Systematic transference of learning"

During every connected unit there is an opportunity for skills to be taught in one subject and applied in another. Skills across all levels can be tracked through the Connected Curriculum Framework for appropriate year groups and taught in a way that enables pupils to revisit key skills more than once in a range of contexts.

3. Experiences – "Bringing it to life"

One central experience is provided as part of every Connected Curriculum Framework unit. This experience must be stimulating, rewarding and motivationally linked to other aspects of pupils' learning. The experience should operate as a facilitating opportunity to provide a real experience for pupils to draw upon.

4. Connectors – "The abstract thread"

The National Curriculum programmes of study and the subject skills are held together by connectors (themes); an abstract hook that acts as a way of thematically linking all learning in that unit. The connector cements the National Curriculum, skills and experiences together.

5. Discrete Subjects – "No tenuous links"

Any subject's programmes of study that do not connect easily should not be forced in under a tenuous link. These elements should be kept out of The Connected Curriculum framework unit and taught effectively in isolation, however up to 70% of the National Curriculum can usually be taught through thematic links.

ORGANISATION OF THE CONNECTED CURRICULUM FRAMEWORK

The Connected Curriculum Framework is built up from units. These units last for six weeks and can be taught during half a term. This equates to two units a term, which in turn means six units over a year. Each unit applies the six guiding principles and shares all the same structural features.

THE VITAL COMPONENTS

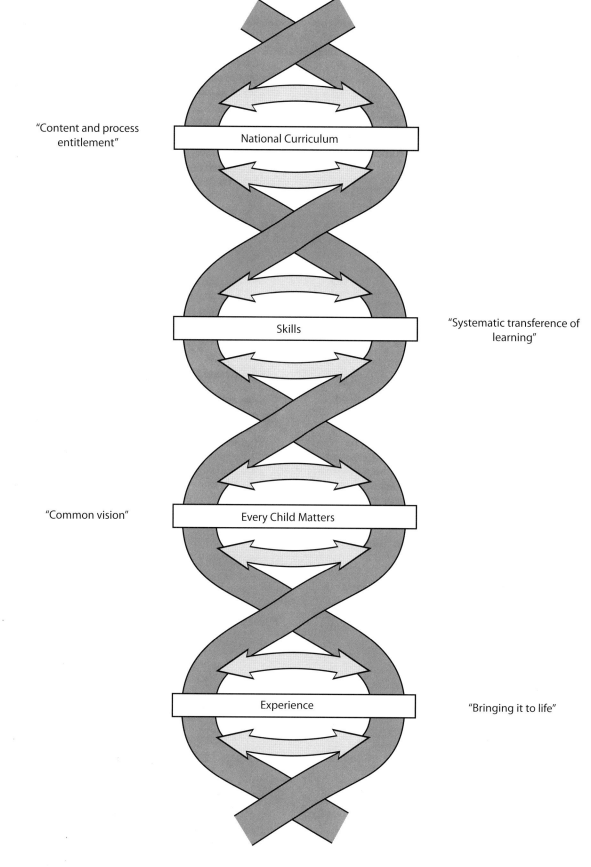

"Content and process entitlement"

National Curriculum

"Systematic transference of learning"

Skills

"Common vision"

Every Child Matters

Experience

"Bringing it to life"

CURRICULUM CONNECTORS

Curriculum Connectors (themes) are critical. They enable pupils to see the cross-curricular links and to apply their learning across the range of subjects, skills and experiences.

In order for pupils to embed their learning they should access and apply aspects of the same information in a range of crucial ways. When we teach pupils in discrete subject-specific lessons without connecting the learning, they often find it difficult to apply these skills, concepts and experiences to other areas of the curriculum. Thematic links provide the bridge between each aspect of learning and enable teachers to include other effective learning opportunities from the wider curriculum.

Below is a short list of possible connectors (thematic titles) that are sufficiently abstracted and may be used to build teaching units. Of course, the complete list is potentially endless.

» Magic	» Moods	» Colours
» Frames	» Treasure	» Elements
» Discovery	» Boundaries	» Adventure
» Power	» Movement	» Strength
» Journeys	» Vehicle	» Holes
» Dreams	» Patterns	» Keys
» Doorways	» Design	» Faces
» Fire	» Changes	» Images
» Tunnels	» Reflections	» Spaces
» Emotions	» Views	» Pathways
» Boxes	» Chains	

SKILLS AND ASSESSMENT

The curriculum model developed for Hopping Hill Primary School deploys the hierarchy of learning skills (see Chapter 11) to identify and track which key skills are being learnt, consolidated and applied. For the Connected Curriculum Framework these skills have been numbered for ease of reference in long and medium term plans.

In addition, use the guiding principles of assessment for learning (see Chapter 3) in order to promote pupil reflection and comment on process elements, content/context or application of skills.

ACHIEVEMENTS AND OUTCOMES

Ensure that core entitlements outlined reflect the aims of 'Every Child Matters'.

FOCUSED EXPERIENCE

Experiences that will ensure that learning "comes alive" and is relevant should be planned in. Experiences in the broadest sense should include: field study and visits, residential visits, visitors, thematic learning days, assemblies, enrichment activities such as World Book Day, Science Week, Sports Events.

CONNECTED CURRICULUM FRAMEWORK AND LONG TERM PLANNING

The models provided in this case study outline one Key Stage One example in detail across one term (Year 2) and one Key Stage Two example in detail across one term (Year 5).

The CCF approach is one model that can be used by schools as a supportive structure for curriculum redesign. The medium term plans that are outlined here have been developed in partnership with Hopping Hill Primary School in Northamptonshire. They reflect generic ways that a school can tackle curriculum restructuring but they must also respect the school's individual situation and position with regards to existing curricular models.

Hopping Hill staff wanted to;

» build in the Primary National Strategies Renewed Framework in Literacy and Numeracy

» use the current Science QCA units and guidance as they felt it was thorough and supported work towards SATS.

» build on successful units of work that they had already created and defined in school e.g. New York topic (English and Geographical cross curricular thematic unit.)

» reference the SEAL project work they were using to support their teaching in PSHE and citizenship

» always keep Religious Education as a discrete subject as any links to other subjects could be tenuous and it deserved a 'unique slot' to develop awe and wonder in its own right.

As a result of the school's 'in-house' decisions the long and medium term plans show;

» English is built into the majority of connected units and follows the Renewed Primary National Strategy guidance for Literacy

» Mathematics is built into themes when appropriate, and some taught discretely when required. All planned mathematics is referenced to the PNS renewed framework materials

» Religious Education (R.E.) is always taught outside of the theme and would usually reflect the local authority's scheme.

» Physical Education (P.E.) is always built into connected

units but additional teaching occurs outside the unit to ensure entitlement to the two hours per week entitlement of all children.

» Science is mainly planned as part of the connected unit and is QCA referenced. Occasionally it is taught outside of the unit

» Information, Communication Technology (I.C.T.), History, Geography, Music, Art and Design and Technology are usually intrinsic to the connected units and coverage occurs as a balance over time. Very occasionally these subjects are taught outside to target specific National Curriculum programmes of study that have not yet been addressed

» Personal, Social, Health and Education (P.S.H.E.) is referenced to the SEAL Project and the citizenship strand is covered through other subjects. In the main PSHE features as part of each connected unit. Each Connected Curriculum Framework unit (six weeks in duration) outlines the five component features

  » National Curriculum subjects included

  » The core skills that will be taught and applied

  » The main experience that will enhance and serve as a learning point of reference

  » The thematic hook (connector) that gels the learning together

  » The subjects that will be taught discretely during the six week unit

CASE STUDY SCHOOL – HOPPING HILL PRIMARY SCHOOL, NORTHAMPTON

Hopping Hill Primary is a large two form entry primary school in Northampton town. In 2005 Hopping Hill was part of the Northampton Town Review and was converted from a lower school into a primary. Recently the school has undergone many changes, including extension into Years 5 and 6. It draws its pupils from the local housing estate which is predominately a low socio-economic, white community. The area is ranked below average on the multiple deprivation index with a significant percentage of adults having no higher educational qualifications.

BACKGROUND

The current Head teacher, Tammy Mitchell joined the school in April 2006 which coincided with an extensive building project, the introduction of the Primary Strategy Renewed Frameworks and the embedding of the 'New Relationship with Schools' providing the perfect opportunity for intensive self-evaluation. One aspect of the self-evaluation was a Stakeholder's Vision Day; where pupils, parents, governors, staff and representatives of the local community identified priorities for future sessions. One of the key outcomes from this inclusive process was that the curriculum no longer reflected the needs and priorities of the evolving school. It

was clear that the curriculum needed to be re-focused and redefined. Tammy felt,

"…in an attempt to raise standards the curriculum has become so segmented that there are too many missed opportunities to practise and apply skills taught in one curriculum area in another. As a result, every time a skill is revisited, it almost seems to be taught from scratch…pupils do not remember or recognise these skills because they have filed them under a specific subject heading"

THE PLANNING AND DEVELOPMENT STAGE

Tammy and the governors took the decision to implement the Connected Curriculum Framework (CFF) model as they felt that it addressed their priorities as well as building on current strengths in their school. An initial meeting that involved senior management and the governors scrutinised the principles, content and processes to ensure that the CCF would address:

» the teaching and application of key skills

» assessment for learning in all areas of the curriculum

» pupil engagement by building on their own interests and motivations

» all current agendas in a meaningful and manageable way

They felt this should, ultimately, raise achievement and attainment across the school.

The staff team made some crucial decisions about what elements of the curriculum were currently working for them. These proved to be a combination of 'in-house' units they have developed themselves, and QCA units that they felt were successful. Senior management were also keen to implement the Renewed Frameworks in literacy and numeracy. Leaders at every level of the school engaged with the managing and leading of this curriculum change agenda.

THE IMPLEMENTATION STAGE

A partnership approach took place in the more detailed development of both long and medium term plans. The model allows for regular reviews and modifications to ensure continuity and progression were maintained within year groups, within subjects as well as across the whole school. The school have been impressed by the rigour and coherence of the CCF units that have sharpened teaching and refined learning. Early indications show pupils have an increased understanding of their own learning journey and standards are continuing to rise,

"We have experience days that help me think. We have skills flags that show me the way, and we have a connector (theme) that helps me see what I've learned"

Lauren Year 4 Pupil

YEAR 2 TERM 1 OVERVIEW - 1ST HALF
Connector: Reflections

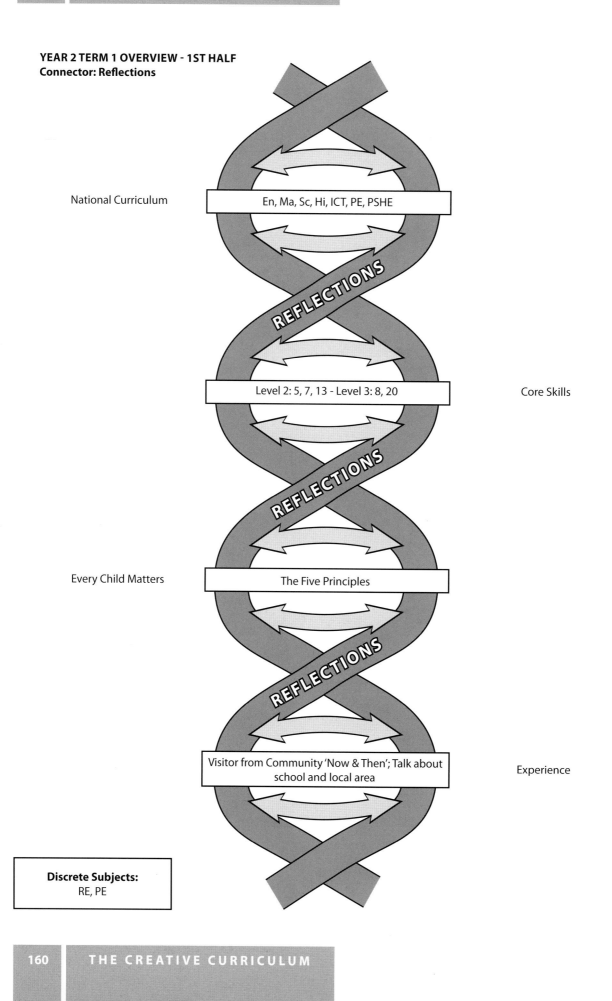

National Curriculum — En, Ma, Sc, Hi, ICT, PE, PSHE

REFLECTIONS

Level 2: 5, 7, 13 - Level 3: 8, 20 — Core Skills

REFLECTIONS

Every Child Matters — The Five Principles

REFLECTIONS

Visitor from Community 'Now & Then'; Talk about school and local area — Experience

Discrete Subjects:
RE, PE

YEAR 2 TERM 1 OVERVIEW - 2ND HALF
Connector: Changes

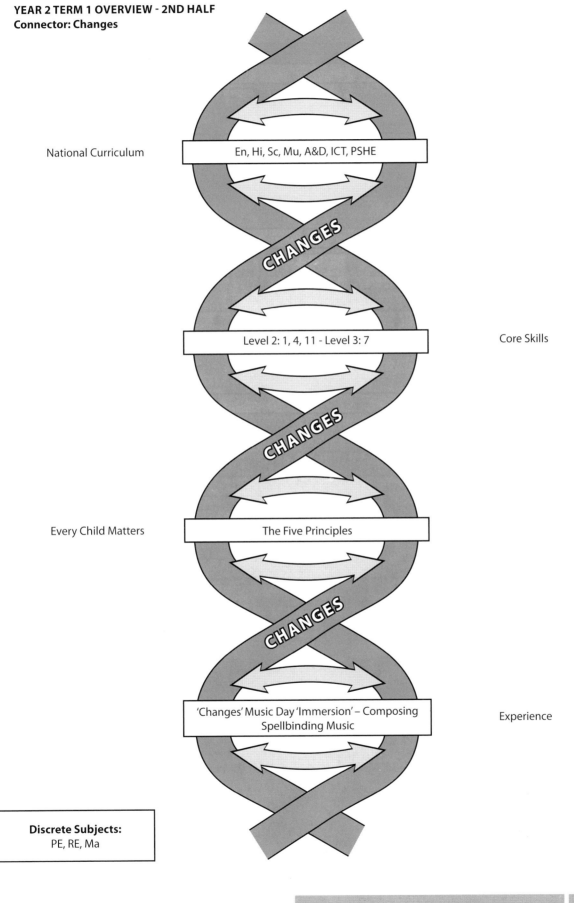

National Curriculum — En, Hi, Sc, Mu, A&D, ICT, PSHE

CHANGES

Level 2: 1, 4, 11 - Level 3: 7 — Core Skills

CHANGES

Every Child Matters — The Five Principles

CHANGES

'Changes' Music Day 'Immersion' – Composing Spellbinding Music — Experience

Discrete Subjects:
PE, RE, Ma

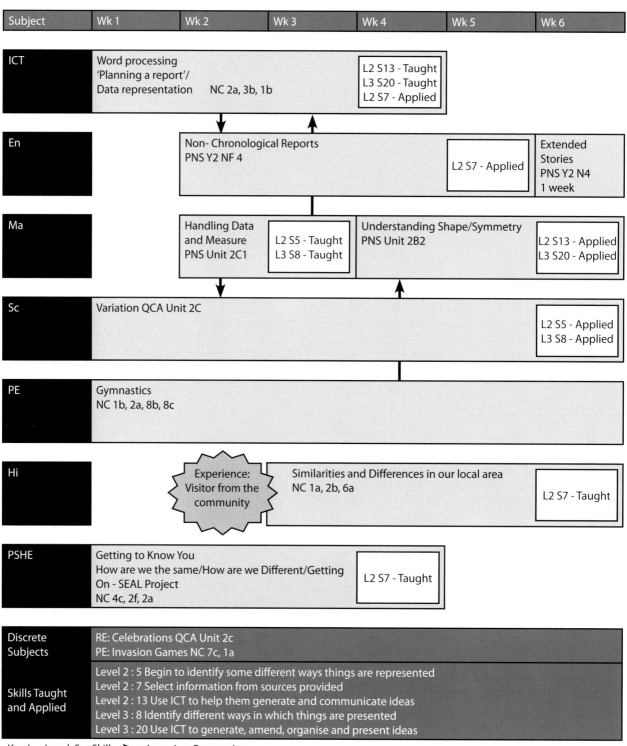

TEACHING

Subject	Wk 1	Wk 2	Wk 3	Wk 4	Wk 5	Wk 6
ICT	Word processing 'Planning a report'/ Data representation NC 2a, 3b, 1b			L2 S13 - Taught / L3 S20 - Taught / L2 S7 - Applied		
En		Non- Chronological Reports PNS Y2 NF 4			L2 S7 - Applied	Extended Stories PNS Y2 N4 1 week
Ma		Handling Data and Measure PNS Unit 2C1	L2 S5 - Taught / L3 S8 - Taught	Understanding Shape/Symmetry PNS Unit 2B2		L2 S13 - Applied / L3 S20 - Applied
Sc	Variation QCA Unit 2C					L2 S5 - Applied / L3 S8 - Applied
PE	Gymnastics NC 1b, 2a, 8b, 8c					
Hi			Experience: Visitor from the community	Similarities and Differences in our local area NC 1a, 2b, 6a		L2 S7 - Taught
PSHE	Getting to Know You How are we the same/How are we Different/Getting On - SEAL Project NC 4c, 2f, 2a		L2 S7 - Taught			

Discrete Subjects	RE: Celebrations QCA Unit 2c
	PE: Invasion Games NC 7c, 1a
Skills Taught and Applied	Level 2 : 5 Begin to identify some different ways things are represented
	Level 2 : 7 Select information from sources provided
	Level 2 : 13 Use ICT to help them generate and communicate ideas
	Level 3 : 8 Identify different ways in which things are presented
	Level 3 : 20 Use ICT to generate, amend, organise and present ideas

Key L = Level, S = Skill, ➤ = Learning Connection

LEARNING

Outcome	Success Criteria	Possible Context	Subject
Word processed report plan	**Do:** enter & store information in a variety of ways **Know:** how to organise information **Understand:** how to interpret information	Life in the 1970s in Duston	ICT
Non - Chronological Report	**Do:** write a non-chronological report **Know:** how to organise information **Understand:** the textual and language features of non-chronological reports	Life in the 1970s in Duston	En
Organise and present data	**Do:** collect data using a tally **Know:** how to present information in different ways **Understand:** how to make sense of data presented in different ways	Car ownership - Then (1970s) and now	Ma
Investigation - using results to draw conclusions	**Do:** observe and measure differences between plants and animals **Know:** that humans are similar to each other in some ways and different in others **Understand:** what their block graphs and charts show	Similarities and differences between classmates eg eye colour	Sc
Gymnastic sequence in pairs	**Do:** repeat simple skills and actions with control **Know:** how to choose and apply actions in sequence **Understand:** the impact of a display on the audience	Symmetrical sequence	PE
Chart showing similarities and differences 'Then and Now'	**Do:** place events in chronolgical order **Know:** differences in ways of life over time **Understand:** the influence of people and events to bring change	Timeline and charts about Duston	Hi
Celebration tree - similarities and differences	**Do:** recognise and respect similarites and differences between people **Know:** that people belong to different groups and communities **Understand:** that differences make you special	Celebrating the talents of others	PSHE

MEDIUM TERM UNIT   **YEAR 2**
CONNECTED CURRICULUM FRAMEWORK
CONNECTOR: REFLECTIONS   **TERM 1 - 1ST HALF**

TEACHING

Subject	Wk 1	Wk 2	Wk 3	Wk 4	Wk 5	Wk 6
En	Extended Stories PNS Y2 N4		Traditional Stories PNS Y2 N2			L2 S1 - Applied
Hi	Non- Chronological Reports PNS Y2 NF 4					L2 S1 - Taught L3 S7 - Applied
Mu	Experience: Immersion day - Spellbinding music	Changes NC 1b, 2b, 4c, 1c, 4b				
A & D	Changes Colour mixing / Light and dark NC 4a, 5c, 2a					L2 S5 - Applied L3 S8 - Applied
Sc	Grouping and Changing Materials QCA Unit 2d					L2 S11 - Taught
ICT					Imaginary situations Storybook Weaver / Kar2ouche NC 2d, 3a, 5b	
PSHE	Valuing the Individual New Beginnings - SEAL Project NC 1d, 1e, 5b, 5f			L2 S4 - Taught		
D & T	Change - Mixing and Making Food Technology NC 1b, 2f, 5c					L2 S11 - Applied

Discrete Subjects	RE: Visiting a place of Worship QCA Unit 2d PE: NC 2b, 2c, 7b Dance NC 3c, 6a, 6b
Skills Taught and Applied	Level 2 : 1 Include relevant details in ideas or events (orally) Level 2 : 4 Discuss work using appropriate language Level 2 : 11 Describe their observations Level 3 : 7 Begin to give reasons for and results of main changes and events

Key L = Level, S = Skill, ➤ = Learning Connection

LEARNING

Outcome	Success Criteria	Possible Context	Subject
Traditional Story	**Do:** write a traditional story **Know:** a range of traditional stories **Understand:** the textual and language features of a traditonal story	Ugly Duckling : Change occurs in main character	En
Non - Chronological Report	**Do:** use common words and phrases relating to the passing of time **Know:** why people did things and what happened **Understand:** why we remember significant people	Influence of important public figure eg Winston Churchill	Hi
Personal composition	**Do:** explore, choose and organise sounds **Know:** how to express ideas through music **Understand:** how sounds can be made in different ways	Musical contrast, eg silence vs loud	Mu
Abstract piece	**Do:** use a range of materials and processes **Know:** what happens when colours are mixed **Understand:** how to create effects using light and dark and express yourself	Strengths of individuals as colours	A & D
Design and execute fair test about changing materials	**Do:** predict what will happen and record observations **Know:** how to choose and apply actions in sequence **Understand:** how to set up a fair test for simple comparisons	Chocolate/Ice/ Flour at different temperatures	Sc
Visual Narrative	**Do:** explore and create imaginary situations **Know:** how to use specific ICT tools **Understand:** information can be presented in a variety of forms	Re-tell a well-known story	ICT
Pen portraits of others	**Do:** recognise their strengths and the strengths in others **Know:** how to feel positive about themselves **Understand:** the importance of developing positive relationships	Relationship building	PSHE
Follow a recipe	**Do:** follow a recipe **Know:** the importance of accurate measurements of ingredients **Understand:** that when certain ingredients are mixed together a new mixture occurs	A decorated cake	D & T

MEDIUM TERM UNIT
CONNECTED CURRICULUM FRAMEWORK
CONNECTOR: CHANGES

YEAR 2

TERM 1 - 2ND HALF

YEAR 5 TERM 1 OVERVIEW - 1ST HALF
Connector: Elements

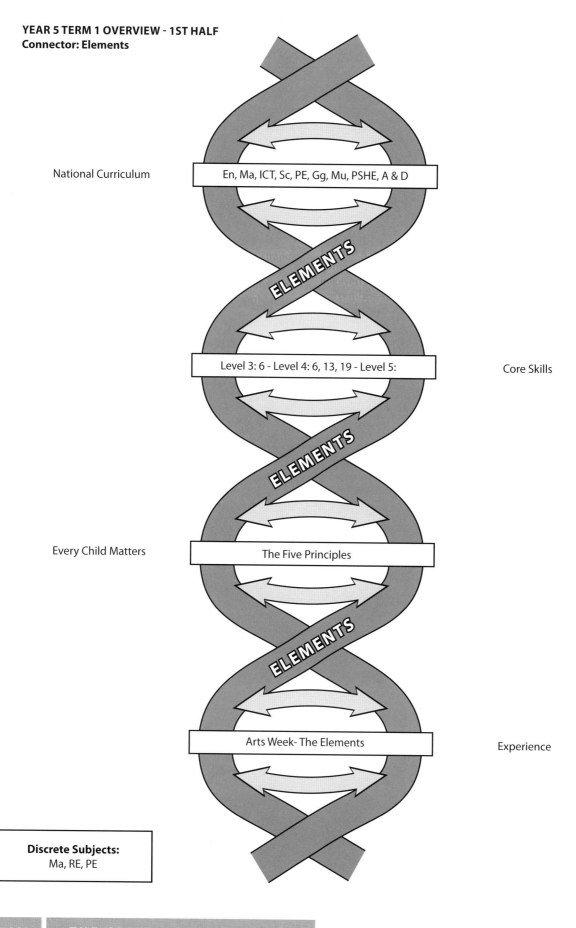

National Curriculum — En, Ma, ICT, Sc, PE, Gg, Mu, PSHE, A & D

ELEMENTS

Level 3: 6 - Level 4: 6, 13, 19 - Level 5: — Core Skills

ELEMENTS

Every Child Matters — The Five Principles

ELEMENTS

Arts Week- The Elements — Experience

Discrete Subjects:
Ma, RE, PE

YEAR 5 TERM 1 OVERVIEW - 2ND HALF
Connector: Doorways

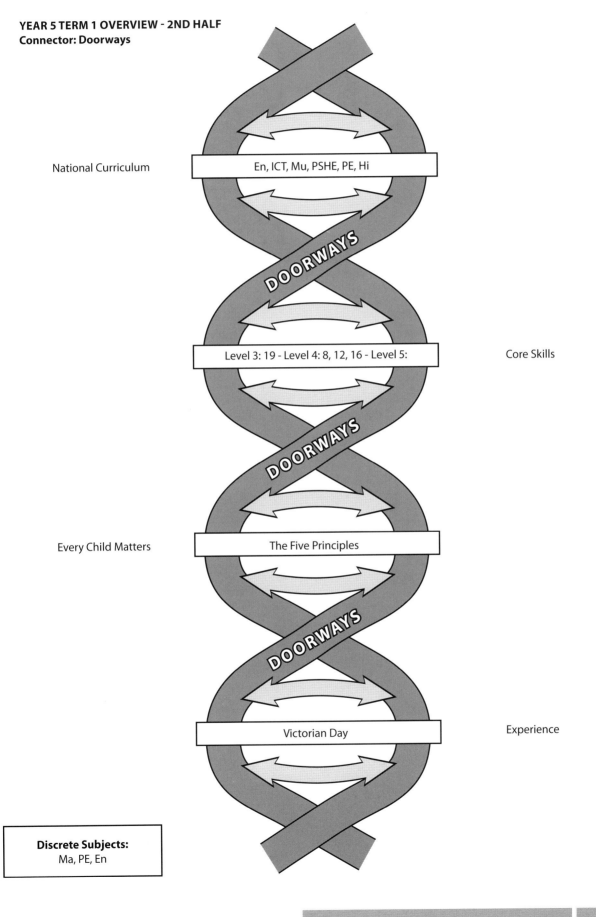

National Curriculum

En, ICT, Mu, PSHE, PE, Hi

DOORWAYS

Level 3: 19 - Level 4: 8, 12, 16 - Level 5:

Core Skills

DOORWAYS

Every Child Matters

The Five Principles

DOORWAYS

Victorian Day

Experience

Discrete Subjects:
Ma, PE, En

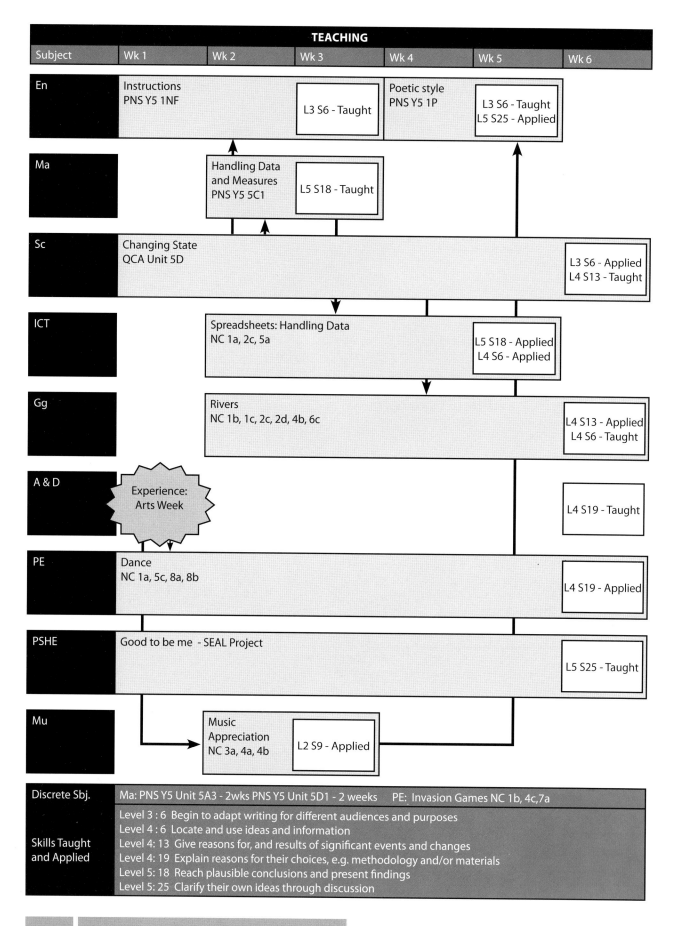

	TEACHING					
Subject	Wk 1	Wk 2	Wk 3	Wk 4	Wk 5	Wk 6
En	Instructions PNS Y5 1NF		L3 S6 - Taught	Poetic style PNS Y5 1P	L3 S6 - Taught L5 S25 - Applied	
Ma		Handling Data and Measures PNS Y5 5C1	L5 S18 - Taught			
Sc	Changing State QCA Unit 5D					L3 S6 - Applied L4 S13 - Taught
ICT		Spreadsheets: Handling Data NC 1a, 2c, 5a			L5 S18 - Applied L4 S6 - Applied	
Gg		Rivers NC 1b, 1c, 2c, 2d, 4b, 6c			L4 S13 - Applied L4 S6 - Taught	
A & D	Experience: Arts Week				L4 S19 - Taught	
PE	Dance NC 1a, 5c, 8a, 8b				L4 S19 - Applied	
PSHE	Good to be me - SEAL Project				L5 S25 - Taught	
Mu		Music Appreciation NC 3a, 4a, 4b	L2 S9 - Applied			

Discrete Sbj.	Ma: PNS Y5 Unit 5A3 - 2wks PNS Y5 Unit 5D1 - 2 weeks PE: Invasion Games NC 1b, 4c,7a
Skills Taught and Applied	Level 3 : 6 Begin to adapt writing for different audiences and purposes Level 4 : 6 Locate and use ideas and information Level 4: 13 Give reasons for, and results of significant events and changes Level 4: 19 Explain reasons for their choices, e.g. methodology and/or materials Level 5: 18 Reach plausible conclusions and present findings Level 5: 25 Clarify their own ideas through discussion

LEARNING			
Outcome	Success Criteria	Possible Context	Subject
Instructional text	**Do:** write an instructional text **Know:** the key features to include in instructions **Understand:** some of the downfalls in writing instructions	Make a kite	En
Collect and display data in different forms	**Do:** collect data and present differently **Know:** how to read and analyse different data formats **Understand:** that data may be better presented in one form over another	Represent data from science investigation	Ma
Instructional text	**Do:** write an instructional text **Know:** know a range of science instructional text **Understand:** the importance of accuracy when describing equipment, quantities and method	Science Invest. States of matter: reversible/ irreversible	Sc
Excel spreadsheet and related graph	**Do:** practise using Excel spreadsheets **Know:** how to input data into the spreadsheet **Understand:** that ICT can support information representation	Represent data from science investigation	ICT
Study of locality in country less economically developed	**Do:** compile information on an area where the river has an influence **Know:** how that river has influences on the people of that locality **Understand:** the impact a river has on its community	Nile/Egypt	Gg
A class textured collage	**Do:** produce a class collage **Know:** that different materials create different effects **Understand:** how mixed-media art can be a powerful form of expression	The elements - use mixed-media	A & D
A dance sequence	**Do:** sequence travelling movements **Know:** how to change movements to reflect different elements **Understand:** the audience's viewpoint in understanding/ enjoying the sequence	Fire, Air, Water, Earth - Music and movements	PE
A poem	**Do:** write a poem about themselves **Know:** what learning is important to them **Understand:** that their feelings can be communicated in different ways	Key aspects of their learning about themselves	PSHE
Compose a musical piece to communicate a different effect	**Do:** combine musical elelments to create a musical structure **Know:** how different musical moods can be created **Understand:** the importance of pitch, duration, texture and silence	Catergorise music to element types and design own	Mu

MEDIUM TERM UNIT
CONNECTED CURRICULUM FRAMEWORK
CONNECTOR: ELEMENTS

YEAR 5

TERM 1 - 1ST HALF

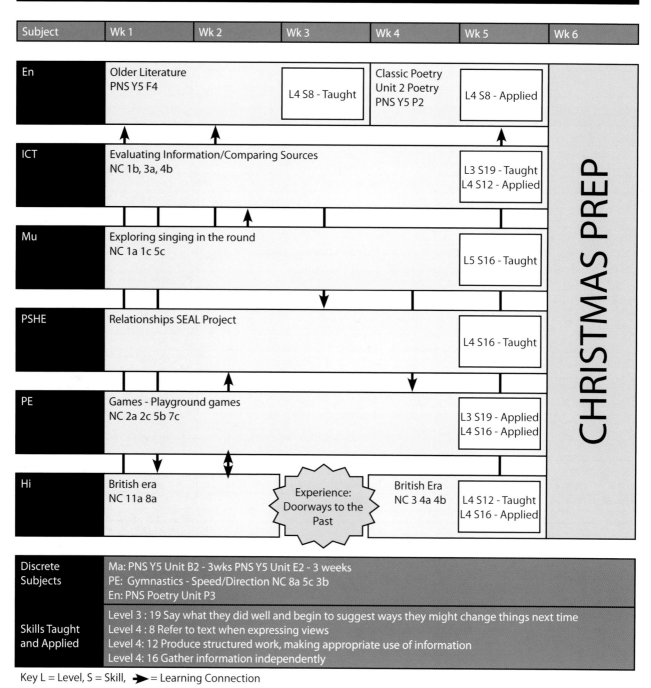

TEACHING

Subject	Wk 1	Wk 2	Wk 3	Wk 4	Wk 5	Wk 6
En	Older Literature PNS Y5 F4		L4 S8 - Taught	Classic Poetry Unit 2 Poetry PNS Y5 P2	L4 S8 - Applied	CHRISTMAS PREP
ICT	Evaluating Information/Comparing Sources NC 1b, 3a, 4b				L3 S19 - Taught L4 S12 - Applied	
Mu	Exploring singing in the round NC 1a 1c 5c				L5 S16 - Taught	
PSHE	Relationships SEAL Project				L4 S16 - Taught	
PE	Games - Playground games NC 2a 2c 5b 7c				L3 S19 - Applied L4 S16 - Applied	
Hi	British era NC 11a 8a		Experience: Doorways to the Past	British Era NC 3 4a 4b	L4 S12 - Taught L4 S16 - Applied	

Discrete Subjects	Ma: PNS Y5 Unit B2 - 3wks PNS Y5 Unit E2 - 3 weeks PE: Gymnastics - Speed/Direction NC 8a 5c 3b En: PNS Poetry Unit P3
Skills Taught and Applied	Level 3 : 19 Say what they did well and begin to suggest ways they might change things next time Level 4 : 8 Refer to text when expressing views Level 4: 12 Produce structured work, making appropriate use of information Level 4: 16 Gather information independently

Key L = Level, S = Skill, ➤ = Learning Connection

LEARNING

Outcome	Success Criteria	Possible Context	Subject
Narrative	**Do:** write a narrative **Know:** well known stories that use doorways to another world **Understand:** how writers heighten contrast between two worlds	Doorways to another world	En
Group research file	**Do:** find information from suitable sources **Know:** how to access, edit and save information **Understand:** how to use and interpret relevant information	Victorian Housing	ICT
Compose and perform own 'round' song	**Do:** sing songs in two parts **Know:** the importance of diction and musical expression **Understand:** the effect on the listener	Oranges and Lemons, Ring a Ring of Roses - Linked to playground games	Mu
School garden re-planted	**Do:** discuss, design and plant garden on a theme **Know:** there are different types of relationships **Understand:** how to develop skills to be effective in relationships	'Special Relationships'	PSHE
Play a range of pair and team games	**Do:** work with others to organise and keep games going **Know:** the rules for different activities **Understand:** the similarities and differences between team games of today and Victorian games	Victorian playground games	PE
Showcase at local museum (Y5 as guides for Y3)	**Do:** study British era of the past **Know:** the impact of individuals, events and change on the community **Understand:** the similarites and differences between now and then	Victorian Britain	Hi

MEDIUM TERM UNIT   **YEAR 5**
CONNECTED CURRICULUM FRAMEWORK
CONNECTOR: DOORWAYS   **TERM 1 - 2ND HALF**

ACKNOWLEDGEMENTS

Jane Considine	Consultant
Michelle Wraith	Consultant
Michael Thorp	DHT/Consultant
Gail Newton	Head Teacher
Peter Smith	Chair of Govenors
The Head Teacher	Parkinson Lane Primary
Sheridan Earnshaw	Consultant
Keith Bardon	Registered General Inspector
Maureen Janane	Administrator
Aaron Marshall	Fire Circle

The pupils, parents and staff of Linthwaite Clough JIN School

The pupils, parents and staff of Parkinson Lane Primary School

The pupils, parents and staff of Hopping Hill Primary School

Text contributed by:

Jane Considine

Gail Newton

Peter Smith

Michelle Wraith

Photographs: Linthwaite Clough JIN School

'The greatest tragedy is that education is now so difficult to enjoy. Every minute of every day is spent in bondage to the great god examination, while standards fall and literacy becomes a lost art'

Ann Widdecombe, MP, May 2007